The Woman I Was Born to Be

**Center Point
Large Print**

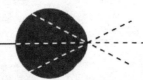

**This Large Print Book carries the
Seal of Approval of N.A.V.H.**

The Woman I Was Born to Be

Born to Be

My Story

SUSAN BOYLE

CENTER POINT PUBLISHING
THORNDIKE, MAINE

This Center Point Large Print edition
is published in the year 2010 by arrangement with
Atria Books, a division of Simon & Schuster, Inc.

The text of this Large Print edition is unabridged.
In other aspects, this book may vary
from the original edition.
Printed in the United States of America
on permanent paper.
Set in 16-point Times New Roman type.

ISBN: 978-1-60285-956-2

Library of Congress Cataloging-in-Publication Data

Boyle, Susan, 1961–
  The woman I was born to be / Susan Boyle. — Large print ed.
    p. cm.
  ISBN 978-1-60285-956-2 (library binding : alk. paper)
  1. Boyle, Susan, 1961– 2. Singers—Scotland—Biography. I. Title.
ML420.B763A3 2010
782.42164092—dc22
[B]
                                                    2010030881

For my mother

Contents

Part Three: *Britain's Got Talent*

Part Four: Who I Was Born to Be

Prologue

My name is Susan Boyle. A year and a half ago, if you weren't from Blackburn, the village in West Lothian, Scotland, where I have lived all my life, you would almost certainly never have heard of me. Today you've probably heard all sorts about me, some fact, some speculation, some pure invention, so I'm writing this book to tell my story from my point of view, and I hope you'll enjoy reading it.

Every story has a beginning and maybe mine started when I was in my pram forty-nine years ago. Whenever my mother put on a record, she noticed that I would sway slowly in time with the ballads, and jiggle faster to the rhythm of the quicker tunes. Or maybe it started with the toy banjo she bought me when I was a wee lassie. I used sit in front of the television mimicking Paul McCartney when the Beatles were on *Top of the Pops*. But I'll go back to all that a bit later.

For you, my story probably started on 11 April 2009 when I first appeared on television, but it was actually a couple of months before, on 21 January, that they recorded the Glasgow audition for *Britain's Got Talent*.

I've been on quite a journey since then, and it was actually quite a journey getting to the audition itself . . .

I'd had one of those sleepless nights that seem endless when you know you should be resting but you can't find a comfortable position. Your stomach's all butterflies, then, just as you've nodded off, it's time to get up and you're in a rush. It was still dark outside and my bedroom was cold. Any other day, I might have been tempted to close my eyes and cosy down in the warmth of the duvet, pretending I'd overslept, but I had a bus to catch, and there was no way I was going to let this chance slip away from me.

The air in the bathroom was so chilly my breath steamed up the mirror as I stood there barefoot on the cold lino, trying to make myself beautiful. My hair has never done what it's told, and that day it looked like a straw hat. When I tried to style it with a hairdryer, I ended up resembling a fluff ball. I could hear the rain sheeting down outside, so I was going to have to wear a headscarf anyway. There was nothing to be done about it.

At least I had a nice frock, even it was a wee bit dressy for six o'clock in the morning! Gold lace, with a gold satin ribbon at the waist, I'd bought it for my nephew's wedding the previous year. I'd found it in a shop in the nearby town of Livingston and it had cost a tidy penny, but it was a special occasion and I thought I looked good in it. At the reception, I'd worn the dress with a white jacket, white shoes and natural-coloured tights, but the morning of the audition—I don't know what possessed me—I decided to pull on black tights. Black tights and a gold dress with white shoes, for God's sake, Susan, do not match! But I didn't know that then.

I put my head round the living-room door to say good-bye to my cat, Pebbles, but she was sensibly fast asleep in the hearth. Just before leaving the house I touched the gold chain round my neck that has my mother's wedding ring on it. Wearing it makes me feel she's close.

"Here we go then," I said, closing the front door behind me.

Sometimes when I look back at that moment, I feel there must have been some sign that my life was about to change, but if anything it was the opposite. There was nothing auspicious at all about that rainy, grey dawn. In fact, it felt like one of those days when the sun never seems to come up.

They call this part of Scotland the Wet Valley because we get more than our fair share of rain. Some people say the next generation is going to be born with webbed feet! Sling-back, peep-toe white shoes are certainly not the most suitable footwear on a rainy winter morning and the water was seeping in through all the gaps.

There were one or two lights on in the neighbours' upstairs windows, but it was still too early for most people to be up and about. A dog that had been out all night shivered in the dripping shelter of a doorstep. I saw a couple of men leaving their houses for the early shift, their coat collars up, lunch boxes under their arms. They didn't take any notice of me, which was just as well because, teetering along on heels like stilts, I was in quite a mood.

Was I completely mad? All the doubts I'd had about what I was doing began to resurface as I walked down the road I used to take to school towards a challenge that was more daunting than anything I'd ever faced before. The comments my brothers and sisters had made at Christmas, when I told them I'd got an audition for *Britain's Got Talent*, kept repeating in my head.

"Do you know what they do on *Britain's Got Talent*? They laugh at you! They boo you! They buzz you! Can you take all that?"

"If you put yourself in the arena, you've got to take the chance, haven't you?" I'd defended myself.

"Oh my God! Don't go there! Not with that Piers Morgan!"

"Just leave it," I'd told them.

"Well, don't be surprised if you don't get through."

"Thanks for your faith in me. Smashing people, you!"

I'd stuck up for myself all right, but inside I'd been thinking, Oh my God! What have I done?

As I hurried along, dodging puddles and

potholes, half of me was wanting to turn back to the safety of my nice warm home and the other half was desperate not to miss the bus. When I reached the main road, the bus was nearer to the stop than I was and I had to run like mad, which is not easy with cold, wet feet in three-inch heels. The doors opened with a hiss and I climbed on, my chest heaving, face pink, and my hair plastered down under my scarf.

"Well," I said to myself, sinking gratefully into my seat. "My worries are over now."

The bus from Blackburn took me into Glasgow, where I had to change and get another bus to the Scottish Exhibition and Conference Centre (SECC), an enormous complex of halls in the middle of the city beside the River Clyde. The rush-hour traffic was building now and the bus wasn't making much progress. I kept looking at my watch, then out of the window. I could see the conference centre in the distance, but it seemed to be inching further away, not closer. It suddenly dawned on me that I was on the wrong bus and I had to push through the crowds to get off.

I got on the next one that came along, but that was going in a different direction as well.

Now I was beginning to panic. Calm down, Susan. I told myself the logical thing to do was cross the road and take a bus going the other way.

"There's plenty of time," the bus driver told me.
"There's not!"

"The world's not going to blow up."

"It's OK for you, but I've got an audition to go to!"

He gave me a look.

It was lucky I had a bus pass because I travelled on six buses that morning before I finally arrived!

There was a queue outside and a young lad next to me was shivering in a short-sleeved shirt.

"I tried for *The X Factor*," he said, "but I got nowhere."

"Well, never mind," I told him. "Perhaps you'll do better in this."

Then the doors opened and everyone cheered. As we all went in, there was a great banner saying "Welcome to *Britain's Got Talent!*"

The letter I had received about my audition said it was at 9:30 and I was there by 9:30, just, but the lassie at reception looked at her list, her eyes running up and down several times before she said that she hadn't got me down for the 9:30 audition. She suggested I go home and come back later.

"And go through all that rigmarole with the buses again?" I protested. "You've got to be kidding!"

"Well, you'll have to wait in the holding room," she said, looking at me warily. "We'll try to fit you in. But it may be some time," she warned, as she handed me my number.

The concourse was light and warm and buzzing with energy and noise. There were crowds of people, like a great big circus: dance groups with bright costumes and feathers, singers, kids, magicians, cats, dogs, even rabbits. I saw people weeping, I saw people shouting, I saw people fighting, I saw people laughing—the lot! I sat in the corner minding my own business. I'm quite a shy and reserved person if you can believe that, but people spoke to me and they were generally very friendly. The banter was good. The atmosphere was good. I chatted to a nice guy in a white suit who sang with a funny voice. I think he got through to the semi-finals.

From time to time they'd call a list of acts to go through to the audition and those people would get themselves lined up. The air would be thick with nerves and a hush would fall for a wee while as they left. One by one, you'd see them come back, some crying, some snarling with anger, others screaming with joy! It was a great feeling to see the Yeses being put through, but as the day went on I started to wonder how many Yeses there were and whether there would be any left for me.

As I'd had such an early start and hadn't thought to bring any food with me, I was beginning to get very hungry. I could feel my stomach going, but I said to myself that I'd better stay put in case they wanted me. I couldn't risk going and getting myself something to eat in case my name was called while I was gone. When one of a group of dancers standing quite near me opened up her lunch box, I must have looked over, because she asked, "Would you like a sandwich?"

I said thank you very much. It was a nice salad sandwich and it went down a bomb! I didn't realize I was being filmed as I sat there munching away, but the camera stayed on me for some reason. I thought they'd forgotten all about me, actually.

I could see Ant and Dec wandering around, which was exciting at first, because I'd seen them on *Saturday Night Takeaway* and they looked just the same—better, in fact, but don't tell them that!—but they didn't seem to be interested in me. I watched them talking to the guy in the white suit. I saw them interviewing lots of other people, and I was starting to think that maybe they didn't want me. The funny thing was that, instead of making me feel depressed, it seemed to put me in a fighting mood. I thought, I'm not going home now—why should I? They're not going to get rid of me that easily!

Finally it was my turn to be interviewed. I told them that I lived alone, with Pebbles of course. Then, I don't know what possessed me, but I mentioned that I'd never been kissed. It was not, as I said at the time, an advertisement! That really got me into trouble, and I'll tell you all about that later. I've learned to be a wee bit more reserved when I'm interviewed now.

At about 7:30 in the evening I finally heard my

name called out among a whole list, so I took my turn in the queue and handed over the CD of the backing track that I'd brought with me. I hadn't actually felt nervous most of the day, but now my tummy started going nineteen to the dozen. After all that waiting, suddenly there wasn't any time at all and I was standing at the side of the stage with Ant and Dec. They asked me if I was nervous and I told them I was in a fighting mood, but my hands were shaking, my mouth had gone dry and I was wishing I'd gone to the toilet. Then they told me to go on.

I said to myself, "Well, you can either be damn cheeky or you can be nervous and let yourself down, but for heaven's sake get yourself out there somehow!" And so I marched on to the stage, hand on hip, this wee wifey from Blackburn with the tousled hair and the gold dress, knees knocking.

The glare from the lights meant I couldn't see the judges at first, but when Simon Cowell spoke to me he was to my right, with Amanda Holden in the middle and Piers Morgan on the left. Simon started on the usual stuff about who I was and where I was from.

"My name is Susan Boyle," I told him. "I am forty-seven years old."

And then I added, "And that's just one side of me."

And I did a wiggle, which was aimed at Piers, because I like Piers. He was one of the reasons I wanted to do the show. Piers just stared at me, his lips pursed.

I could see that they were thinking, "Oh my God, who is this apparition?" But I hoped that maybe they were also thinking, "At least she's different!"

Simon asked me where I was from and whether Blackburn was a big town, and my mind went blank. I was so nervous I forgot the word for village, and I could see his eyes were rolling. I learned later that the judges were in a bad mood because it had been a long day and they'd seen very few talented acts. Simon was ready for a cup of tea.

I could hear a few titters in the audience. I was aware that I was being laughed at, but I've been ridiculed a lot in my life so I've learned how to be resilient. Instead of being hurt and saying, right, I'm coming off, I thought I'd show them what I could do.

Simon asked me what my song was, so I told him it was "I Dreamed a Dream" from *Les Misérables*. I'd chosen that song because at the time I could identify with a lot of the emotions in it. I had recently lost my mother and I was still getting over the shock of being alone, because she'd been with me all my life. So I was lonely and depressed because I didn't think my life would change. It's a powerful song.

Simon said, "Are you prepared to do another song?"

They cut this bit out of the video that appeared on television.

That threw me. My second song was "The Power of Love," but I didn't think I sang it as well as "I Dreamed a Dream." I didn't want to miss my chance, but "I Dreamed a Dream" was the song I wanted to sing. So I looked Simon in the eye and said, "Well, I'm prepared to sing another song if required, but what's in the machine is 'I Dreamed a Dream' from *Les Mis*."

To my relief, he heaved a weary sigh and told me to go ahead. I gave Ant the thumbs up.

As I listened to the pretty opening notes of the introduction, I became aware for the first time of the size of the audience in front of me. There were thousands of people, row upon row banked up behind the judges, and they were all watching me in anticipation. I knew what they were thinking. "Just look at her! She's got a bum like a garage, a head like a mop, I'm not too sure if her teeth are her own, and she's claiming to be a singer! She cannae sing. She cannae! Well come on, let's hear you then . . ."

So I opened my mouth and showed them what I could do . . .

Part One

When I Was a Child

1
Welcome to the Boyle Family

My story really starts on 1 April 1961, the day I was born. Whenever I go past it now, Bangour Hospital looks a sad, deserted place, because it has been closed down and all the services transferred to St. John's Hospital in Livingston. The listed Victorian buildings stand derelict and abandoned awaiting development into flats, if the local economy ever starts to turn around.

In 1961, however, Bangour was a thriving model hospital built in the form of a village on a hillside. It led the world in some medical fields and the maternity unit served the whole of West Lothian. When my mother arrived there in labour, the hillside was bright with golden daffodils and the sight of spring lifted her spirits for a moment. She was apprehensive. Having given birth to eight children over a period of twenty-three years, she had been advised not to have any more because of physical complications, but when she was forty-five along came yours truly. The doctors considered the danger so severe that they offered a termination, but, as a devout Catholic, that would have been unthinkable for my mother. She wanted to give this new life a chance.

It was two weeks before I was due and my mother was suffering from high blood pressure and edema. During the birth it was touch and go for her as well as for me, but, eventually, I was born by emergency Caesarean section.

When my mother came round from the anaesthetic, the doctor was looking at her very seriously.

"You have a girl," he told her. "She's very small and she needs help with her respiration, so we have her in an incubator."

There was none of the usual, "Congratulations, Mrs. Boyle! A beautiful baby girl!"

When my father appeared at my mother's bedside, she knew immediately that something was wrong.

"She was starved of oxygen for a wee while," he said.

Although the words hadn't yet been spoken, my mother was an intelligent woman and she knew what that meant.

"She's all arms and legs, like a wee frog!" my father told her, smiling.

It was a few weeks before my parents were allowed to take me home. The doctors had explained that it was likely that I had suffered slight brain damage caused by perinatal asphyxia.

"It's probably best to accept that Susan will never be anything. Susan will never come to anything, so don't expect too much of her."

I'm sure they had the best intentions, but I don't think they should have said that, because nobody can foretell the future. What they didn't know was that I'm a bit of a fighter, and I've been trying all my life to prove them wrong.

In those days, people like my parents thought that doctors knew everything. It must have been very shocking news, especially as my mother was still fragile after the birth. They'd had eight kids who in their eyes were perfectly "normal," although their second little girl, Patricia, had died in infancy. Then along comes this baby with problems. How on earth were they going to cope with that at their late stage in life?

To make matters worse, although I was just a tiny wee thing, I had a pair of lungs that would frighten the French!

When they brought me home from hospital, I used to keep my dad up all night with my bawling. He'd roar at me to shut up, so much that a neighbour actually spoke to him about it, but the poor man was a miner and had to get up to do a hard day's work. My father actually helped a lot with looking after me because my mother had suffered a kind of mini-stroke and had temporarily lost the use of her right hand. He was quite good at getting me to sleep in my pram during the day, but only if he was wearing his red sweater. I seemed to be able to distinguish between colours at that early age. Funnily enough, red is still my favourite colour, but the family were all sick of looking at that red sweater.

In the mornings my oldest sister, Mary, who, at twenty-three, had recently qualified as a teacher, used to bathe me and dress me, and during the long summer evenings she would push me round Blackburn in my pram. When I was settled, I was a smiling baby with a head of soft, dark curls. Neighbours used to look into the pram and coo over what a lovely wee curly-haired thing I was— the ones who weren't within earshot at night, that is.

The Boyle family were fairly recent newcomers to Blackburn. It's a small town about fifteen miles outside Edinburgh, just off the M8. My parents originally came from Motherwell, a larger industrial town on the outskirts of Glasgow. My father, Patrick Boyle, served in the army during the war, but afterwards he found employment as a miner. Every night he used to catch a bus from Motherwell to the pit near Whitburn, the next town along from Blackburn.

My sister Bridie tells the story of him tucking them up at night, saying, "It's all right for you lassies going to your bed when your daddy's going away on a cold, cold bus . . ."

And she and Mary chorusing, "Don't go, Daddy, don't go!"

In 1949 the bus was discontinued and my father

had to decide between unemployment or moving closer to the pit. I don't think my mother was very happy about leaving her roots in Motherwell, but she had no choice.

Blackburn was like a lot of small communities. If you haven't got ancestors in the graveyard, you don't belong, and so my father and mother were always very anxious to be seen as respectable members of the community. My mother, whose Christian name was Bridget, was Bridie to her friends in Motherwell, but she was always Mrs. Boyle in Blackburn. She dressed and behaved like a lady. My parents lived in a brand-new council house with a garden and a lawn that my dad tended so carefully that his growing family of children weren't allowed to play on it.

At the time, Blackburn was a wee village with no streetlights, and to Mary and Bridie and their younger siblings Joe, Kathleen, John, James and Gerard, who arrived at regular intervals throughout the forties and fifties, it was a country playground. They used to roam the nearby fields, dig up potatoes and bake them in little campfires. As teenagers they used to reminisce about the idyllic times they'd shared in their first house, and I used to listen entranced, wishing I'd been around when they were all having so much fun together.

When my mother fell pregnant with me, the family needed more room, and this is how we came to move to Yule Terrace and the house where

I have lived ever since arriving back from Bangour Hospital in my Moses basket. It's a standard semidetached council house with a dining room at the front, a living room at the back, a small kitchen downstairs and three bedrooms and a bathroom upstairs. My four brothers were in the back bedroom, my three sisters in the small room at the front. It was the beginning of the sixties. Elvis Presley was on the radio. You can imagine the noise. And that was before I arrived!

Traditionally, as a ninth child, I should have been baptized by a cardinal, but a new Catholic church was being built in Blackburn and it wasn't ready, so instead I was baptized Susan Magdalane Boyle by our local priest, Father Michael McNulty. My godmother was my sister Mary.

During the day, my white Moses basket was set in the corner of the living room at the back of the house. My babysitter was a budgie called Jokey. I can't remember him, of course, but my mother insisted that the wee bird used to know when I was about to cry and he would ring his bell. That would distract me as I looked to see where the noise was coming from. You could call it my first musical training.

There is a photograph of my mother holding me, taken when I was about six months old. I am still small for my age. I'm wearing a bonnet and a white matinee jacket and booties. Unusually, I am asleep. My mother looks very thin and frail. You can tell she has not been well, but there is determination in her eyes. She looks like a woman who has not had an easy time, but has found the strength to go on. She has both hands firmly clasped around me. For me, the photograph sums up our relationship. My mother guided me and I relied on her. She was the lodestone of my life.

2
Bel Air and Beehives

Memory is like a jukebox: push the right button with a song, a photograph or even a smell and you're transported straight back to a time and a place.

The contrast between my life now and my life before *Britain's Got Talent* could not be greater. One of the many things that's different—one of the nice things, actually—is having my hair and make-up done. It's quite calming to sit in a chair getting pampered. What woman wouldn't want to get used to that? When the finishing touches are being made to my hair, the sweet, sticky scent of the hairspray always takes me back to the choking cloud of Bel Air in the girls' bedroom at home.

My sister Bridie used to kneel on the bed so she could see herself in the dressing-table mirror as she backcombed her hair and got herself ready to go out. The bedroom was just big enough to fit a small wardrobe, the dressing table and the double bed, in which Mary, Bridie and Kathleen slept top to toe. Bridie was a sixties chick, with a pink shift dress and beehive hairdo. In the photos of the time, she looks like a model. Even though she was grown up and working at the Plessey electronics factory, she still had to ask Dad if she could go out in the evening.

"Where are you going?"

"Don't know," Bridie would tell him, with a defiant shrug.

But she did know. She was going out dancing to the Palais in Bathgate.

"What time will you be back in?"

"Don't know."

"Well, I'll tell you what time you'll be back," says my dad. "You'll be back at ten o'clock!"

Sometimes he wouldn't allow her out at all. It was tame by today's standards, but the Palais had a reputation for fights and my dad was protective. Once, when he thought Bridie was safe upstairs, she put a mirror up on the grill of the cooker to check her make-up and, with a quick whoosh from the squeezy bottle of Bel Air, she hoisted up her mini-skirt and climbed out the kitchen window!

I can still feel the tingle of terror and anticipation when my dad discovered that she'd gone out, and the rest of us kids tried to cover for her. She got a row when she came in! One day, she didn't dare to come back but spent the night at a pal's. When my dad found her, she told him she wasn't coming home because she wanted to be able to go out dancing. Not many people were brave enough to stand up to my dad, because he could make a bit of noise, but he told her, fair enough, you can go out. He wasn't an ogre or a bully and he was only strict because he loved his children and wanted to do the right thing.

31

• • •

One by one, my older siblings began to spread their wings and leave home. A year after I was born, Mary was married and moved to a flat of her own. She raised a family of five children as well as teaching at our local primary school, Our Lady of Lourdes. My oldest brother, Joe, who is the most academic of the Boyle children, went to university, married and moved away. He was training to be a teacher too, but was put off when some of the pupils at the school where he was doing teaching practice trundled a piano down a corridor and pushed it into the swimming pool. That's when he decided teaching wasn't for him.

As the youngest child, I watched with curiosity as the older ones got themselves dressed up, ready for exciting adventures in the world outside. It was a mystery to me what they were doing, because my experiences of the world outside our house weren't very pleasant at all.

Every so often I was taken for hospital appointments, and as the time approached, the atmosphere at home would change. My mother, who always used to sing as she did her housework, fell silent and she was a wee bit less patient when I pestered her with questions. I think she probably worried about what the doctors might be going to tell her. My screaming had become worse with teething and I suffered fits and febrile convulsions. It took a long time for me to learn to walk. I had to undergo all sorts of tests at the Royal Hospital for Sick Children, including a lumbar puncture for suspected meningitis and a brain scan for epilepsy.

At that time, the word "Edinburgh" to me meant a silent journey, dressed in my best clothes, in a car that felt as if it was crammed with words that couldn't be spoken. It always seemed to be raining, and as I peered out through the rivulets running down the window, dark sooty buildings rose like straight-sided crags, so high I couldn't see the sky above, however much I craned my neck.

Inside, the hospital smelled funny, and there were long corridors with squeaky floors.

It was always, "Be quiet, Susan!" and "Don't do that, Susan!"

I didn't like it at all.

Sometimes the doctors would give me toys to play with and watch what I was doing, but then they'd take the toys away. If that was designed to make me scream, it worked.

One day, as a treat afterwards, we went for a walk by the sea in Portobello, one of Edinburgh's coastal suburbs. A salty sea breeze blew the nasty hospital smells from our clothes. My dad bought me a wee teddy bear. I called it Boo Boo and I hung on to it for dear life. I wasn't going to let anyone ever take Boo Boo away from me.

I was diagnosed as hyperactive, and I was slower at learning things than other children because I was easily distracted. Nowadays it would probably be called Attention Deficit Hyperactivity Disorder, but in the sixties they didn't have the knowledge that they have now and if you were hyperactive it was treated as a mental illness. I believe it was wrong to give me that label, because it had a particular resonance for my mum and dad. There was much more stigma attached to learning disability in those days. My mother had a younger brother, Michael, who suffered from learning and emotional problems. He had been sent to a special school and then kept in an institution for most of his life. I think my parents assumed that I would be like him, and that narrowed their expectations for me.

But I'm not like Uncle Michael—not that he wasn't a very nice man. You'll meet him later on.

3
The Sound of Music

There was always music in our house. My mother was always singing as she went about her chores, and in the front room the piano stool was full of sheet music—mostly Irish songs, because my mother's family, the McLaughlins, came from a wee village outside Derry in Northern Ireland. My mother had taken piano lessons in her youth and given recitals in Motherwell, so sometimes she would play and my father would sing. He had a lovely tenor voice, but he never got the chance to perform professionally, which is a pity, because I think that is what he would have most liked to do. In those days there weren't the opportunities for ordinary people. During the war, he did try to apply for the entertainment division of the forces, ENSA, but he was informed by his commanding officers in the Royal Engineers that he was needed for the war effort and threatened with a charge if he tried to apply again. Even though he was disappointed, my father took pride in being a good soldier and went on to become a sergeant major. He did manage to sing once on Radio Hamburg, in a show the forces put on, but for the rest of his life his audience was his family.

I must have been about four when *The Sound of*

Music came out. Dad bought the record and got us all singing along. My sister Mary has a beautiful voice and now sings in a choir. The boys were good singers too. John has something of Gene Pitney in his voice, while Gerard is more like Neil Diamond. It's something the Boyles do particularly well. We were like the von Trapps. Like the Captain, my father was a military man. The only thing he didn't have was the whistle, but he didn't need one to keep us all in line!

Singing was a sign that my father was happy. On Saturday evenings he used to sit singing in his chair in the living room. As we ate our tea in the dining room, my mother would smile and tell us, "That's him getting ready to go for a pint!"

The song we all remember him singing is "That Lucky Old Sun." The song had been a hit for Frankie Laine in 1949, and I suppose to my father, it was one of the pop songs of his youth. He didn't have much time for the pop songs of our youth, but he did like the Shadows, because he said they were the only ones who could play their instruments. My father used to spend what spare money he had on LPs. He was a great admirer of Josef Locke, and he also loved to listen to Caruso and Mario Lanza.

My brother Joe bought a guitar when he was at university, and, like a typical student, mournfully strummed the chords of "House of the Rising Sun" by the Animals and wrote songs in his bedroom.

John, James and Gerard used to take turns to play as well. The boys' bedroom was a no-go area in our house. Four teenage boys create quite a hum, and I don't mean in the musical sense. They used to put their socks on the windowsill outside to try to keep the atmosphere fresh. It didn't really work!

At the end of the week, Bridie would often come in from work and go straight to the red-and-white Elizabethan record player in the living room, take the lid off and put on the latest Elvis single she'd bought with her wages. Bridie was mad about Elvis.

Thursday was the night when all the kids gathered round the telly to watch *Top of the Pops*. One of the first presents I can remember is the toy banjo my mother bought me. It was yellow and red and I used to hold it like Paul McCartney, strumming along with the groups on the screen. Our love of pop music cut across age differences. A truce was called on bickering as we all focused on the screen, watching the latest bands and waiting excitedly to see who was going to be at the top. There were some great artists around then, like Cilla Black, Dusty Springfield, and two very odd-looking types with long hair and funny jackets called Sonny and Cher, who sang "I Got You Babe." Some of the songs from that time are still classics today, like "You'll Never Walk Alone" by Gerry and the Pacemakers. It became the anthem of Liverpool Football Club, but the supporters of the football team in Blackburn used to sing "You'll Never Walk Again," because they were hackers!

Neither of my parents was very big. My father was a strong, sturdy man, but not tall, and my mother was a wee, spritely woman. But when they sang, their presence filled the house. My mother sang songs from musicals as she cooked and cleaned, and at night she would softly sing songs like "The Dream Man Cometh" to lull me to sleep. The one I heard most often was "Babes in the Wood":

> *Oh don't you remember*
> *A long time ago*
> *Two poor little babes*
> *Their names I don't know,*
> *They strayed far away*
> *On a bright summer's day,*
> *These two little babes*
> *Got lost of their way?*
>
> *And when it was night*
> *So sad was their plight*
> *The sun it went down*
> *And the moon gave no light.*
> *They sobbed and they sighed*
> *And they bitterly cried*
> *And long before morning they*
> *   lay down and died.*

And when they were dead
The robins so red
Brought strawberry leaves
And over them spread
And all day long
On the branches did throng
They mournfully whistled
And this was their song:

Poor babes in the wood
Poor babes in the wood!
Oh don't you remember
Those babes in the wood!

It's a very sad song, but my mother had a wicked sense of humour and she used to sing it to all her children, and later on her grandchildren, to see which of them would be the first to break into tears.

I didn't cry. I didn't go to sleep either, but sat up in bed asking "What happened to them?" "What were they doing in the wood?" "What did they die for?" "Is it because they didn't behave themselves?"

My mother would sigh wearily and try to think of another strategy.

From birth to the age of about three, I seemed to be able to defy sleep—but if I wasn't tired, everyone around me was. My mother tried everything but a hammer to get me to go off. Once, in the midst of her repertoire of lullabies, she was suddenly aware that the room had miraculously fallen silent. My eyes were closed, my breathing was even. Very tentatively she rose from the end of bed and tiptoed slowly across the darkened room. She was within inches of the door and daring joyfully to anticipate a few hours of peace, when she stepped on a toy sheep I called Larry the Lamb which had a squeak.

Up I sat.

"I want another song!"

4
The Girl with the Curls

There was a little girl, who had a little curl . . .
When she was good, she was very very good
But when she was bad, she was horrid.

When I was child, I was a bonny wee thing with curly hair. I existed in my own little world, like most children do. I had my toys and my constant companion, Boo Boo. That was all I knew. I wasn't aware of being slightly different from other children. The only difference I knew about was that, as the wee bairn, I wasn't allowed to do things that my older siblings could do, like stay up late, and that made me cross.

In every family the baby gets teased, and I was as gullible as any other child. My brothers invented a character called Peter Noddy and told me he was out the back of the house waiting for me. I used to trot out to see this Peter Noddy and then one of my brothers would jump out and roar at me. I fell for it every time and it made me scared.

When the older ones used to chat away about places they had been and things they had done, I didn't know what they were talking about, and that made me feel excluded.

41

With ten people in a small house, it's difficult to get yourself heard. But I found a way. I used to scream. Then people knew I was there.

Terrible twos is a phase most children go through, but unfortunately mine extended to terrible threes and fours as well.

"If you don't stop that screaming you'll go to Wall House," my mother used to threaten.

"What's Wall House?"

"That's an orphanage where they send the wee bairns."

That made me scream even more.

My brothers and sisters would tell you that my parents were inclined to indulge me more than they did their other kids, partly because I was the baby and partly because they put my behaviour down to the slight brain damage I'd suffered at birth. It caused some resentment, because the older ones saw me getting away with behaviour they were never allowed, but if they tried to criticize me my mother gave them a row.

"You be quiet. You know she can't help it."

There were also times, however, when my siblings used my screaming to their own benefit.

My brothers were great fans of the Rolling Stones. My mother and father didn't approve. On Thursday nights we'd all be watching *Top of the Pops* when Dad came in from a long day at work and he did not appreciate the noise. He used to walk across the room and turn the volume down decisively. I'd start to cry and my brothers would goad me on when Dad was out in the kitchen.

"Keep on doing that, hen, and we'll get to see the programme!"

And more often than not, my father would decide that the sound of *Top of the Pops* was preferable to the racket I was making.

There was one place that I did not scream so much and that was in church. My mother and father were very devout Catholics. My mother used to go to church every morning and every evening. Before we went to bed each night we always used to get down on our knees to say our prayers. My mother believed that a family that prays together stays together and on Sunday mornings we always walked to Our Lady of Lourdes for nine o'clock Mass. There must have been rainy Sundays, windy Sundays and snowy Sundays, but the only Sundays I can recall are sunny days when the sky was a fresh blue and the air full of birdsong.

Nobody could call our council estate in Blackburn a pretty place. The houses are unadorned and utilitarian, their exterior walls rendered in pebble-dash in grim shades of grey or brown. Some folk make an effort with their front gardens, but mostly they are laid to scrubby lawn or turned into spaces for the dustbins. But sunshine can turn pebble-dash render honey-gold and make geraniums in a window box as bright as stained glass.

My father always dressed smartly for church, in a suit and tie; my mother wore a dress and a mantilla. She had such a petite frame that she had all her clothes made for her. All of us kids were nicely turned out. I was lucky, because the boys and the older girls had all had to wear hand-me-downs, but being so much younger I was bought brand-new clothes. My favourite was a blue-and-white polka-dot dress that I wore with a white cardigan with a brown pattern on it. With my ringlets and my white knee-high socks, I looked like a wee Shirley Temple.

Catholicism is more than a religion to Scottish Catholics. It is also an identity, and my father was very proud to lead his fine family along the street to Mass. It was a great disappointment to my parents when two of my siblings married people who were not Catholics, and it caused a lot of arguments and tension at home that I was far too young to understand.

Our Lady of Lourdes church in Blackburn was completed in the year of my birth. Inside it seemed enormous to me. Light poured in through the high windows and the air was cool, with a scent all of its own of flowers and floor polish and hymn books. As we walked through the door the constant hubbub of life was suddenly stilled. The ceiling was very high and there was a slight echo that made our responses during the Mass sound as if they were going up to heaven where Jesus stayed.

I found the ritual and repetition of the Mass very soothing, and I liked it when the organist played the first notes of a hymn and then everyone started singing. My father always sang more softly in church than he did at home, and even at a young age I understood this as a sign of his humility in God's presence, although I wouldn't have known the word then.

In a wee side chapel to the right of the altar stands a statue of Our Lady, carved from wood and looking very kind and beautiful. My mother, who had a great devotion to Our Lady, explained to me that she was the mother of Jesus.

"Did Mary laugh? Did Mary play with Jesus like we do?" I asked her.

"I'm sure she did," replied my mother.

"Did Mary give Jesus a row?" I asked.

"No, because Jesus behaved himself!"

My mother tried to explain how Mary was an ordinary woman, but that being chosen to be the mother of Jesus had put her on a different plane that made her a very special model of faith and charity for everyone.

"For me too?" I asked.

"Of course for you," said my mother. "If you pray to Our Lady, she will help you."

I loved my mother very much and trusted her above everyone else. I thought it was a great idea that there was another maternal presence who would look after me as well.

I think the beginning of my faith derived from that knowledge.

After Mass, the family walked home together and my mother would cook our Sunday lunch. In the afternoons we sometimes went for a drive. My dad was working at the British Leyland plant in Bathgate by then, and he'd bought an old Bedford van with a sliding door. It was a bright turquoise-blue colour outside and had red leatherette seats inside. You could have your tea in the back. That van took us everywhere, although there was always something wrong with the engine. It used to splutter and backfire. Once it broke down. My dad looked under the bonnet and asked if any of us had any chewing gum. One of the boys dutifully removed his gum from his mouth and my dad used it to block up a hole until it could be properly fixed! On Sunday afternoons our destination was usually Motherwell, to see my mother's brother Michael, who lived in a wee room down a long corridor in a great big hospital called Hartwood.

Sometimes, in the summer, we'd head for the coast. Our family didn't have holidays as such because there wasn't the money for it, so our jaunts to the seaside on Sunday afternoons were special times. Like most children, I loved the beach. I can remember the sensation of the freezing cold sand between my toes as I paddled, then the firm hands of my father swooping in and grabbing me just in time to stop me plonking my bottom down in the water and ruining my polka-dot dress.

On Sunday evenings my father often sang his party piece, "Scarlet Ribbons." Though it has the sound of an old Irish folk song, and has been recorded by many artists, including the Fureys, Sinéad O'Connor and my father's favourite, Jim Reeves, the song was actually written in America in 1949. Whenever I sing it now, it reminds me of my father's strongly held faith and his love for his children.

I sometimes wonder if my dad had a particular affection for the song because it tells of a small miracle that happens to a wee sleeping lassie.

5
Sticks and Stones

As I grew older, I became aware that there was a place called school that all my brothers and my sister Kathleen disappeared to during the day. I liked it when they left because then it was just me and my mother together. While she cleaned and tidied our house, singing all the time, I played with my doll's house, which had a red roof that came off. Once a week my mother took me to the library, where she always took out four big books, which she would read and exchange for new ones the following week. I don't know how she found the time, but she was a great reader who devoured history books and biographies as well as novels. I was introduced to reading at an early age, because my mother bought me a magazine called *Once Upon a Time*. There were great stories and illustrations in it, as well as little bits of history. The stories I liked best were about a cheeky rabbit called Brer Rabbit who was always tricking people.

My mother was a storyteller too. She had not had an easy life, having lost her father in the First World War and her beloved mother to cancer when she was only nineteen. She was employed as a shorthand typist for a while, then at twenty she married my dad. They had been at the same school together. Sometimes my father used to joke that he'd been shanghaied into marrying her, but in the wedding photo he looks like the cat who got the cream, with my mother looking very pretty in her pale blue wedding dress and big picture hat. In those days, people didn't go on honeymoons—there wasn't enough money—so my parents went to the pictures on their wedding night, and that was that. Not exactly a fairytale beginning.

The wedding was in 1936 and all too soon there was another war. My father went away to serve in the forces, leaving my mother with two bitsy bairns, Mary and Bridie, to rear all on her own in Motherwell. It must have been terrifying for her during the bombing raids, but the stories she told were always about how people kept their spirits up. There was a funny one about a neighbour during an air raid who wanted to run back home to retrieve her false teeth. "Those are bombs they're dropping, not pies!" people shouted at her. My mother and the two wee lassies, sheltering under the kitchen table, could hear the clip clop of frightened horses who'd broken loose on the cobbles outside. She sang songs to keep them all calm. My mother could sing "Lili Marlene" just like Marlene Dietrich.

I think I must have picked up the ability to mimic from her. In the afternoons, when children's television came on, I liked to stand in front of the television imitating what was happening on the screen, shouting "Bobbob Bill! Bobbob Ben! Bobbob, Little Weed! Weeeed!" at the end of *Bill and Ben the Flower Pot Men*. And singing "Here We Go Looby Loo" when *Andy Pandy* was on, although my dancing was more like the clumsy Teddy than the rag doll Looby Loo. At the end of the programme, when they sang "Andy Is Waving Good-bye!," I sat transfixed, waving at the screen, with my mother hee-hawing behind me.

The daftest programme was *The Woodentops*. It was obvious that they were puppets because you could see all the strings! Spotty Dog had ears that went up and down, and Mrs. Scubbit had a duster attached to her hand, so she probably had to sleep with it at night as well. They spoke a language my mother called the Queen's English, which sounded very different from the way we talked. When I imitated them, my mother used to laugh until there were tears in her eyes.

My mother had a brilliant sense of humour herself. People used to say that she could make a cat laugh. When Bridie brought home a wee black-and-white cat called Twizzle to stay with us, I watched her closely but I never did catch her hee-hawing.

I would have been very happy to continue for ever being on my own with my mum, playing with Twizzle and my toys, but one day we had to make the journey to the Royal Hospital for Sick

Children so that I could have something called an assessment.

"What's an assessment?" I asked.

Although she was very protective of me, my mother never talked down to me, so I developed quite a grown-up turn of phrase for my age.

"It's a test to see what sort of school you can go to," she told me.

I didn't like the sound of that at all. Tests were when they gave you toys, then took them away. Today there was one to do with putting shapes through holes in a box. I was feeling tired because I'd been up all night as usual, and it seemed to take for ever to get the shapes to go in the right places. I wasn't helped by this bald-headed man who was staring at me as I tried, and writing words on a piece of paper.

Afterwards, I listened to him talking to my mother. The word he kept using was "borderline." Then he shook my mother's hand and said, "I bet my bottom dollar that Susan can be as good as anyone else. It's just that she's tired."

My mother seemed very happy about that. The frown had gone from her face and she bought me some sweeties on the way home, a quarter of strawberry bonbons, weighed out from a big jar and covered in pink dust that made my fingers sticky. When my father came home from work that evening and she told him the news, he picked me up in the air and gave me a very tight squeeze.

"What's borderline?" I asked my mother that night when she kissed me goodnight.

"It means you can go to the same school as your brother Gerard," she told me. "You're not special-school material."

In other words, it meant I had passed my test. But I didn't understand that until much later.

The following September, when I was four and a half years old, my mother dressed me in a wee grey pinafore dress, combed my hair into two tight bunches, and held my hand firmly as we walked to school with Gerard tagging along behind us.

Our Lady of Lourdes Primary School is situated literally just round the corner from our house, but when my mother let go of my hand and left me there, it felt like a foreign country. The playground was buzzing with children rushing around. I wasn't used to the company of children my own age. Although I had lots of brothers and sisters, because I was so much younger than they were my upbringing was much more like that of an only child. I didn't know what I was supposed to do.

"There's to be no bawling, or screaming. You don't do that at school," my mother and my sister Mary had warned me on many occasions.

The last thing on my mind was bawling and drawing attention to myself. I wanted to be invisible, but sometimes the more you try to disappear, the more you stand out. One by one, they stopped their games and started staring at me. I stood there, feeling like the wee antelope surrounded by lions that I'd seen on a wildlife programme on television.

The bell rang. The others lined up, but I just kept standing where I was until our teacher, Mrs. Monaghan, came and took my hand and led me in. She was a tall woman with red hair. I didn't dare say a word, but just sat with my head down, staring at the floor. It was agony trying to keep still. I stared at the clock above the blackboard, trying to remember what my mother had said about the big hand and the little hand. When they were both pointing straight up I could go home for my dinner, but they weren't moving at all. Eventually there was a clanking sound in the corridor outside and we all stared at the door as a man came in carrying a crate of milk cartons. Mrs. Monaghan gave us one each with a straw to stick through the top.

"I'm not thirsty," I told her, trying to be polite.

I hated the taste of milk. My mother was always trying to make me drink it at night to make me go to sleep, but it didn't work because it made me feel sick. The milk they gave us at school tasted even worse, warm and slightly off, as if it had been left standing in the sun.

"You have to drink your milk to make you grow, Susan," Mrs. Monaghan said.

When you're little and a teacher has a cross voice, it's scary, so I started crying, but one of the little boys jammed his straw right through the top of his carton, sending a fountain all over his jumper, and that was funny.

In the playground, the yells and shrieks of all the other children swirled around me like a whirlwind. Wherever I stood, I was in somebody's way. A boy thumped me hard on the arm and shouted, "You're it!"

I ran away to the edge of the playground and stood close to the fence so no one could come up behind me. The gate wasn't locked. Seizing the opportunity, I crept out into the street and ran all the way home.

My mother tried to look cross when she opened the door and saw me standing there, but she couldn't stop herself laughing.

"Oh, you wee terror!" she exclaimed.

"I don't want to go to school," I informed her.

"You want to be a big girl, don't you?"

I shook my head.

"Everybody has to go to school, Susan," she said.

When she said my name like that, it was a sign that I wasn't going to get my own way.

The children stared at me even more when my mum brought me back, but I didn't feel as frightened when she was there. We marched straight across the playground and into the school to see the headmaster.

I realize now that she wanted to make it known

to him that I had managed to escape without anybody noticing; at the time, I thought I was going to be in trouble.

Instead of being cross with me, the headmaster, whose name was Mr. Jordan, smiled kindly at me. "I'm sure if I lived close by I'd be nipping home as well," he said.

Later on I often tried to sneak off early, but there was always a grass who would point out my escape bid to the teacher.

"Put the chair down, Susan! It's not time to go home yet!"

For the first few years of school, I was usually at the back of the class for some reason, either because of my behaviour, or because I was last. My ability to learn seemed to follow a different pattern from other children's.

Reading wasn't a problem. I had learned to read at an early age, as my parents had discovered one day when we were out at the shops.

"I want an ice cream!" I'd demanded.

"There's no ice cream shops here," my mother tried to fool me, as parents often do.

"Yes there is!" I told her, pointing at the distinctive yellow sign. "Look—it says 'Wall's Ice Cream'!"

What I found difficult was writing my letters. My hands felt clumsy and I used to have a habit of trying to bunch the letters all up together. I don't know why. The page was a mess. It was as if there was a lack of coordination between my brain and the hand doing the writing, and that made me the slowest in the class. It took a long time before I could write properly.

I also suffered from what psychologists call cognitive difficulties. Even at a young age, I often knew the answers to questions, but I couldn't seem to get what I was thinking out of my head and into my mouth. I knew what I wanted to say, but I just couldn't say it. It was as if my thoughts kept coming up against a barrier and there was never enough time to find my way past it. It was very frustrating and it made fury boil up inside me. Sometimes that would burst out as anger, more often as tears.

At playtime, I didn't understand the hierarchies that operated in the playground. I was naturally outgoing and I didn't know why some of the other children didn't want to be my friend. There was one boy who wouldn't let you join in a game unless he told you you could. If I brought a book into school, he would tell me who I could show it to and who I couldn't, then if I got it wrong I wasn't allowed to play. The adult turn of phrase I'd picked up from spending so much time with my mother didn't really help. When I tried to please people by acting out television characters, they laughed at me, not with me. I was never sure how to express my needs or communicate in a way that would make the other children accept me. If I was excited, I laughed a bit too noisily; if I was sad or angry, I was straight into tears or a tantrum.

You know how kids are. They're very quick to perceive weakness and it was good fun to try to get a rise out of me, so they laughed at me and called me ugly names. Unfortunately, that meant that I stopped trusting anyone and became a very shy person instead.

My difficulties were exacerbated by certain medical problems that singled me out from the rest of the class. I had a very dry scalp, so when the nit nurse came round she took longer going through my hair than anyone else's. All the others gathered round peering at me, assuming I'd got nits. When I told my mother what had happened, she was straight up to the school to give the nurse a row. "I hope you haven't been saying she's got nits, because this is a clean house!"

When we were given our vaccination for polio on a sugar lump, I reacted badly to it and ended up in hospital. There always seemed to be something different about me.

To make matters worse, I had been prescribed tablets to slow down my hyperactivity, and these often made me sleepy and even slower, so that was another excuse for teasing. The medication was fairly quickly shown to have dangerous side effects, causing respiratory problems, and my doctors stopped prescribing it, but the bullying continued because it produced results. I cried, or I lashed out, and then my tormentors had the excuse to kick lumps out of me.

When you're a child, grown-ups always tell you that "sticks and stones will break your bones, but words will never hurt you." They say it as if it's a kind of spell that's going to protect you. I've never seen the logic of it. Cuts and bruises quickly heal and disappear. You forget all about them. The psychological wounds that bullies inflict with words go much deeper.

Even now, I don't like to think about those times too much, in case the scars begin to open up and hurt, making me feel useless all over again.

I don't want to give the impression that my problems were ignored, because my teachers did the best they could. My teacher in Primary 3, Mrs. Stein, could see that I wasn't stupid, and she had a lot of patience with me and got me some extra help. On Wednesdays, my mother used to pick me up at lunchtime. We'd have some soup, or my favourite spaghetti on toast, and then my dad, or my brother John if my dad was working, would drive us to Edinburgh to see a child psychologist in Royal Bank Terrace. He told my mother that I wasn't a happy child because I was very much aware that something was wrong with me and I felt guilty for being a nuisance. I think he must have been a clever man, because I can identify with what he was saying now, although I was too young to understand it then.

My parents didn't know anything about psychology. They had been told that my difficulties came from the slight brain damage I had suffered at birth and so they assumed that I couldn't help how I behaved and they always stuck up for me. Other members of the family thought that a bit less sympathy and a bit more discipline would have worked wonders—but that's the trouble with having a sister who's a teacher!

6
The Lisbon Lions and a Bear Called Bruno

It's a full-time job being my postman. A year ago, I didn't get any letters on my mat for weeks, and then it was only a bill. Now letters and gifts arrive every day from kind-hearted people all over the world. Several times each morning there'll be a knock on the door with a new delivery of flowers, or a shiny helium balloon with a cheery message. I can never get used to the excitement of tearing open packages to see what's inside. I've received poems, paintings and prayers, and each one of them means so much it can sometimes be overwhelming. People are very thoughtful. Recently, someone in America sent a wee toy cat for me to stroke when Pebbles isn't here. He's grey and white with blue eyes, and he's very soft. Actually he's much better behaved than Pebbles! I can hardly sit down on my sofa for teddy bears.

I've always loved the comfort of cuddling soft toys and when I was small I used to take them all to bed with me, along with a doll my mother had bought me for Christmas called Pouting Pretty, whose mouth turned down in a pout when you held her upside down. I always pleaded for a doll I'd seen called Giggles, who laughed when you pressed her tummy. I can now understand why my requests were denied. I made enough noise as it was. It was difficult enough for me to get to sleep with my collection of toy companions, but I wasn't the only person in the bed. When Bridie left home, I had moved out of my parents' bedroom and into the girls' double bed with Kathleen.

Not many teenagers would appreciate having their hyperactive wee sister and all her toys in bed with them, but Kathleen was a very special person. My sister Bridie had inherited the same fair colouring as my mother, but my sister Kathleen, with her darker hair and sparkling Irish eyes, was more like my mother in nature. She was gentle and compassionate, and as the middle one of the children, she was like the centre of our family.

My other sisters and brothers always thought they had the right to tell me what to do because I was the youngest, but Kathleen never told me what to do, nor gave me a row. If I was cross, Kathleen spoke to me kindly, pulling me out of a mood with her smile.

"What's the matter, hen? You'll spoil your pretty face."

Like my mother, Kathleen seemed to have the ability to see things from my point of view, and she always had time to talk to me.

There was one day, however, when another teddy joined the menagerie of toys in our bed, and even for someone as patient as Kathleen, that was a bear too far.

That year, 1967, was an eventful one for the world. It was the year of the first heart transplant, and the Biafran war. In the United Kingdom abortion became legal, and the pound was devalued. Sandie Shaw won the Eurovision Song Contest singing "Puppet on a String" in bare feet, and *Sgt. Pepper's Lonely Hearts Club Band* was released. In America young people found a new way of protesting for peace—Flower Power. But for our family, the most momentous event took place on Thursday, 25 May 1967.

My dad was mad about Celtic Football Club, and they were playing Inter Milan at the Estádio Nacional in Lisbon in the final of the European Cup. We all crowded into the back room to watch the game on our small black-and-white television. Celtic were the underdogs and nobody, apart from fans like my dad, believed they could win.

Manager Jock Stein's instructions ahead of the game were simple: "Go out and enjoy yourselves." But in the opening moments a penalty was awarded against Celtic and Inter took the lead. The atmosphere in our living room was electric. None of us dared speak as the game went on and Milan's defence stopped every Celtic attack on goal. My dad was up out of his chair a dozen times, only to sink back down in dismay.

Even the woodwork was against us. My dad kept shouting at the television, cursing the referee, urging the players on. Then, after almost an hour's play, the boot of Tommy Gemmell equalized the score. After that, Celtic outclassed the Italians and went on to win 2-1.

Jock Stein summed up the mood of half of Scotland: "There is not a prouder man on God's earth than me at this moment!"

Suddenly all of us and all the neighbours spontaneously poured out of our houses to celebrate. Our street was throbbing! Every window had green-and-white scarves waving from it. Cars drove past beeping their horns. Everyone went mad! My dad went off to the pub. I think he must have drunk the place out of beer.

Usually when my dad had a wee bit too much to drink, we all used to keep out of the way because he'd sit and feel sorry for himself, going over and over all the injustices done to him in life. Sometimes my mum got so fed up with it that she'd tell him she was going to make him a bed up in the road. But that night my father was the happiest I had ever seen him. We could hear him coming down the road cheering and singing, and when my mother opened the door we saw he had brought home a new friend—an enormous pink-and-white teddy bear.

"Here you are, hen! This is for you!" He presented me with the bear.

I'd already had my birthday and it wasn't Christmas for a long, long time.

"Nae bother!" said my dad. "This is a special day!"

I've been a Celtic supporter ever since.

I called the bear Bruno, and from then on Bruno had to sleep in bed along with me and Boo Boo and the rest of the animals and dolls. I had quite a routine, where I had to get all the toys settled in a row down the middle of the bed before I could get in too. Kathleen slipped in later on. She sometimes used to wake up with a start and find this great bear's face with his glassy eyes staring at her.

One night I woke up with a thud on the floor. I'd been kicked out of bed.

"Oh, I'm so sorry, Susan—I thought you were Bruno!" said Kathleen, as she picked me up and tucked me back in.

At least that was her excuse!

7
Craic

In the summer of 1967, excitement was running high in Yule Terrace because, just like Cliff Richard, we were all going on a summer holiday. It was the first proper holiday I had ever been on, and things are always a wee bit more exciting when you don't know what to expect. I knew we were going to Ireland, where my mother came from, and while we were there we were going to visit our Irish relations. So even though it was a new place, there would be people who knew us, so there wasn't anything to be frightened of, my mother assured me. We packed up suitcases and put them into the boot of the car we had then, a grey Austin Cambridge with a white stripe down the side, and then we all crammed in. My father was driving and my mother sat at the front. On the back seat there were four of us: Kathleen, me, James and Gerard.

The first leg of the journey was the drive to Stranraer to catch the ferry to Larne. I had never been on a boat before, but on television I'd seen Francis Chichester's yacht sailing into harbour after his single-handed voyage round the world, so I thought it would be like that, with a sail and all of us standing with the wind in our hair as we sped across the water. But the boat we were sailing on wasn't that sort of boat at all. In fact, I didn't even know we were on it until my father told us to get out of the car. The car deck smelled of engine oil and looked more like a garage. Upstairs on deck, a raw wind was blowing, and the floor under my feet had an uneasy rocking motion that made me feel peculiar. That was before we set sail. As soon as the ferry was out of the harbour, I felt so ill I was sure I was going to die. All the nervous anticipation about the holiday seemed to swish around in my tummy, spewing bile up into my throat along with my breakfast. Mercifully, once we were off the ferry, I fell asleep for the journey across Northern Ireland.

I woke up feeling much better, with only a sour taste in my mouth to remind me of my ordeal. Someone had opened the car window and a mild breeze was blowing on my face. Portrush, the town we had come to, was built on a little peninsula that stuck a mile out into the sea. In the harbour, fishing boats with coloured hulls and yachts with white sails bobbed on the glinting water. The distinctive call of seagulls filled the air, along with wafts of an unmistakably mouth-watering aroma. Fish and chips. My favourite meal!

There were beaches on both sides of the town and, leading down to them, terraces of pretty houses all painted different colours—sky blue, rose pink, lemon yellow—that looked like the squares of paint in a paintbox. And we were going to stay in one of those houses, called Dungevin House, which was run by a nice lady called Mrs. Docherty. The bedrooms had that distinctive, slightly musty smell that houses near the sea often have.

"Look!" said Dad, picking me up so I could see out of the window.

There was nothing but sea and sky as far as my eyes could see. There aren't many views in Blackburn. When you look out of the front windows you see the front of the houses opposite, exactly the same as ours. And out the back there's a small yard, my dad's garage and the backs of houses just like ours. The endless stretch of blue in front of me made me feel excited, as if the world was full of possibility.

"Look at the white horses!" Dad said, pointing.

I couldn't see any horses.

"Scotland's over there." He pointed into the vast blue beyond. "When it's a clear day, you'll see."

I squinted my eyes together, but all I could see was milky blue.

On days when the weather was good, we played on the sandy beaches, or strands as they're called in Ireland. When you were close to it, the ocean looked powerful and dangerous, with great white rollers surging towards you over the flat sand and a salty spray blowing in your face.

The strand was dotted with other families like ours, with children fetching pretty stones and ribbons of seaweed to decorate their sandcastles. My father, who never normally played with me, helped me fill my bucket and tried to teach me the technique of turning it over quickly to make the turrets of a castle. His always turned out better than mine. My brothers dug holes: holes so deep they could hide in them, and shallower holes with a little bit of water in the bottom for me to paddle in. Sometimes children from other families jumped in and paddled with me. On a beach, there didn't seem to be the same rules as in the school playground, where other children decreed whether I was allowed to join in games or not.

Not many holidaymakers were brave enough to pit themselves against the giant waves. Sometimes there were flags up indicating it wasn't safe to swim. One morning, however, Gerard announced at breakfast that he was going in.

"Look! That's him!" My mother pointed as we watched him from the guest-house window, a solitary figure striding confidently across the sand. The tide was out and it was a long walk. We could see him in the distance like a wee stick tiptoeing into the icy water, then suddenly he turned and sprinted up the beach with a wave chasing him.

One afternoon we went for a drive to see the spectacular sights of the Antrim coast. My dad and two brothers went clambering over the basalt columns of the Giant's Causeway while the three of us watched, my mother holding one hand, Kathleen the other. My physical coordination wasn't very good. I found it impossible to hop on the spot, let alone go climbing on tall pillars by the sea.

"That's a staircase the giant made," my mother told me. "So he could walk over to Scotland."

"What giant's that?" I asked, looking round suspiciously.

"It was a long time ago," said Kathleen, quickly.

On the way back to Portrush, my dad stopped the car so we could get out and look at the ruined castle of Dunluce that rose forbiddingly out of the cliff.

That's where the giant lives, I thought, shivering in its dark shadow.

As my mother had promised, we paid visits to relations in a village called Claudy outside Derry. Their name was McLaughlin, just as my mother's had been, and there were lots of children younger than me. My mother told me to go outside and play with them while the grown-ups talked.

I quite liked the feeling of being the oldest one. It meant I could tell the wee children what to do, instead of always being told. Since I was in charge, I decided that I would do a television show for my cousins, so I sat them all down and I made up a story about a wee princess being chased across the sea back to Scotland by a giant. I acted all the parts, putting on different voices. My cousins watched me and laughed when I wanted them to. Encouraged by their reaction, I made the princess's screams of terror so loud and convincing that my mother came out of the house to see what was happening.

"Keep that noise down!" she said, but there was a smile on her face.

In the evenings, after Mrs. Docherty had cooked us a typically Irish supper like boiled ham and colcannon, or fish with parsley sauce and potatoes, the tables were cleared and there was a sing-song in the lounge. All the grown-ups would take a turn at singing, but the best was my dad. Tucked up in our beds upstairs, we could hear his melodious tenor voice belting out the Irish songs, and feel the wooden floor reverberating with all the clapping and cheering that followed.

The Irish word for having a good time is *craic*, and Irish people said lots of things differently from us, like "it is" instead of "aye," but after a wee while we all started sounding Irish ourselves. It didn't feel like a holiday at all. It felt as if we belonged there.

8
Our Lady of Lourdes

I felt more alone than ever in the playground when I went back to school, because Gerard had moved on to big school, St. Mary's. When some girls in my class tried to be kind and asked me to join in their skipping game, I hung back because I wasn't any good at timing my jumps over the rope and I thought my foot would get caught and people would laugh at me falling over.

There was a new intake of young children, with grey shorts and pinafores bought a size too big to grow into, some of them dashing about confidently, others looking lost. I remembered entertaining my little cousins in Ireland. The children in my own year group didn't like my play-acting or my funny voices, but the wee children did, so I played with them from then on.

Discomfort seems to dwell longer in memory than happiness, but there were lots of things about school that I enjoyed. Our Lady of Lourdes was a strictly Catholic school and religion was very much part of the curriculum. Every morning we had catechism and the priest, Father McNulty, used to come in once a week to see how much we knew. There was a book called *Light of the World*, with readings and prayers, and I always liked those lessons because it reminded me that God was there protecting me.

I knew, because my mother always told me, that God had given me a path to follow and I would gradually find out what it was. I liked the idea of being on a special journey that God had created just for me. I always tried to remember that other people's opinions about me didn't matter. What mattered was the path that God had laid out for me.

The best part of the day for me was when we listened to stories about Jesus's life, and sometimes the teacher would read us stories about saints whose special day it was. The one I liked best was about a wee girl called Bernadette, who lived in a place called Lourdes, which is where the name of our school and our church came from.

Bernadette had lived a long time ago and she was the daughter of a miller. It was a large family with nine children, just like the Boyles, except that some of the children had died when they were little, just like my sister Patricia had done.

Unlike the Boyles, Bernadette's family were so poor that they all lived in a single room. One winter day, when all the family were shivering, Bernadette was out gathering firewood with her sister and a friend when she saw a little lady standing in a niche in the rock. "Look!" she exclaimed to the other girls.

But they could see nothing.

The next day Bernadette went back to the same

place, and the lady was there again. She was very beautiful and she was wearing a white veil, a blue girdle and had a golden rose on each foot.

It was Our Lady!

I knew that straight away because of the statue in our church, but Bernadette didn't know. When she told the village people about what she'd seen, some people thought she was making it up; others thought she was mad and said she should be put in an asylum. Each day, Bernadette went back to the grotto as the lady told her to, and on the thirteenth visit the lady said to her, "Please go to the priests and tell them that a chapel is to be built here."

So Bernadette went to her parish priest, but even he didn't believe her. He told Bernadette that she had to ask the lady to prove she was real by performing a miracle, so Bernadette did.

The lady told her to drink from the spring that flowed from the rock. Bernadette was mystified because there wasn't a spring, but she scratched the earth where the lady was pointing. A few drops of water trickled out and Bernadette got her face muddy trying to drink them. When she returned to the village, people laughed at her even more with her dirty face, but over the next few days a spring began to flow and it was found to have healing properties.

Finally people believed Bernadette. They built a chapel and ever since then pilgrims have visited Lourdes and been cured of illness.

I think I loved the story so much because I could identify with that wee lassie with all the people laughing at her. Her story proved what my mother always told me. It was sometimes difficult to understand the way God worked, but if you kept on believing, then it would all become clear.

The teacher told us that one day we might be lucky enough to visit Lourdes ourselves and I added that thought into the prayers I said with my mother every night.

I don't want to give the impression that I was a wee angel, because I most definitely was not. I was just as capable of being naughty as any other kid.

Father McNulty prepared us for First Communion. He was a very strict, unbending priest, and he terrified our class when he told us that we would have to confess our sins to him, but even that didn't stop me from making mistakes. I made some honeys!

Every little girl gets excited about First Communion, because it is a special day and you get a very white beautiful dress. Mine was knee-length with a stiff petticoat that made the skirt stick out, and a ribbon at the waist. It was hanging under a paper cover on a special padded pink silk hanger in the wardrobe in my parents' bedroom. I was forbidden to go near it.

One Saturday around that time, I heard an ice cream van coming down our street, the tinkle of the jingle getting louder as it approached. My mouth began to water at the thought of one of those delicious swirls of cold ice cream on a crispy cone. My parents were in the back room talking to Bridie, who'd come round. I knew that if I asked my mum she'd say no. If she bought an ice for me, she'd have to buy one for everyone and we didn't have that kind of money.

There wasn't a lot of money in our house. I knew that because I'd been watching television recently when my mother came in and pulled the aerial out of the back of the television.

"What's going on?" I cried, because I was a telly fiend.

"There's a reason for that, Susan," my mother told me in a firm voice. "There's a detector van in the street and we haven't got the money for a licence."

I'd seen Bridie's handbag was hanging over the banister at the foot of the stairs. Her purse was just peeking out. I could hear the jingle at the corner now. One more minute and it would drive away. The temptation was too hard to resist.

The white moustache around my mouth was a dead giveaway.

"Where did you get the money from?" my mother demanded to know.

"Found it!"

I wasn't much of a liar.

"You'll not be able to wear that white dress!" my father threatened.

"That dress is made of special fabric," Bridie added, "that knows if you've done wrong and rots your skin!"

I was very ashamed.

In the end, of course, I was allowed to wear the dress. But I never took money again!

My First Communion was in June, and as we walked to church, it was another beautiful day. All of my class lined up outside the church, the girls in their white dresses, the boys in suits with white sashes. We walked in together and sang "Mary, Dearest Mother," as we had rehearsed. The sun shone in through the stained glass and it felt very special. Inside the church I was very well behaved, and when I looked over at my parents and my sister Mary, who is also my godmother, their eyes were shining with pride.

In my white dress, white shoes and a wee white veil attached to my head by a crown of flowers, I must have looked very pretty. My hair was long and my mum had styled it in long sausage ringlets.

Unfortunately, there is no record of this, because I didn't like having my photograph taken. It was such a special occasion, my parents booked a photographer to come to our house a couple of days later.

"You'll be happy to wear your beautiful dress again, won't you?" Mary told me, in a voice that sounded more like an order than a question.

"No!" I replied.

The photographer tried the gentle art of persuasion.

I made silly faces at the camera.

The photographer got cross with me.

I made even sillier faces.

My dad came in and gave me a row.

I bawled.

So that was the end of that.

Forty years later, a sudden memory of that day made me smile at another camera. I was doing a photographic shoot for *Harper's Bazaar* in Cliveden House, of all places, which is a very select hotel near Windsor. I had been pampered and groomed and helped into a beautiful gown.

"Straight at the camera! That's lovely! And again! Little smile!"

The photographer used all the same phrases, but on this occasion, I'm glad to say, there was no need for anyone to come in and say, "For God's sake, Susan, sit on your bloody arse and do as you're told!"

9
Special

My report card at the end the summer term of Primary 4 in 1970, the year when I became nine, makes interesting reading. My oral English is marked "Very Good" as is my achievement in History, Geography, Natural History and Science. Maths and Arts and Crafts are considered "Good." My teacher that year was Mrs. Byrne. She had a voice that would frighten anybody, but she was a kind-hearted person. She knew when to be strict and when to be gentle, and she obviously saw some potential in me because she got me remedial help. I didn't like being separated from the rest of the class, but it was only for a few weeks, and given a little confidence and some extra help, I began to catch up with the others. My attendance that year was a hundred per cent. My conduct gets S for "Satisfactory." In other words, could be better, but, hey, nobody's perfect!

The headmaster's remark says "Commendable effort," and it is signed Mr. Green. He was the new headmaster and he was going to play a very important part in my life.

That summer we went to Ireland again, this time to Donegal. We stayed in a boarding house called

Castleport House near Dunglow. My mother's family had roots in Donegal. We visited a wee cottage where her grandparents had lived and went on to a holy shrine called Doon Well. There was a spring there, and my mother told me that the water was miraculous. On a bush beside the spring, the sick and the injured had left their bandages behind after their injuries had been healed. Under the bush were walking sticks and crutches. None of us had any wounds or injuries, so I didn't know why we had to walk round the spring and take a bottle of the holy water away with us, but I can still remember the sensation of the wet grass under my bare feet.

There was a longer journey we embarked on, and that was to a place called Knock, in County Mayo.

My mother bought me new clothes in Dunglow for the trip: a reddish-orange poncho, which was very fashionable at the time, to go over my dress, and a smart cream tammy to wear on my head, so I knew we must be going somewhere special. My mother explained that Knock was a place where Our Lady had appeared about a hundred years ago.

"Like she did to Saint Bernadette?" I asked, immediately interested.

"Something like that."

"Are we going on a pilgrimage?" I asked.

I knew that pilgrims often had to travel enormously long distances, and this car journey seemed never-ending, especially when my dad went the wrong way round the one-way system in Sligo.

My mother just smiled.

We arrived late in the afternoon. The surrounding countryside was flat and there wasn't anything to indicate that Knock would be different from any other village, until I spotted the basilica, Our Lady, Queen of Ireland, which had only recently been built. It was more modern than any other church I'd ever seen. From a distance it looked like three gigantic white blocks with a very tall spire on top; inside it could hold ten thousand people. I was always surprised by how much loftier Our Lady of Lourdes felt inside than when you saw it from the street, but this church was so vast that the priest's voice was relayed through an echoing loudspeaker that made it feel as if the words were not just being spoken to me, but were all around me, enveloping me in their power.

Knock wasn't as crowded then as it is now, because the airport hadn't yet opened, but there were a good few people attending Mass with us. Afterwards, we processed to another church that looked, from a distance, like an ordinary grey stone church. Beside the south gable, where the apparition had taken place, a chapel had been built, with a sloping glass roof so that sunshine could pour in on three white sculptures of St. Joseph, St. John the Evangelist and Our Lady.

Fifteen people had witnessed the vision, and some of them had been children as young as me. They described the Blessed Virgin Mary looking very beautiful, standing a few feet above the ground. She wore a white cloak and a brilliant crown of glittering crosses. Her eyes were raised to heaven. Even though it was raining, the ground beneath her remained completely dry. As night fell, she shone with bright white light.

We knelt in front of the statue, and as I closed my eyes, I prayed very hard that Our Lady would appear, smiling and beautiful, to me too. As I've grown older, I've come to understand that she is there guiding me, even if she doesn't appear to me as she does to some very privileged people.

I wasn't aware then, because I was only nine years old, that my mother took me to Knock as a healing experience. She was haunted by the diagnosis I'd received at birth and she believed that I would get better only with Our Lady's help.

When you look back on events with the benefit of hindsight, you can sometimes see connections. When I remember our wee pilgrimage to Knock now, it's interesting to note that it was shortly after that that I sang publicly for the first time.

Mr. Green, the new headmaster at Our Lady of Lourdes Primary School, arrived with some progressive ideas. He believed that children should be encouraged to be creative as well as academic and should be given the opportunity to express their different talents.

As primary-school children, we had always sung together, especially carols at Christmas time, but now Mr. Green wanted to have concerts every term. Some children were picked out to perform solos. The first song I can remember performing on my own was the hymn "Child in the Manger" in a Nativity play. I sang it to the tune of "Morning Has Broken" and I was very nervous at the thought of singing on my own, so I hid behind some of the other children in the choir. When I opened my mouth to sing, however, all the trembling stopped and I felt very still as I sang the notes.

As I finished, there was a moment of pure silence. I was aware of the other children turning to look at me with their mouths hanging open. Then all the teachers started clapping and smiling at me. I'd seen other children doing well and getting praised, but I had no idea what it actually felt like to be good at something. It was as if I was a balloon filling with air and floating up into the sky. The parents in the audience were applauding too. I had a gift, people kept telling me afterwards. I knew it must be a precious gift because it made everyone smile.

My friend Lorraine Campbell remembers the first time she heard me singing, and I didn't even know her then! She was in Primary 4 and I was in

Primary 5. Mr. Green had entered the school in a Burns' Day competition with independent judges from outside the school. The teachers selected children who were good at singing to enter. The competition took place in the school hall, but so that all the other children could hear it was played through the tannoy in each classroom.

I was quite pleased with myself when Mr. Green came to our classroom that morning and called out my name, because I was getting time off from doing sums. I couldn't resist smirking a little as I pushed my chair under my desk and sashayed across the room to go along with the headmaster.

There were about ten of us from different classes. The hall felt empty and much colder than it did when the whole school came together for assembly. My nerves started to kick in. I'd rehearsed my song with the music teacher and practised it at home, but now I couldn't remember what note was supposed to come out of my mouth, and it was so dry it was likely no sound would emerge at all. What were the words? In lessons, I was always forgetting things. Sometimes I'd put my hand up, but then when the teacher pointed at me the answer had already gone. I was so scared, it was all I could do to stop myself peeing on the stage as my name was called.

I stood in front of the table of three people I'd never seen before.

"Your name is?"

"Susan Boyle." My bare knees were knocking together.

"How old are you?"

"I'm ten years old."

"And what song are you going to sing?"

" 'Ye Banks and Braes.' "

"In your own time."

Behind the judges, in the wee windows in the doors at the back of the hall, I could see small, grinning faces appearing momentarily, as naughty boys, who had been sent out of class, jumped in the air to try to sneak a peek at what was going on. If I ran away, they were sure to report back that I'd been a scaredy cat; if I sang with a squeaky voice, the class would hear me through the tannoy system. Either way, when I returned to the classroom everyone was going to laugh at me.

The music teacher gave me a big nod with her head and raised her hands above the piano keys to start playing. I glanced at Mr. Green. He wasn't allowed to speak to me, but his head was nodding and his whole face was encouraging me, as if to say, "Go on! Have a go!"

I didn't want to let him down, so I opened my mouth.

> *Ye banks and braes o' bonnie Doon*
> *How can ye bloom sae fresh and fair?*
> *How can ye chaunt, ye little birds,*
> *And I sae weary, fu' o' care.*

Ye'll break my heart, ye warbling birds
That wanton through the flowery thorn,
Ye mind me o' departed joys,
Departed, never to return.

Oft hae I roved by bonnie Doon
To see the rose and woodbine twine,
And ilka bird sang o' its love,
And fondly sae did I o'mine.
Wi' lightsome heart I pu'd a rose
Fu' sweet upon its thorny tree,
But my fause lover stole my rose,
And ah! He left the thorn wi' me.

In Primary 4, Lorraine listened to the sounds floating through the box on the wall near the door and thought, "That Susan Boyle . . . she's got some voice!"

When I finished, one of the judges said thank you and the others were writing on their notepads, but I could see that Mr. Green was happy.

It was a boy called Charles Kelly who won the competition. He had a lovely voice and I sometimes wonder if he did anything with his singing. I came second, but when I returned to my classroom the teacher said, "Well done, Susan!" and started clapping.

Then all the class joined in, even the naughty boys!

At the Easter Special concert at the end of term I

sang the jolly number "McNamara's Band" as a member of the choir, but my sister Mary says that you could hear my voice soaring out among the others. In the Summer Concert I ventured out on stage by myself to sing "The Hills Are Alive" from *The Sound of Music* and raised my hands, just like Julie Andrews does in the film.

The fear before a performance was always the same, but if I could find the courage to start, the excruciating grip of nerves would loosen as the singing took over, and I never forgot the words. For the duration of the song, I was special. Not the kind of "special" people talked about when they really meant I was a nuisance, but special in a nice way.

My singing silenced the bullies, but better than that, it silenced the demons inside me. When you've been jeered at, told to shut up, sit still, stop being silly, there's a cacophony of noise constantly rolling around inside your head. When I was singing, it was peaceful.

10
Uncle Michael

I was ten when my sister Kathleen got married. My mother bought me a trendy hat with a wide floppy brim and a lovely pink dress with lace down the front for the occasion. The sun shone and Kathleen looked radiant in white. Her husband, Joe, was from a Catholic family and they married in Our Lady of Lourdes church. My dad walked her proudly down the aisle. Afterwards there was a reception in the Bowling Club, which is near the church, and everyone was happy, but when I came home afterwards I cried and cried. Our bed was still full of toys, but it was cold and empty without my big sister.

Kathleen was my mentor and my friend. She supported me emotionally and spiritually. Kathleen was my sponsor when I received the sacrament of confirmation and the gentle weight of her hands on my shoulders reassured me as I waited my turn to be anointed by His Eminence Cardinal Joseph Grey.

Kathleen only went as far as Whitburn, the next small town along the valley. She and Joe moved into a terraced house on a council estate. It was a small house but there was always a big welcome there, and if ever there was a birthday or some other celebration in the family, Kathleen's house was the place we all gathered. It was the social hub of the family. When I was a wee bit older, I often used to go along to babysit Kathleen's baby, Pamela, and Kathleen was always popping along to see us in Yule Terrace. She was like a breath of fresh air coming into the room, but whenever she left after a visit, our house felt as if someone had switched off the light.

Kathleen was the last of my sisters to leave home. My brother Joe was married with two daughters, Gwendoline and Kirsty; James was married and working as a toolmaker; John had a job in Hepworth, the tailor's shop in Bathgate. Gerard and I were the only two left in the house, and Gerard was a teenager, so he wasn't around much.

When I came home from school, I used to switch on the television and watch on my own. I was addicted to cartoons like *Top Cat* and *Wacky Races*, I liked *Blue Peter*, but my favourite programme was *Crackerjack* on Friday. It was a great way to end the week because it had lots of games, like the one where three children stood on boxes on the stage while the host, Leslie Crowther, asked them questions. If they got the answers right, then they were given piles of presents to hold, but if they gave an incorrect answer, they were given a cabbage, which was really difficult to balance, and so the presents would fall down.

Sometimes my mother would hear me laughing and stand in the door behind me. If I guessed the answer right, my mother would say "Present," and if I got it wrong, she'd say "Cabbage." Once, when I got several answers in a row correct, I asked her, "Can I go on *Crackerjack?*"

The show was in a theatre and all the audience were children too, shouting and calling out. I thought it must be great to be on television. It wasn't just the presents that appealed—I wanted to meet Leslie Crowther and his sidekick, Peter Glaze, because they were so funny.

"That's in London," my mother told me.

"Where's London?"

"A long way away."

My mother was very good at quiz shows herself because she had gained so much knowledge from reading books. She possessed the ability to absorb information like a sponge. She loved watching *University Challenge*, which in those days was hosted by a man with the strange name of Bamber Gascoigne, who wore glasses and was very intellectual.

"Do you fancy him or something?" Dad used to say to my mum.

And my mum would go, "Shush!"

The contestants were students, so they were supposed to be clever. I couldn't even understand the questions, but my mum would call out the right answers and my dad and I would look at her in astonishment. My mother had never been anywhere near a university. She was very intelligent, and would have been a great teacher herself, but in her youth you had to pay for education and so it was only upper-class women who ever got the chance.

One day, around this time, I overheard my mother and father discussing new arrangements for the dining room.

"What's up?" I asked.

"Your uncle Michael is coming to stay with us, Susan," my mother told me.

"Smashing!" I said, thrilled that there would be another person in the house to talk to when I came home after school.

I knew Uncle Michael because we sometimes visited him at weekends. He lived in a great big Victorian building called Hartwood near Motherwell. The sheer size of the place looming above us always terrified me as we drove in. Inside, we had to walk down a long corridor with all these different people and nurses wandering around. There was that horrible disinfectant smell that hospitals always reek of. Uncle Michael shared a room with another man who couldn't speak very well, so it usually took a little while before Michael himself would talk to us. Although he was old, like my parents, he came across more like a child, because he always asked if we'd brought him any sweeties. He liked sweeties.

At the end of our visit, Michael would watch us walking away down the long corridor, and even though there were lots of other people milling around, I used to think that he looked completely alone, standing there. I could tell that he would have liked to come home with us. In the car after, my mother was always quiet, and I knew that she didn't like leaving him there either, so I thought it was a great idea that he was coming to live at our house instead.

Michael was my mother's younger brother and he had had a very difficult start in life. In 1917 my mother's father, John McLaughlin, went to fight in the First World War and died in the Battle of Ypres. Just after the news of his death came back, my Granny McLaughlin discovered that she was pregnant with Michael. The shock and grief of her terrible loss probably affected the baby in her womb, because Michael was born with learning and emotional difficulties. By all accounts, he was a mischievous little boy. One day, when he was barely more than a toddler, my Granny McLaughlin was at Mass when she suddenly realized that Michael was no longer standing beside her. Looking around frantically, she couldn't see him anywhere, but then suddenly his wee face popped up in the pulpit!

Michael went to a special school for his education, but when he was eighteen my Granny McLaughlin died and he was sent to Hartwood, which was then known as an asylum. In those days they thought it best to segregate people with learning and emotional disabilities rather than integrating them into the community. It wasn't until 1959 that the law changed, and even then it took another forty years for all of those big Victorian institutions to be closed down.

None of us kids knew the exact nature of Michael's problems before he went into Hartwood, but it was always said that poor Michael got "twenty years for breaking a few windows." My mother would have liked to have done more for him, but with a husband of her own who was in the army and then nine children, she had a lot to cope with as it was.

We made a bedroom for Michael downstairs in the dining room. He took time to settle into our family life because he wasn't used to mixing with people in a normal environment. He used to spend a lot of time in his room and I could hear him in there muttering to himself. He could be prickly, and it was a wee while before he understood that my father was the man of the house.

Sometimes he used to challenge my father to a fight.

Michael's room was below mine and I'd hear him getting worked up. Then his door would slam and he'd march into the living room, where my dad was watching television.

"Come out the back and fight, you coward!"

My father would ignore him for a while, but when Michael didn't stop, he'd heave a heavy sigh, put down his paper and get to his feet, rolling up his sleeves and pretending to square up. Then you wouldn't see Michael for dust!

Most of the time, Michael was a gentle soul, and he and I used to have great chats. We always got on very well together and Michael used to say to my father, "The wee girl can be nice to me, how come you can't?"

He didn't understand that my dad was being very good having him to stay in the house. At times it could be stressful for my mother.

Michael gradually gained in confidence. My mother used to give him pocket money so that he could go and buy his own sweeties. Like my mother, he was a great reader and used to borrow lots of books from the library, particularly adventure stories by Alistair MacLean. He started to go out for long walks on his own, whatever the weather, and became well known as "the walking man" by the kids who took buses from the outlying villages to school. Many times, when it was lashing down, various family members who saw him would try to give him a lift in a car, but he refused to get in. He didn't like that idea at all. Instead, he came back dripping.

"Look at you, you're soaking!" my mother scolded.

"I'll do what I like!" Michael told her, relishing his newfound freedom.

Now, when we went out for drives on a Sunday, it was always the four of us. Mum, Dad, Michael and me. In the evenings we would watch television together. My father always had to watch the news. He was a shop steward in his union, and the unions were always in the news. There was a lot of stuff about Northern Ireland too, and my mother used to worry about her relations in Claudy, because that was one of the hotspots of the violence. She liked a good drama, such as *Upstairs, Downstairs* or *Colditz*. Gerard was a great fan of *Monty Python's Flying Circus*, but he had to be secretive and watch it when my parents were out, because they didn't approve of that kind of subversive humour.

Spending all my time in the company of older people gave me different interests from my peers at school. Because I was a natural mimic, I used the phrases that my mother used and talked about things that other children weren't interested in.

When I was twelve, my father bought me a radio of my own so I could listen to it in my bedroom. While the other children listened to Radio 1, I used to like Terry Wogan on Radio 2. I don't know whether it was the soft Irish accent, or that he was really good at punning and making up nicknames, but there was just something about the guy. So while the other children talked at school about Tamla Motown, I talked about Terry Wogan.

"Who's Terry Wogan?"

"He's a man with black hair, and he's Irish and I like the stuff he plays on his show, like Frank Sinatra—"

"You cannae like Frank Sinatra—he's a reject!"

"I think he's brilliant."

I used to get ribbed about it rotten.

"Terry Wogan's old, you cannae like him!"

"I think he's funny. He calls Charles Aznavour 'Charles As No Voice'!"

"Charles who?"

That sort of conversation didn't exactly make me popular with my classmates, but I wasn't lonely because I had discovered the company of books. Up in my room, I used to immerse myself in novels I'd borrowed from the library, like *What Katy Did*, *Little Women* and *Lorna Doone*, enjoying the heroines' triumphs and crying my eyes out at their tragedies.

I used to make up stories myself, borrowing characters from television programmes I'd seen, or books I'd read, and practising in front of the dressing-table mirror. When I acted them out at school, it used to drive people mad. There she goes again! I can see now that, in essence, it was improvisation, which wasn't bad for a ten-year-old kid, but I didn't know that until much later when I went to acting school.

I began to write stories myself and took some of them into school. My English teacher gave me an A, but she observed, "There's always a character called Sue who's an extrovert. Are you hiding something?"

I said, "Maybe . . ."

When you're introverted you tend to imagine yourself in different situations. Putting a character called Sue in my stories was my way of compensating for the fact that nobody understood me. It was a kind of escape.

Once, I was asked to read my ghost story out to the class. It frightened the life out of everyone, including me!

The hero of the story was called Terry Wogan.

"Terry Wogan?" said my teacher. "Isn't he a bit old for you?"

I think everyone thought my creative writing was a wee bit eccentric, but in other ways I was just a normal adolescent girl with a pair of hot pants— sky blue with a bib and a pink blouse underneath, in case you're wondering—and my long hair in bunches.

One Thursday evening, when I was watching *Top of the Pops*, the camera panned round to a young singer sitting on a high stool, who looked almost the same age as me, and, like thousands of lassies all over the country, I fell in love for the first time.

11
Puppy Love

If I'm going to be absolutely honest, when I first saw Donny Osmond on *Top of the Pops*, with his glossy long hair and his high voice, I mistook him for a lassie.

Don't worry, Donny—I soon realized you were a boy!

Maybe part of his appeal to an innocent teenage girl like me was that having a crush on Donny wasn't much different from wanting him to be my friend. When I imagined what it would be like to meet Donny, the most intimate thing we ever did was hold hands. That clean-cut, wholesome image is probably why my parents allowed me to plaster my bedroom walls with any and every photo of him I could find.

"As long as there's no pock marks in my wallpaper!" my dad warned.

"No, Dad, I'll be careful," I promised, trying to cover over all the holes I'd already made.

Every penny of my pocket money went on magazines like *Pop Swap* and *Fab 208* that carried features on the Osmonds. I liked all of the brothers, Wayne especially, and little Jimmy Osmond, but it was Donny who floated my boat. I scoured the pages for articles that speculated about matters of sublime importance, such as what kind of boyfriend Donny would be (sensitive and shy, but friendly, obviously!), and what sort of clothes Donny preferred girls to wear (floaty, romantic maxi-dresses, but my dad would have had something to say if I'd worn one of those!).

If a magazine had a photo of Donny on the cover, I bought it, and when a girl at school called Anna, who was as Osmonds-daft as me, informed me that there was a magazine called *Osmonds' World*, I was straight off to the newsagent.

"What do you want to waste your pocket money on those stupid magazines for?" my mother cried in despair.

She put her foot down when it came to the Osmonds' fan club. I wasn't allowed to join, but Anna was, so I heard all the news from her. A shared passion for the Osmonds gave us something in common, although I knew that I'd have to watch out for Anna if the Osmonds were ever to turn up in Blackburn—a totally unlikely scenario, but one we fantasized about all the time.

I loved Donny's beautiful dark eyes; I loved his friendly, white smile. When Tony Blackburn was presenting *Top of the Pops*, he said if you turn down the brightness on the television you'll see nothing but a set of teeth, and he was right! But what I most loved about Donny was his voice, and the sincerity of the emotion he could bring to a song. Every time I heard him sing "Puppy Love," I thought he was singing it just to me.

I remember reading one of those cartoon stories they used to have in *Jackie* magazine about a girl who had a crush on Donny and dreamed, as I did, of meeting him. When a guy moved into her street who looked just like Donny, she fell in love with him instead. I thought that was stupid. Someone who looked like Donny wasn't the point. Someone who could sing like Donny, now that would be a different matter . . . but nobody could sing like Donny.

There's always a moment just after I wake up each morning when I look up at the same lampshade, hanging from the same ceiling I've stared at ever since I was a child, and I think, Of course it was only a dream. It had to be!

Sometimes, there's even a ripple of relief across the flood of disappointment. But then, as my eye travels down to the floor, I see my framed triple platinum disc propped up against the skirting board. I've pinched myself so many times, my arms are black and blue!

I've done incredible things this year, seen beautiful places and met wonderful people. Luckily, I don't have to pick out one moment to keep and treasure for ever—but just say I did, that moment would have to be when I met Donny Osmond in Los Angeles. He was so exactly as I had imagined him, it felt as if time had simply collapsed. I was a teenager again, my heart was going nineteen to the dozen and I was unable to say anything sensible because I kept giggling.

Even though I haven't seen her for years, I couldn't help myself remembering my friend Anna and thinking, Oh my God! If you could see me now!

Christmas morning is a magical time for any kid. At school, we made paper chains, sang carols and listened to the best story of all, the story of Jesus's birth. At home, my mother prepared a crib in our living room and a tree with tinsel branches that made pretty patterns of light on the walls when winter sunshine caught them during the day, and glowed with tiny coloured fairy lights when it was dark outside.

As a wee child, when I woke up on Christmas morning my first thought was presents, and I'd be straight out of bed. When I became old enough to accompany my parents to Midnight Mass, I would awake with a joyous feeling inside me that I wanted to hold onto for a few moments before joining the fray downstairs.

Our living room was filled with the scent of tangerines and overnight it had miraculously turned into Santa's grotto. My mother never wrapped what she'd bought for us—I don't think people bothered with that so much in those days, or maybe we couldn't afford the paper—but we each had our own wee pile of gifts in its own particular place, with a tangerine, or satsuma, on top. My pile was always in the left-hand corner by the window and when I was little I had to squash through past my brothers. As the older ones left home and organized their own family Christmasses, there wasn't quite so much shoving, jostling and squealing, but it was still exciting.

The best Christmas I can remember was when I was thirteen. I was barely dressed before Kathleen, her husband and their new baby, Pamela, arrived at the door. Kathleen loved her family so much she always came home on Christmas morning for a wee ginger wine with my parents and a Christmas hug with me. The children were allowed a nip if they wanted, or black currant cordial, which I preferred. My mother did not drink alcohol, although once, not realizing how strong it was, she'd had a couple of Drambuies at a friend's house and couldn't stop giggling. She never repeated it.

Gerard eventually emerged from his bedroom, yawning. He'd left school by then and was working in Hepworth, the same tailor's shop in Bathgate as our John, but he was still living at home.

All the grown-ups watched me open my presents. Underneath the pile of books and games from my mum and dad there were two LPs from Gerard. The first was *Portrait of Donny*, which included my favourite track, "Puppy Love"; the other was *The Plan* by the Osmonds.

"Thank you!"

Standing up and slipping the LP out of its sleeve, I went over to lift the lid off the Elizabethan record player.

"Hold on," said Gerard. "Have a look at what's underneath."

"What is it?" I asked, kneeling down again, and pulling the flaps up from a large cardboard box.

"Now we won't all have to listen to the Osmonds!" Gerard joked.

Two LPs was already a very generous present, but I was overwhelmed to discover that my brother had also bought me my very own portable record player. It had two speeds, 33 and 45, so you could play LPs or singles. You could stack singles up so they played one after the other. That seemed like the height of modern technology at the time.

It was the best present I have ever received. However, it didn't stop everyone hearing the Osmonds, because from that moment on, if you ever came into our house, you'd hear not only the Osmonds but me singing along with them too. The sound-proofing wasn't great. My dad would often come up and bang on my door, so I'd turn the volume down for a couple of minutes, before turning it up again. On Sunday mornings there'd be another noise as well, and that was Gerard shouting, "For heaven's sake, will you turn that blessed record player down! I'm trying to have a lie-in!"

Or words to that effect.

Now that I had a record player in my bedroom, I could watch myself singing in the same dressing-table mirror where Bridie used to do her make-up. My hairbrush was my microphone and I used to spend hours perfecting the movements and gestures I'd seen on *Top of the Pops* with an imaginary audience around me.

People talk about the innovation of sixties' music, but there was also a great variety around during the seventies, from "Tie a Yellow Ribbon" by Dawn to "Metal Guru" by T. Rex. I used to buy K-tel compilation albums with all the songs on, and I was equally at home singing "Tiger Feet" by Mud, "Billy Don't Be a Hero" by Paper Lace, or "Vincent" by Don McLean. I don't know whether it was the endless repetition, or just that your memory's better when you're younger, but give me the name of a hit from the seventies and I can still sing you all the words.

In those days I had the ability to make my voice sound just like the record. My sister Mary, who has a very good ear, says that if she came to our house and listened, it was impossible to tell whether it was me singing or the artist on the record. One moment I would be the New Seekers teaching the world to sing, the next I'd be Michael Jackson with one of my favourite-ever songs, "Ben." I hadn't yet found my own voice, but for the duration of the song, I became the star.

12

St. Kentigern's

Just before Christmas 2009, I was pottering about at Yule Terrace one morning when my phone rang.

"Hello? Is that Susan Boyle?"

"Who's calling?"

I have had to learn to be circumspect when I'm talking on the telephone because you never know who has got hold of your number.

"It's Stephen Campbell. I'm the headteacher of St. Kentigern's Academy."

You know how it is sometimes when you haven't done anything wrong, but you feel guilty as if you might have? That's how I felt with the headmaster on the line. I waited for him to speak again.

"We're opening the new extension to the school next week," he went on. "We've got Cardinal Keith Patrick O'Brien coming along, and we'd love it if you could join us . . ."

I didn't need to be asked twice. His Eminence had been very supportive of me and I'd been lucky enough to meet him in person a couple of times. When a cardinal of the Catholic Church asks you to do something, you don't ask questions.

"Of course I will!" I agreed.

On the day, the headmaster drove his car round to pick me up. I'd deliberated for ages about what would be suitable to wear for the occasion. I wanted to be smart, but not too formal, so eventually I decided on a patterned dress with a tailored black jacket over it. It was only when I arrived at the school and saw the children in their black blazers that I realized I'd unconsciously put the uniform back on!

In the hall, Stephen Campbell read out a list of the people who were there to open the new buildings as if it were a school register. At the end, he said, "And a certain Susan Magdalane Boyle . . ."

And I walked out on to the stage.

The pupils went wild. My appearance had been kept as a surprise for them. After the Cardinal had officially opened the refurbishment, we all had a look around and many of the students came up with work books for me to autograph.

It was quite surreal to be celebrated in a place where I had known so much despair.

St. Kentigern's Academy is a large comprehensive school on the outskirts of Blackburn that serves all the surrounding villages. It was opened in 1973 and I was one of the first intake. It was a terrible wrench for me to leave Our Lady of Lourdes, where everything was familiar, to transfer to St. Kentigern's. The walk to school was much longer and the buildings were bigger. There were hundreds of faces I didn't recognize. Instead of remaining in one classroom all day, we had to trail round to different rooms for the various subjects. I seemed to spend half my time trying to remember how to get to where I was supposed to be. Once I was in the right place, my brain would try to switch from History to Science or whatever it was, but I found it very difficult to focus, and before I could concentrate, we'd be off again to the next lesson.

I'd had my curls cut into a short, grown-up style to go to St. Kentigern's and the uniform was a smart black blazer then as it is now, but I was at the bottom of a school again, and there were no little ones for me to look after and play with. Nobody at St. Kentigern's was interested in being entertained by me. It sometimes felt as if nobody was interested in me at all. When I was unhappy at primary school, people tended to know about it because I made a noise, but by the time I was twelve I had stopped letting all my problems out and turned my emotions inwards. I became very quiet and withdrawn.

There was a drama club, but I didn't dare join because I wasn't very good at mixing and I knew the other pupils would make a fool of me. I joined the choir because I could feel safe as part of that, but there weren't the musical concerts every term that there had been at Our Lady of Lourdes, so there was no forum for me to express myself.

At breaktimes, the boys played football. They were big lads now with strong legs, so you wouldn't want to get in the way of a shot. The girls hung around talking about make-up, or doing quizzes in magazines with questions about kissing and other things I didn't know about. I stood on my own in the playground just watching, knowing from experience that if I tried to join in I would be laughed at, so I decided not to bother. I didn't really mind being on my own because I found it interesting to observe what the others were doing. The only part of the day I truly dreaded was the long walk home.

At primary school, my mother used to pick me up, or I would wait for my sister Mary to finish her teaching duties and walk me home. At big school, I had to walk home by myself. There was some unspoken selection process I didn't understand whereby children split into gangs and ambled along together chatting. It didn't occur to me that if I walked along beside a group they might just start talking to me too. I was certain that if I found the courage to ask to join in, they were bound to say, "No, we don't want you with us, Susan Boyle, you're stupid!"

When you're walking by yourself and there's a crowd of mates behind you yelling and joking, it always feels as if they're laughing at you. I probably didn't help myself by looking round and quickening my step. At the corner of our street, I always ran the last hundred yards to our house. Standing in the hall with the front door closed safely behind me, I could feel trickles of sweat under my white school blouse and my heart thumping as the fear gradually ebbed away.

Playing records in my bedroom upstairs was my escape. When I was singing, I could forget all about being Susan Boyle and assume a different identity. The early seventies saw the advent of musicals like *Jesus Christ Superstar* and *Godspell*. My parents, as traditional believers, worried that pop songs about Jesus might be blasphemous, but I welcomed them as a new and very personal way of expressing my faith.

In my jukebox of memories, "I Don't Know How to Love Him" is one of the most-played songs.

"Don't you ever go out to youth clubs, or discos?" my sister Bridie asked me.

Bridie had moved to England when I was about nine years old. Her husband came from Motherwell, and they ran a Scottish club in Coventry called the Tam O'Shanter. Every Easter they used to organize a coach from Coventry to bring a whole crowd up to the Fir Park Club in Motherwell for a good old reunion and sing-song. When she was back in Scotland, Bridie always came to visit my parents, along with her daughter, my wee blonde niece Joanne.

It was incomprehensible to a sociable person as Bridie that a teenager wouldn't be out socializing with friends.

"I do go to discos," I replied defensively.

There was an annual disco at school. I went a couple of times and sat on a chair at the side with my glass of lemonade. I liked listening to the music.

"Who are your friends?" Bridie wanted to know.

"I don't need friends," I told her. "I like my own company."

I was aware that people of my age met up in the evenings at the community centre, or went down to Murrayfield for Penny Night when the travelling fair—which we call the shows—came to Blackburn. I never did any of that. When I was fourteen, Bay City Rollers-mania hit Blackburn. I liked the music as much as the other girls in my class, and sang along in my room with "Shang-A-Lang," but I wouldn't have dreamed of pestering my parents to allow me to go to a gig in Glasgow with a bunch of girls dressed in tartan and half-mast trousers. My parents would never have allowed it anyway.

The bullying at primary school had left me unable to relate to people of my own age. It was almost as if I had missed some of the lessons life teaches us about building friendship, and never quite managed to make up the ground. The only people I knew how to trust were adults, and, at school, that meant the teachers.

Some of the teachers at St. Kentigern's were interested only in the bright children, but others were very kind to me and I found I could talk to them. There were those who knew how to handle my neediness, but others were alarmed in case I was taking crushes. One of the male teachers asked my games teacher to take me aside and try to establish whether it was a sexual feeling I had.

"Of course it's not!" I told her, flushing with embarrassment. "How could I have a sexual feeling at my age?"

I'd been so sheltered from the facts of life that when the Biology teacher at St. Kentigern's asked how many of us had had their first period, I said I didn't know what that meant, and everyone laughed at me.

The attention I sought from the teachers didn't go unnoticed by some of the other pupils. I think they thought that I was telling tales, but I wasn't. I just wanted to talk to someone.

One afternoon, a gang of girls and boys started chasing me. I set off, trying to get a head start, running as fast as I could along the main road, thinking that if I could just get to the turning up into our estate, I would be safe. But they turned left into the lane after me, and then I realized how stupid I'd been because there was the narrow bridge and the bit of waste ground to cover before I got within sight of the first houses, and it was uphill and I was never going to make it. I would have been safer on the main road, but I couldn't turn round now because I'd run straight into them. My lungs were burning in my chest and my feet were pounding one in front of the other, but it was like one of those nightmares where you're trying to run and your limbs won't move fast enough. They caught me up on the narrow bridge, grabbing my bag. I yanked it away. I'm only wee, but I've got a sturdy physique like my dad, and I thought I was fighting for my life. I managed to make it over the bridge, but there were too many of them. This time they grabbed my bag and swung me round so I toppled down the bank towards the stream, landing flat on my face in a patch of nettles. The ringleader, whose name I won't mention, stepped forward, took her cigarette from her lips and stubbed it through the back of my blazer.

"That'll teach you to lick up teachers' backsides, Susan Boyle!"

With my arms covering my head, I lay numb in the dirt, too scared even to whimper, listening to the clatter of their footsteps receding into the distance, praying that they would just keep going. For a long time I couldn't tell whether I could still hear the cackle of their laughter, or whether it was just an echo inside my head.

Eventually trusting the silence, my senses began to return. I could hear the swish of cars on the main road; I could feel the nettles stinging through my socks. I sat up and took off my blazer to examine the damage. It was only then that the tears began to fall.

The perfect round hole the cigarette had burned seemed to sum it all up. All I was good for was stubbing out a cigarette. I was no use to anyone.

There was no way I was going to be able to hide that hole from a mother who took pride in my appearance and always made me do a little twirl, like Anthea Redfern on *The Generation Game*, just to check everything was in place before I left the house. My mother was bound to be angry, not with me, but with the school, and she'd go and give the headteacher a roasting, and that would make things even worse.

I couldn't tell the teachers, because that's what started it in the first place.

It was all my own fault.

But I hadn't done anything!

Suddenly, the clarity of anger burst through the blur of tears.

It wasn't fair!

My face set in a scowl as I picked myself up out of the dirt muttering, under my breath at first, then louder, the impotent battle cry of the humiliated, "I'll show you! I will! Just you wait! I'll show you!"

For many years, I tried to block those malevolent memories, but a few months ago they all flooded back when I was recording a song for my album. The unexpressed rage that burned inside my teenage soul seemed at last to flow out from my head and into my voice.

The song is by Madonna. It's called "You'll See." When I was singing it in the studio, I felt that I'd finally found my own way of responding to those bullies.

St. Kentigern's is a totally different school now, with new staff, fantastic new buildings and a vision to help all young people in the community achieve their fullest potential academically, personally and spiritually. There are expanding facilities for music and dance that never existed when I was there, as well as a fabulous social area for the pupils. It feels like a safer, more caring environment where every member of the school can be valued. I spent several hours there on my visit to the opening of the new extension and was made to feel very welcome. I was given a guided tour of the school and was very glad to see that these days the school tries to integrate children with autism and learning difficulties, so that, with a bit of extra patience, they can achieve their potential. Kids with disabilities shouldn't be made to feel that they have to be segregated, because if they weren't segregated, they might grow up to be perfectly normal, whatever "normal" is.

At the buffet after the opening ceremony I spotted an elderly priest and walked over to him. "I know you, Monsignor Lawson," I told him. "You taught me History."

"Did I?" he smiled.

"You did, and you must have been a good teacher because I got an O-grade in it!" I informed him.

History was one of only two O-grades I passed. The other was English. I loved reading, especially the big classics like *Wuthering Heights* and *The Mill on the Floss*, where you could lose yourself in the story, or Jane Austen's novels, where the heroine always ended up with the man she loved. I'm a bit of a romantic at heart!

The problem was that I couldn't handle exams. Even though I wasn't stupid and I wasn't lazy, I somehow couldn't cope with the pressure of having to get my knowledge onto paper within a time limit. It was the same feeling I'd had all my school life: my brain possessed the facts, but I couldn't find a way of delivering them. There was an invisible, impenetrable wall.

Years of bullying had been toxic to my self-esteem, and after my O-grade results, things only seemed to get worse. The time when I would have to leave school was fast approaching. Like all children, I'd had ideas about what I wanted to do when I grew up. Sometimes I thought I'd like to be a teacher, like my sister Mary, helping the slower children to learn. Other times I thought I'd like to use my writing skills to be a journalist and see my name in the paper. I found out about a course in journalism, but you needed four Highers to get on to it. I knew that wasn't going to happen. I was beginning to realize that all these futures I had constructed for myself were meaningless. I had stopped in the middle of nowhere. I looked all around, but couldn't see a way forward.

I don't seem to have the same filtering system that other people have that processes anxiety, so worry stacks up on insecurity and my brain becomes overloaded. The first few times I fainted, it was put down to teenage hormones, but it started happening so regularly that I was tested for epilepsy again. When that was ruled out, I was referred to a psychologist called Mrs. Fell. She gave me an IQ test, and afterwards she told my mother, "There's nothing wrong with her intelligence. The questions she does best in are in music. I think our Susan could maybe benefit from a career in music."

We couldn't work out who was crazier, me or the psychologist. I couldn't even play an instrument! I could hold a note, but so could everyone in my family. That wasn't something that could earn you a wage.

At the time, Gerard was trying to make a career for himself as an entertainer in the evenings. Not only does he have a great voice, but he is also a very talented comedian. Using the stage name Paul Brookes, he performed in the local pubs and clubs. You needed to be an outgoing, flamboyant type of character to survive in that environment, with the drunks and the fights, and Gerard fitted the bill. He was used to dealing with a wee bit of heckling at home. At the time, his long curly hair stuck out in an Afro style and he wore a moustache. I used to call him Pedro as a joke. When he appeared one day sporting a new cream velveteen jacket with fawn braiding round the lapels, my dad told him he wasn't going out in that—he looked like an ice cream man! Or words to that effect.

Gerard could shrug the insults off, but the working men's clubs and pubs were no place for a shy wee lassie like me. My mother wasn't the sort of person who would ever go to a pub, let alone allow me to go to one.

Nobody knew what to do with me, but it was clear that I was too troubled to continue at school, so I left St. Kentigern's with two O-grades and a kick in the pants.

13
The Taste of Defeat

The song that was playing all summer was "Summer Nights," from the film *Grease*. I was helping in a nursery just down the road in Blackburn and it was the tune the wee children liked to dance to. I liked being with children and they could relate to me because I'm just a big kid myself in some ways. We played that song so much, I'm surprised the record didn't wear out.

The chorus was very catchy and the kids used to shout it out. They knew all the actions as well. In my memory, "Summer Nights" is the soundtrack to images of children dancing with happy abandon, their joy so very distant from what I was feeling.

Every night I went to sleep and woke up crying.

Our doctor put me on Valium, but my mother had never been happy about me taking medication since the pills they had given me for my hyperactivity had been shown to produce side effects. She thought I was far too young to be taking tranquillizers.

What I really needed, she decided, was a nice break and some fresh air. We'd always enjoyed our holidays in Ireland, so now we packed up the car and set off, my mum, dad, Uncle Michael and me, to a place called Buncrana, situated on Lough

Swilly, an inlet on the shores of Inishowen, County Donegal.

The light on the north-west coast of Ireland is particularly luminous and uplifting, the air fresh and salty. We went for drives and gazed at wonderful views. Buncrana was a seaside town, with shops with spinners of postcards outside and brightly coloured windmills that twirled in the breeze. There were plenty of places to buy ice cream, whipped swirls with strawberry sauce or multicoloured scoops balanced precariously on top of pale wafer cones, and sweeties galore for my Uncle Michael. In the evenings, the air was filled with the appetizing smell of fish and chips, and when you walked down the cobbled street to the harbour, snatches of Irish music wafted out of pubs along with the cigarette smoke and the bitter tang of beer.

I was aware of all these sensations, but unable to experience them. I looked at views and felt no exhilaration; I ate food but it had no taste; I heard music but felt no desire to sing. There was a cinema just down the road from the cottage where we were staying. Uncle Michael liked action films and they were showing *Star Wars*. In those days there were continuous performances and my uncle sat through the film several times. One evening I joined him, but I didn't laugh at Harrison Ford's wry one-liners, and I didn't jump at any of the surprises. On Saturdays there was a wee parade through the town. I watched the bands and the children happily marching past, but my foot didn't tap to the rhythm and my face was unable to smile.

When we came back to Blackburn I went on the Youth Opportunities Scheme and became what was known as a Yopper, which was the worst thing you could call a teenager in those days. For a few months I had a job as a catering assistant in the kitchen at West Lothian College in Livingston. It was menial work, cleaning and cooking, which I wasn't best suited for because in our house my mother was cleaner, cook and chief bottle-washer. To be honest, I'd been a bit spoiled. I probably flooded the floor more often than I served a meal, but the job made a change from sitting at home in my room, even if it wasn't exactly the vocation I'd always been hoping to find.

I think the disappointment showed on my face, because on the bus home people were always saying to me, "Cheer up. It may never happen!"

If I'd had the confidence, I would have retorted, "Yes, and that's the problem."

Instead, I just scowled.

A gloomy mood seemed to have taken over the whole country that winter. It was known as the Winter of Discontent. In May 1979 a new political force swept into power under the slogan "Labour Isn't Working." Unfortunately, under Mrs. Thatcher's new government, unemployment rocketed, and I was one of the first casualties. My job hadn't exactly been inspiring, but at least I'd had some money to buy records. Now there was nothing and no prospect of change. I felt as if there was something missing in my life. Everyone else who had left school had slotted into jobs. What was wrong with me?

Anyone who has experienced depression knows that it is very different from being unhappy. When you are unhappy, you can be cheered by love and support, but when you are depressed it's like being cut off from the rest of the world. Alone in my room, I cried constantly. I wasn't able to sing. Nothing, not even music, could comfort me.

It was like being trapped in a cold, dark place. I could see the light of God's love shining outside, but I was unable to feel its warmth on me.

It must have been almost as frightening for my parents as it was for me. They had known hardship in their lives, and suffered pain. They had adapted to the unpredictability of my disability as best they could, but they'd never seen me like this. Sometimes my mother looked at me with a peculiar frown, as if she had no idea who I was any more.

I don't know if the right word for what I experienced is an emotional breakdown. I don't find the labels people put on things very helpful.

Eventually, I was referred to another psychologist.

At first, I was sceptical. Psychologists I had seen

over the years had given me tests, then talked to my mother as if I wasn't there, although I always listened to what they were saying as I pretended to be playing. Now I went to see Miss Bakie on my own. For the first few sessions I sat with my mouth firmly closed.

My insistence on keeping myself to myself because I was frightened to trust people meant that I had never experienced the release of sharing my problems with someone else. I had never learned that everyone needs relationships. If you don't engage with other people, they can't hurt you—but they can't help you either.

More importantly, if you cut yourself off from society, you don't allow yourself the chance of helping other people, which is the best therapy of all.

"How would you feel about going along to Bangour Hospital?" Miss Bakie asked me one day.

"What do you mean?" I asked, immediately suspicious.

Bangour General was the hospital where I had been born, but Bangour Village was renowned as what was known then as a mental hospital—that had been its original purpose when it was built at the end of the Victorian era. I didn't like the idea of going there one bit, until Miss Bakie explained that she wasn't recommending me to go as a patient. Her idea was that it would be good for me to get involved in voluntary work. One of the biggest hurdles I needed to climb was simply talking to other people. She felt that it would be a kind of social therapy for me to talk to young people who had problems of their own.

Growing up a Catholic, I had always known that it was my duty to help less fortunate people. But it was only when I tried counselling that I began to realize that offering comfort to others is not a selfless act, but something that gives meaning and value to life.

Part Two

A Song in the Breeze

14
Healing

Those who do not enjoy the fullness of what is called a normal way of life, through either mental or serious physical handicap, are often compensated in part by qualities which people often take for granted or even distort, under the influence of a materialistic society: such things as radiant love—transparent, innocent and yearning—and the attraction of loving and selfless care. In this regard, we often find in the Gospels the refreshing example of Jesus himself, and the loving bond of affection between him and the sick and disabled: how many were his exertions for them, the great words of faith addressed to them, and his wonderful interventions on their behalf, "for power came forth from him."

—from Pope John Paul II's speech made at St. Joseph's Service care homes, Rosewell, Scotland, 1982

The sun was up, but it was still early enough in the morning for breath to make clouds in the chilly air as we chatted quietly in the church car park. The group were mainly teachers, including my sister

Mary. My mother was invited and she had asked for me to come along too. When the coach turned off the main road and ground towards us, a small cheer went up. I was standing next to my mother, my tummy a tangle of apprehension. I'd never been as far away as London before, let alone further afield.

"It'll be worth it when we get there," my mother whispered reassuringly. She had the ability of putting herself in another person's shoes and she always seemed to know what I was thinking, sometimes before I did.

We stopped at Knutsford service station on the motorway for something to eat. It was evening by the time we arrived in London. Our hotel was a skyscraper on the Cromwell Road. I lay in bed listening to my mother's even breathing and the noise of the streets outside, unable to sleep in the persistent orange haze of city light.

In the morning, we all trailed our suitcases along the noisy street, down steps and into the busy Underground station. I'd never seen so many people on a platform, their faces breaking into sudden yawns as they tried to shake off sleep. We stood guarding our suitcases in the train, hauling them off and up more steps at Victoria.

When the boat train finally trundled out of the station, there was a sigh of relief that we'd managed to negotiate the first leg of our journey, but there was still a whole day and night's travelling by sea and rail in front of us. Watching the grimy streets of South London flashing past the window, I remembered our long car journey to Knock ten years before. It was nothing compared to this pilgrimage.

When we finally arrived in Lourdes, the train station didn't look any different from the others we'd passed through on the journey. It was too dark to see anything on the way to the hotel, and I was exhausted, but filled with anticipation.

I had always longed to come to the place where Bernadette, the poor girl with no fancy robes and no scholarship who had been chosen to spread God's message, had seen Our Lady. Now we were here, and I didn't think I would be able to sleep, but as soon as my head rested on the long sausage of a pillow, I fell into a dreamless sleep.

Lourdes is a pretty market town surrounded by wooded peaks, and the morning air had the crispness of altitude, but the southern sunlight fell kindly on my face. France smelled different to Scotland. The milk in our tea at breakfast had a funny taste. The squares of toast were dry all the way through, like sweet stale bread. Outside, as we walked down the street, we breathed delicious almond-scented wafts as we passed patisserie windows with perfect lines of beautifully decorated cakes.

It was almost Easter, and as we approached the bridge to cross the milky green river to the

Massabielle—the rock where the sanctuary buildings are situated—we found ourselves among great crowds walking with us towards the basilica, many pushing wheelchairs carrying the sick and the injured. There was a feeling of expectancy in the air, like an excited whisper rushing round. People had travelled many miles to celebrate their faith, and now the wait was almost over. I glanced at my mother and caught her looking at me with that expression she sometimes wore when she couldn't understand what was going on with me. It suddenly dawned on me that we were here for healing too and I smiled at her. Her eyes flashed with surprise and I realized it was the first time that I'd smiled in ages.

The Mass was celebrated in a cavernous modern underground basilica. I had never been to Mass with so many people. There were dozens of priests in white robes, and rows of people in wheelchairs at the front. The words repeated in many different languages sounded awesome magnified through the loud speakers and the responses rumbled through the basilica like an echo in a giant cave. It was very profound and very humbling to hear the familiar rhythm of prayers murmured in one voice from thousands of pairs of lips.

Afterwards, we stood in a queue to go into the wee grotto where Our Lady appeared to Bernadette. The Basilica of the Immaculate Conception built above it is very ornate and beautiful, but the cave is a very simple and natural chapel in the rock.

Outside in the queue there was a respectfully soft whispering of conversation, but inside the coolness of the cave there was an air of great peace. When I closed my eyes, I could hear only the soothing gurgle of water from the spring that Bernadette scratched. There were many people all around me, but I felt still and quiet, as if it were just me there, with Our Lady listening to my prayers.

My mother and I were lucky enough to get into the baths. "You mustn't dry yourself off when you get out," she instructed.

"Why?" I wanted to know.

"Because the water is miraculous."

As the water dried on my skin, I felt an indescribably wonderful physical, psychological and spiritual sense of warmth, like a holy embrace.

When I look back on my life, I can see turning points that I might not have recognized at the time, and for me it is clear that my first visit to Lourdes was such a moment.

The voluntary work suggested by the psychologist was a practical step towards finding a solution to my problems, but the visit to Lourdes arranged by my mother began to restore me spiritually and to give me back a sense of purpose.

My mother noticed it first. She said I was easier

to talk to, and I became more confident, more willing to have a go at things.

I'd wanted to be a teacher, but I recognized I wasn't good enough at exams. That didn't mean I couldn't contribute to society, so I started doing voluntary work with young people at Blackburn Community Centre. There were various sports activities laid on at the centre and sometimes we'd put on discos. For most of the young people it was just a place to hang out with their mates in the evenings.

I had never been allowed to go there as a teenager because my parents worried about the types I'd be mixing with. In the meantime the whole punk era had happened. The eighties is a decade people associate with shoulder pads and yuppies, but there weren't many of those in Blackburn. The kids who came down to the centre wore their hair in Mohican hairstyles, livid green and fluorescent pink, with torn T-shirts, leather jackets, nose rings, the lot. I don't know how their parents let them go out like that. But teenagers are never as hard as they look, and being that bit older, I was like a big sister to them.

Because I was acting in a supervisory role, rather than being in charge, I think the kids found me easier to talk to. They used to come and tell me about their problems and confide their worries. It turned out that I was quite good at the counselling side of things and I got a lot of satisfaction out of being there for them. I began to think that maybe there was an opportunity here, and perhaps a career in social work might be the thing for me.

I made some enquiries and found out you could get a formal qualification on in-service courses at a teacher training college called Moray House in Edinburgh. The idea of going to college was daunting, but I remembered a conversation I'd had just before my O-grades with a teacher called Mr. Kavanagh, who had taken me to one side and asked me a question.

"What is worry, Susan?"

"I don't know, sir, what is worry?"

"It's unproductive," he said.

"It's all right for you, sir," I told him. "You're clever."

"You're looking at someone who failed at school," he told me. "I went to Night School. I wasn't always a teacher."

Mr. Kavanagh had found a different route. Maybe I could too.

But there was another big obstacle in my way. I'd never been to Edinburgh on my own. The image I retained from childhood was of grim, dark institutions looming over me.

One day I said to myself, "Come on, Susan, you've been to London and survived. It can't be as bad as that."

So I got on the bus to Bathgate and took a train into the city. When I emerged from Waverley

Station I didn't recognize the place at all. In front of me was a beautiful park; on my right, adorned with well-tended flowerbeds and hanging baskets, Princes Street with its elegant department stores; to my left, the old town. As I climbed a flight of steps up to the centre, the tall medieval buildings with their steep, gabled roofs that had seemed so forbidding when I was a child now looked picturesque, like the illustrations you might see in a book of fairy stories.

The Royal Mile was buzzing with buskers and jugglers dressed like court jesters, and groups of tourists on sightseeing tours. A whole vibrant world of music and performance was happening just half an hour away from where I lived, and I'd never been aware of it before. I walked over the cobbles with the lightness of step that comes from feeling you've arrived in a place you were meant to be. I had a strong sense that I had turned a page in the story of my life.

If I hadn't had the courage to go to the big city on my own, I never would have been in Edinburgh when Pope John Paul II came on a pastoral visit. All of us young Scottish Catholics felt that he came specially to see us, because the first thing he did was address a huge congregation of Scottish youth at Murrayfield. I took myself up to the Mound to see his procession. There were so many people, I didn't think I had a hope of getting a glimpse because I'm not very tall, even when I stand on tiptoe, but somehow I found myself on a corner just as he was passing in his white Popemobile. As he came round he turned, and for a moment, he was looking directly at me. I felt so privileged that I bowed.

I didn't know then that His Holiness was on his way to visit St. Joseph's in Rosewell, which was a home for mentally and physically disabled people run by the Sisters of Charity of St. Vincent de Paul. There he would meet a man called Frank Quinn, who was later to become my teacher and my friend, but I'll tell you about how I met him later.

15
Happy Valley

"I'm just going for a walk," I called out as I opened the front door.

My parents were watching television in the back room. I could hear the canned laughter.

"You'll be back before it's dark?" my mother called back.

I often went for walks on my own and she was fine with that. People knew me in Blackburn. I wasn't going to come to any harm. Sometimes Uncle Michael came with me, but he was a very fast walker. He devoured the ground like an express train. That evening, they were all firmly glued to *It Ain't Half Hot Mum*. My dad had been a sergeant major in the army and they loved that programme because it was a chance for them to have a good laugh at his strictness without making him cross.

I closed the door behind me, breathing a sigh of relief. I didn't want Michael's company that evening. I was being truthful when I said I was going for a walk, but I was only intending to walk as far as the Happy Valley pub and I knew what my mother would think about that. In my family, pubs were for men. My father went for his pint with his mates every Saturday and blew in late on a cloud of cigarette smoke and the sour scent of beer. My mother never went to the pub. It wasn't a suitable place for a lady.

The Happy Valley is a small hostelry on Blackburn's main street. I must have passed it thousands of times on my way to the shops, or to church, but I had never been inside. Now I stood on the pavement looking at the silhouettes of drinkers against the glow of the window, listening to the slew of noise and random laughter. If I pushed open the door and stepped in, I wondered if all the noise would suddenly stop and people turn and stare at me.

"Are you coming in, Susan?"

Perhaps I would never have plucked up the courage if Jim Murphy hadn't come out for a breath of air and found me there. James Murphy was a man I'd known all my life. He came from a very musical family in Blackburn. His brother had been in Bridie's class at school and had gone on to play in a local band. Every Thursday evening Jim compèred a sing-song at the Happy Valley and he was always asking whether I'd like to come along.

"It's good fun. You'd enjoy it."

Nervously, I followed him into the lounge, but nobody took much notice. One or two people said, "Hello, Susan!" as if it were perfectly normal for me to be there.

Jim found a chair for me and asked what I wanted to drink.

"A lemonade, please."

"Sure you don't want anything in that, Susan?"

I shook my head. At twenty-three I was old enough to drink alcohol, but I felt guilty enough being in a pub without my mother's knowledge.

In those days, everybody smoked. I almost wished that I did, so that I had something to do. I wasn't very used to making conversation. When people asked me questions, I answered yes or no. I always forgot to ask them something back, and by the time I'd thought of something to say, they'd turned away to talk to someone else.

Fortunately, when Jim switched on the mic and started introducing the people who were going to sing, most people stopped chattering and looked at him.

The music ranged from folk to pop, with some hits from the musicals in between. There were some who could hold a tune and some who couldn't, but everyone who wanted to sing got a turn. I enjoyed listening. The atmosphere was a bit like one of the family gatherings we always had in Motherwell at New Year where everyone did their party piece.

"Would you like to sing something, Susan?" Jim was asking me.

The words "OK, then" came out of my mouth.

As I walked to the mic, I was conscious of a ripple of surprise going round the room. Most people knew me, but they'd probably never seen me without my mother before. I could tell that they didn't quite know what to expect.

I closed my eyes and imagined that I was on my own in my bedroom with my record of *Jesus Christ Superstar*.

"I don't know how to love him . . ."

The murmur of pub conversation suddenly stopped and I felt myself trembling because everybody had gone so quiet. I'd started now; I'd look even more of an idiot if I stopped. I kept my mind fixed on what the words were saying, and that steadied my voice, making it clear and strong. By the time I reached the end I was so involved in the emotion of the song that I had virtually forgotten that anyone else was there.

I opened my eyes.

The room was completely silent, and then somebody cheered, another person whistled and the place was rocking with applause. It was a very nice surprise.

I handed the mic back to Jim. His eyes were shining like Mr. Green's when I was at primary school.

"Are you not going to give us another song, Susan?" he asked.

"Go on!" someone shouted.

Others clapped and stamped their feet.

I took back the mic and sang "Take That Look Off Your Face" from *Tell Me on a Sunday* by Andrew Lloyd Webber. That's not a song you can sing with your eyes closed. At home, I looked in the dressing-table mirror when I sang it, imagining I was Marti Webb wearing a blue shiny jumpsuit and staring into the camera as I'd seen her do on television. I'd never sung the song to an audience. On family occasions I might have had people watching me, but I never made eye contact with anyone. Now I found myself picking out faces, singing the words to them. To my surprise, they smiled back at me. It felt as if they liked me.

I had finally discovered a way of communicating, and it was a nice way, because it made people happy! It was like finding the key to a box of jewels that I had never been able to open, lifting the lid and feeling the sparkling reflection lighting up my face.

When I finished singing I sat down on a chair, but my spirits were as high as a kite. I've never taken drugs, but that feeling was addictive.

From then on, I was sneaking out of the house every Thursday night.

My parents must have suspected that something was going on after I'd come back from my "walk" several times smelling of smoke and with a great big smile on my face.

One evening, my dad followed me down the road and stopped me just as I was about to go into the Happy Valley.

"Are you going into that pub on your own?" he called.

"It's OK, they know me," I told him, guiltily.

"You shouldn't be doing that," he said.

"I'm not doing any harm. I'm just sitting on my own with a lemonade."

"You should get somebody to go with you," he said.

"Well, why don't you come in then?"

So he did, and when the mic came round, he couldn't resist getting up to sing himself. He gave them "Scarlet Ribbons."

After that, he let me go on my own because he'd checked the place out and he knew I wasn't going to get into trouble. My dad was a man's man. He didn't want to go to the pub with a woman.

16
On Becoming a Person

Singing gave me a new identity. Instead of being "That Susan Boyle . . . do you remember she was a bit odd at school?" I became "Susan Boyle . . . did you know she can really sing?" As well as The Happy Valley, I often used to sing at the Bowling Club in Blackburn too. Singing was my social life in the evenings, and during the day I started going into Edinburgh once a week for my course at Moray House.

One of the books on the reading list for the diploma I was studying for was called *On Becoming a Person* by Carl Rogers. It's about helping people to discover their path to personal growth. Through reading it, I began to understand more about my potential, my limitations and how other people saw me. It was like opening a window to understanding myself a little better. We also studied Jungian psychology and the idea of life being a journey, and that seemed very relevant to me at the time.

When the opportunity came up for a paid job as a youth leader at the Community Centre, I applied for it, but the authorities felt someone older would be better for the post. I kept doing my voluntary work because I had taken on board that life is not about solving problems once and for all, but about being part of a process. I was on a journey. I just didn't know where it was going just yet.

You could say that the eighties were a period of trial and error for me. I kept trying to find the right path, but I made the error of looking in the wrong places! At that time I believed that you had to have an academic qualification in order to make a success of your life. I took all sorts of courses because I was desperate to prove that I wasn't stupid. I was reasonably good at doing essays, but I always came up against the same brick wall of exams.

When my voluntary contract at the Blackburn Community Centre ended, I decided to have a go at the Open University. The idea of studying at home appealed to me, as I could work in my own time without the pressure of being in a class with other people. The course I entered was for a BA in Social Work and the elements I had to pass were Social Science Foundation, Psychology and Social Psychology. As somebody who left school with two O-grades, I was quite proud of getting on the course.

In the summer of 1985 I went away from home for the first time in my life to an Open University summer school at Stirling University. My mum and dad took me to the railway station and waved me off. Then I was on my own. I thought I looked like a proper student in a pair of pink dungarees with the legs rolled up. Now I think I must have resembled a stick of rock.

It was a nice atmosphere on the course, and I met people from all different backgrounds and age groups. The following year I went to a summer school for a week at Keele University, which was even further afield. On that occasion I studied English Literature, Art History, Music and Drama as well. Lying in my student bedroom in the halls of residence, I sometimes tried to imagine what it would be like to be a full-time student, being self-sufficient for long stretches of time, but I never took the thought much further, because I knew that the idea of me leaving home would worry my parents. I don't think they would have tried to stop me going, but I didn't want to cause them any more anxiety. Although they never said so, I was aware that I had been a nuisance to my parents all my life. Now they were getting old and my mother wasn't always in the best of health, I didn't want to start making things difficult again.

My sisters thought I had an easy life. As they saw it, I was trying this course and that course, popping into Edinburgh whenever I felt like it, and not doing much around the house.

"I'm not going to make a skivvy out of her," my mother told them firmly.

As the youngest daughter, who didn't look likely to get married, it would have been usual for me to take on the burden of housework, but my mother didn't want that for me. To be honest, I think my sisters were right. I was a bit spoiled.

A lot of assumptions have been made about me caring for my mother, but the truth is that for most of my life my mother was my carer, my supporter and my rock. She looked after me like a bird with a broken wing and wrapped me up in cotton wool when perhaps I would have benefited from a good boot in the backside!

Sometimes I think that making allowances because there was "something wrong with me" did me more harm than good. You can prevent people from developing their full potential by protecting them too much. I've come to realize that you should always try to focus on what people can do, not what they can't do. That being said, my mother never stopped me from exploring avenues that I was interested in, and I never felt that I was being prevented from spreading my wings and flying. Mum encouraged me to do whatever made me happy and I was always quite comfortable remaining in the nest because I felt safe and secure there.

My mother never let me make mistakes about the way I dressed, although I could have done with less interference from my dad. On one occasion I came down with a pair of leggings, a long shirt and a leather jacket over the top.

"Name of God, it's the f. . .ing budgie!" was my dad's assessment.

"What's wrong with it?" I asked him.

"They're not even trousers, they're long johns," he said. "You're not going out like that!"

I did have the occasional rebellion, like the time I decided I'd like to dye my hair a weird and wonderful colour like the fashion designer Zandra Rhodes. I bought a can of pink hairspray and whooshed it on, but it looked ridiculous, so I brushed it out. Unfortunately, my mother used the same hairbrush later that day. Her hair was white, but that afternoon it looked like a stick of candyfloss!

Another time, I thought I'd try smoking, but my dad caught me.

"Oi! What are you doing?"

"I'm having a smoke," I told him.

"Well, I wouldn't mind, but they're my fags. Buy your own!"

My father was overprotective in his own way.

In my late twenties I had a boyfriend called John for seven weeks. I met him at a wedding and it was the first time I was involved with anyone, because I was always frightened of guys at the time, but he was very kind. It was a very chaste relationship that never went further than holding hands and a peck on the cheek. But when I held his hand, I knew it was a very different feeling from holding my mother's hand, and when he pecked me on the cheek, it wasn't like my brother giving me a kiss, because the touch of my boyfriend's lips lingered on my skin for hours. When we were together, it was a completely new feeling, knowing he liked me and I liked him. It made my face smile all the time. I waited for him to call, my tummy all giddy with nerves that became giggles of relief as soon as I heard his voice, and he'd make some joke, or I'd say something funny to him. Once, John took me home and his mother proudly showed me a new fridge she'd just bought.

"That'll do for you when you get married," she told me.

"You want us to live in there? Won't that be a bit cold?" I attempted a joke to cover my embarrassment.

I couldn't decide whether the prospect of making a life with a man was thrilling or terrifying.

Then one day I was upstairs in my room when the phone rang in the hall. My dad got to it first.

"She doesnae want to talk to you," he said, and put down the receiver.

"Who was that?" I asked him, bewildered, as I came down the stairs.

"You're no ready for a boyfriend, hen!" my dad informed me.

I suppose my dad was right and I wasn't mature enough for a relationship. I'd read *Tess of the D'Urbervilles* at an impressionable age. I'd seen Barbra Streisand and Robert Redford in *The Way*

We Were. I thought that love was all about people who should be together not being able to be together. My dad only wanted to protect me from getting hurt, but it did hurt when we stopped seeing each other. The only way I could find to fill the emptiness was singing upstairs in my room. I learned to express my pain through song.

With all that has happened in the last year, it seems obvious now that what I should have been trying to do all along was pursue a career in singing, but until my late twenties the thought didn't seriously cross my mind. I sang socially at The Happy Valley and at the Bowling Club. Sometimes I went down to Coventry to visit Bridie at the Tam O'Shanter Club. I wouldn't have dreamed of asking to go up on stage and sing there, as Gerard often did, but there was one evening when Bridie's husband, Jimmy, who'd had a drink or two, insisted that I was going to sing.

The band had finished playing for the night, but the club was still full. Jimmy took me down, still in my slippers, from watching television in the flat upstairs and announced to the whole room, "I want you to listen to this singer!"

There must have been a thousand people in and it was a Saturday night so all of them were rowdy and full of drink. I didn't think anyone was listening; even if they were, I didn't expect they would be able to hear. But Jimmy was determined, so I did as I was told and sang them "Scarlet Ribbons." At the end, you could have heard a pin drop.

After that, I was sometimes asked to make up numbers in the singing competitions when the Tam O'Shanter came up to Fir Park in Motherwell at Easter. There's a video someone took at the time. I'm singing "The Way We Were." People were always telling me that my singing would bring a tear to a glass eye and occasionally, when I sat down after a song, someone would say, "You're wasted here, hen!" or "Have you ever thought of doing something with your singing, Susan?" but I don't think anybody seriously entertained the thought of me becoming a professional, least of all me. You can see on the video that I was still a very shy wee lassie. I wasn't bad looking in those days, with my curly hair shoulder length and kept under control with clips, but I wore conservative skirts and blouses, chosen for me by my mother. I didn't exactly look the part.

Gala Days are a summer tradition in the small towns and villages of West Lothian. Everybody gets involved. Each Saturday in June it's the turn of a different village and there's always a theme, like the circus, or a zoo, so the schools and nurseries make costumes for the big parade. Bunting goes up in the streets and the whole community turns out to watch the bands and floats going past. Our family always used to gather at Kathleen's house in Whitburn because the procession passed the end of the crescent where she lived.

In the local park there is a caravan where you can buy tickets for your Gala Day box, and on the day you hand in your ticket and get a bag full of treats, like juice, crisps and a Tunnock's tea cake. There are races organized in the park for the children, and, if the weather's good, everyone eats their picnic there. In the evening the teenagers go to the shows—a travelling fairground that stops in every village on its Gala Day. It's a real family occasion, something everybody looks forward to each year.

In the run-up to Gala Day is Civic Week, during which different events are organized on each night to raise funds for the Gala Day committee so that they can have a Gala Day the next year. There are quiz nights and football tournaments, and also singing competitions, in which teams from all the local pubs and clubs take it in turns to host a singing competition each night of the week.

Whitburn Miners' Welfare is a working men's club with a long tradition of live music. In the sixties the Kinks and lots of other famous bands played there. During the eighties, Kathleen used to work behind the bar in the evenings and one year, when they were trying to get a team together for the competition, she put my name forward.

When the compère called me up to the stage I

was more nervous than I usually was because it was a competition and the audience wouldn't necessarily be on my side. Kathleen gave my hand an encouraging squeeze. I didn't want to let her down, so I took a deep breath and pushed past tables full of people.

I sang the Eva Cassidy version of "Somewhere Over the Rainbow." When I finished, there was a moment of stunned silence, then everyone cheered—even the other teams! As I wove my way back to our table, people kept patting me, or shaking my hand.

"Amazing!"

"Fantastic!"

"That's some voice you've got there, hen!"

"Have you thought of taking it further?"

I smiled and shook my head, knowing I would never be able to face an audience I didn't know. Then it suddenly dawned on me that was what I'd just done. I'd sung in a venue where professionals were paid to sing every week, and the crowd seemed to like it!

17
Opportunity Knocks

Every decade of my life has had its own television talent show. In the sixties it was *Opportunity Knocks* with Hughie Green. The audience in the studio judged the acts on a clap-o-meter, but the real result was in the hands of the audience at home, who used to have to write the name of the act they liked in their own handwriting and send it into the programme. Sometimes that method produced shock results, like when the comedienne Su Pollard was beaten by a singing dog. Some great acts came out of that show. I can still remember watching Mary Hopkin with her acoustic guitar singing "Those Were the Days," and that wee Glasgow lassie with the raunchy voice, Lena Zavaroni, whose fairy story later turned into a tragedy.

In our home, it was the one night of the week where the whole family was round the television, laughing at the freaks and cheering on our favourites. As you've probably gathered, we all had our opinions and we expressed them loudly!

In the seventies there was a programme called *New Faces*, in which the acts were judged by a panel of professionals. Some judges, like the disc jockeys Ed Stewart and Noel Edmonds, were generally encouraging; others, like Tony Hatch, could be a bit mean. Remind you of anyone? One of the winners, a tall, red-haired entertainer called Marti Caine, actually went on to present the show. The best thing about those sorts of shows is that they give ordinary people a foot in the door of fame.

It was the only route to success that someone like me knew. I hadn't a clue about how the music industry worked. So, in the late eighties, when the BBC announced that they were reviving *Opportunity Knocks*, which had previously been an ITV programme, I thought I'd have a go. As I said to myself when I wrote off for an audition, "What do you have to lose? Nobody's going to know about it anyway."

The morning of the scheduled audition, I spent ages in our bathroom, trying out different looks in the mirror. I wanted to be taken seriously, so eventually I decided on a black dress. To make myself more glamorous I got a silver scarf and tied that round my neck. In those days, big hair was the thing. Mine was bigger than most, but not in the right way. I'd never got the hang of taming it back from my face into waves that would stay, so I scraped it back into a bun. I thought I looked quite elegant, but when I went downstairs to show my mother, she told me I'd be better without the silver scarf. I took it off, but shoved it in my handbag so that I could put it on again when I got there.

I'd never been to Glasgow on my own, and my mother didn't want me getting lost, so Gerard gave me a lift with a friend of his.

The producer of the show asked me what I was going to sing.

"'I Don't Know How to Love Him' from *Jesus Christ Superstar*," I told him.

I'd chosen that song because it was like a talisman for me. I'd sung it my first time at The Happy Valley, and I'd sung it at my parents' Golden Wedding anniversary party. I didn't know any of the technical terms about registers and ranges then; I just knew the song seemed to use my whole voice and the words meant a lot to me too. People who heard me sing it said that it made the hairs stand up on their arms.

The producer could barely disguise his boredom at my song choice. "You realize you've only got three minutes?" he said. "Start when you see the green light."

I stood where I was told in front of the microphone. A red light came on to show that we were recording, and then the green light. I closed my eyes and found the first note, then I remembered I was being filmed, so I opened my eyes, looked at the camera and sang with all my heart.

What the producer hadn't told me was that you were supposed to stop when the green light went off, but I was only halfway through the second chorus. The crew began preparing for the next audition, but I went on singing until I reached the end of the song.

"Thank you," the producer called in a distracted voice from somewhere in the darkness behind the camera. He didn't even bother to say, "Don't call us, we'll call you."

So that was that.

Gerard said I'd done well, apart from the business with the lights. But I knew I'd made a right codswallop of it.

I didn't say a lot on the way home because I was in a mood.

What an anticlimax! I'd got myself all dressed up for that. I'd sung the song well. I knew I had. What sort of stupid rule was three minutes anyway? Next time, I'd show them. I would. I'd show them!

If I'm being absolutely honest, the best thing about going into Edinburgh for the day had never been the academic courses I took as much as the atmosphere on the streets as I walked to the college. There was always something to stop and watch, from bagpipers in tartan kilts to mime artists in monochrome Pierrot outfits. During the Edinburgh Festival season, you can hardly move for people in sandwich boards handing out flyers for Fringe events, but though I always said thank you very much and took one, I never actually went into a theatre or the upstairs of a pub where a performance was taking place.

I'd never been to the theatre in my life. My family didn't have that sort of money. So I didn't really know how you went about it, but I increasingly found myself outside places like the Assembly Rooms, watching people go in and wondering what it was like inside.

"I was thinking of going to one of those shows on the Fringe." I floated the idea one evening to my mother. "It's with one of the guys from *That's Life!*"

That's Life! was a television programme we all enjoyed. It was a combination of consumer journalism and humorous observations. Simon Fanshawe was one of the presenters and I thought it would be great to see him in real life.

"What time does it finish?" she asked.

"I don't know," I admitted.

"As long as you catch the eleven o'clock train," she said.

It was as easy as that.

Simon Fanshawe's show was full of jokes about what was in the headlines. He was nominated for the Perrier Award that year, and two years later he won it. The material was a lot more risqué than *That's Life!* and I found it hilarious. Afterwards, I saw that some people were going up to say hello to him, so I thought I'd go too. As I shook his hand, he said, "They can't shut you up, can they?"

That made me laugh even more. I gave him a little cuddle, because that's what I'd seen the ones in front of me do.

It was a great feeling meeting someone I'd seen on television, and there was enough time for me to get a burger to eat on the eleven o'clock train home.

After that there was no stopping me. I'd been well and truly bitten by the theatre bug and I saw as many shows as I could. Instead of disapproving, as I'd half expected, my parents were pleased that I'd found a passion. Sometimes, when a show on the Fringe was going to finish after the last train back to Bathgate, my father would even come in to Edinburgh and wait outside the show to pick me up. They thought it was a good outlet for me and a safe way of mixing with people.

"You always did love your play-acting when you were a child," my mother remembered.

As usual, she seemed to know what I was thinking almost before I did. I enjoyed being part of the audience, but the more shows I saw, the more I found myself thinking about what it would be like to be on stage myself.

One of the Fringe venues was in University building on Pleasance and I noticed that it was also the location of something called the Edinburgh Acting School. I applied and got an interview with a lady called Amanda, who was a graduate of Edinburgh's Queen Margaret University herself.

She accepted me, saying that I'd start from the basics and build up, so I began with a leisure class one evening a week with other adults. Part of the training was to act in shows that the school put on, but first of all we had to audition.

The first role I tried for was the part of Puck. He was supposed to be wee and dainty. I am short, but I've never been what you might call light-footed.

Plonk, plonk, plonk.

That was me coming on to the stage.

The director called out, "Can you please lift your feet!"

"I am lifting my feet!" I shouted back.

He said, "You're supposed to be a fairy, not a flaming horse!"

"Well, I'm not wearing these stupid tights, and I'm definitely not flying!" I told him.

"OK, then," he said. "We'll get someone else."

Afterwards he told me, "You're the only fairy I've seen who'd make a hole in the floor!"

I found that I was very good at improvisations. It must have been all that practice in the playground when I was at primary school. I also had a talent for mimicry. Years of copying voices from the television finally found a use when they put me into a comedy magic show for children.

Unfortunately I was in a different sort of trouble for that because my mum and dad decided to come along to see the show.

"Oh dear, who's this? They'd let in any riff-raff

these days," I improvised when I saw them arriving in the middle of it.

That got a laugh from the audience, but it didn't go down too well with my dad.

"Don't you be cheeky like that in public again!" he told me when ~~we got~~ home. Or words to that effect.

I decided to extend my studies at the Edinburgh Acting School to include a special subject— Musical Theatre. During my twenties my taste in music had matured from pop to musicals. The emotions those songs could evoke were deeper and more in line with what I was feeling at the time, especially the musicals of Andrew Lloyd Webber. I bought all the albums and I knew every word and every note. The voice I tried hardest to emulate was Elaine Paige in *Cats*. It was a strong voice and I loved the way she could make a character come alive, even though I'd never seen her on stage.

I'd never seen a musical in my life before I started at the Edinburgh Acting School, but now I began going to productions at the Edinburgh Playhouse because there was a discount for students at the school. The seats up in the balcony weren't too expensive, and when I had a little bit of extra money after Christmas or my birthday, I'd treat myself to a seat in the Circle.

The first musical I ever went to was *Barnum*, and I was lucky enough to see Michael Crawford in the title role. Everybody thought he was great in the sitcom *Some Mothers Do 'Ave 'Em*, but on stage he was even better. There could be no finer example of why we say *give* a performance, because Michael Crawford gave it everything, pouring every ounce of his energy and talent into that show. After that I went to see every musical that came on, including all the ones I'd starred in up in my bedroom, like *Cats*, *Evita* and *Jesus Christ Superstar*. It was at the Edinburgh Playhouse that I first saw *Les Misérables*, and I loved it so much I went back again, and again, and again.

After two years at the Edinburgh Acting School, I auditioned for the musical *Guys and Dolls*, but I didn't get the part, perhaps because I had the dancing skills of a shire horse in a tutu. But I did achieve Guildhall Grade 7 in drama, and that gave me more confidence when I went on stage in singing competitions in the local pubs and clubs. At the time, it didn't seem as if my career as a professional singer was going anywhere, but when I look back I realize I was gradually gaining the skills I would need to become a performer.

In the world of television talent shows, the nineties belonged to Michael Barrymore, who hosted a show called *My Kind of People*. I wrote to LWT for an audition and the first place I went along to was the Forge Shopping Centre in Glasgow.

I was a big fan of Michael Barrymore and when

I met him I was a bit tongue-tied, so I just said, "You're the guy out of *Strike It Lucky*, aren't you?"

"Don't look at my hotspots and you'll be fine," was his smart reply.

I was meant to be singing "The Way We Were," but I tripped as I was going on stage so that wasn't a good start, and I was a bit too nervous to get my words across, so that wasn't very impressive, but I enjoyed the day chatting to the other contestants.

I could see that Michael Barrymore made fun of the ones he thought could take it and he let the really talented ones have the stage to themselves, so now that I understood the format, I thought to myself, If I keep on doing this, perhaps I'll get better.

For the next audition, in a shopping centre in East Kilbride, I got myself dressed up in my mother's best dress and my own bright pink jacket and scraped my hair back into a topknot with a scarf tied around it. At the time I thought I looked sophisticated, but I now know that I looked as if I had a cake on my head. Someone who had a relation singing in the show must have been filming it on a video camera, and when I became famous they put the recording up on YouTube.

"Are you in braces?" Michael Barrymore asked me when I went up on the stage.

"Why?" I asked.

"Because you keep coming back to me!"

"Well, I don't want people to think I'm not a tryer, so I try," I told him.

159

I'd decided to sing "I Don't Know How to Love Him" because I wanted to give it my very best shot. It's a very serious song, and I tried to remember everything I'd learned at the Edinburgh Acting School and channel it all into the words.

Unfortunately, Michael Barrymore had other ideas. When the audience in front of me started laughing, I realized he must be making funny faces behind my back, so I thought I'd play him at his own game. When he knelt on the floor beside me, I crouched down beside him, singing the song to him, but when he lay on the floor trying to look up my skirt, I wasn't sure what to do. People have said it looked as if I was trying to kick him in the face with my heel, but I wasn't, I was just trying to avoid him being rude.

Sometimes things don't turn out the way you want them to, but that doesn't mean you should give up, because there's usually a positive to take from a failure. It's only afterwards that you can look back and see all the steps you have made on your journey.

I didn't get on to television with my audition for *My Kind of People*, but it was very fortunate that I went along to the show, because it was there that I got talking to a very accomplished singer called Trina Reid. She told me about a singing teacher she went to, Fred O'Neil, and she gave me his telephone number.

18
Finding My Voice

It was chucking it down with rain as I walked from the bus stop down a road in a modern estate on the outskirts of Livingston, but I was well protected with a raincoat and a rainhat as well as my umbrella. There wasn't a bit of me that the rain was going to get to.

"Are you Fred O'Neil?" I asked the tall, good-looking man who opened the door as I peered out under the brim of my dripping rainhat. I was keeping my distance because there were a couple of small dogs yapping round his legs.

"I am," he said. "And you must be Susan. Would you prefer me to put these two in the kitchen?"

I think he could see that I'm a wee bit frightened of dogs. You never know if they're going to jump up at you.

"I would," I told him.

I waited on the doorstep until it was safe to go inside.

Fred looked slightly aghast as I removed my outer layers and dripped all over his hall carpet.

The front room was a normal kind of sitting room with a standard lamp and a sofa, except that half of it was taken up with a baby grand piano. The thing I noticed straight away was a framed black-and-white photograph on the wall showing a very beautiful young man dressed in kind of 1920s style and wearing a boater hat.

I looked at Fred's head of strawberry blond hair and then back at the photo.

"Is that you?" I asked him.

"It's from a movie I did when I was twenty-two," Fred told me.

"You've got some make-up on there!" I observed. "You're an actor, are you?"

"I used to do some television and film acting," he said. I noticed that he had a slow, considered way of speaking. "The way I describe myself now is a singer and a singing teacher."

I tried to work out his age. He looked younger than I expected a teacher to be.

"How old are you?" I asked.

"I'm thirty-four," he said.

"I'm thirty-five," I told him.

"Well, here we are!" he said.

I decided that I liked the guy.

"Are you going to teach me to sing, then?" I asked him.

"Let's start with a few scales."

Fred and I were reminiscing recently about our first meeting, so I'll let him describe it from his point of view.

"We did some scales just to see what your voice was like. I pretend I'm working out people's range, but I'm really seeing what their tuning's like. And of course your tuning was great, Susan. What I heard was a lovely round sound and some crystal top notes which were just plucked out of the air. An A1 instrument, the best kind of instrument, and I was excited. There's no point in saying, oh I knew this person was going to be a superstar, because anyone who says that is lying. None of us knew. I'm also very wary—no matter how wonderful a singer is—about trying to hoist a dream on to someone, because that can cause them a lot of hurt in their life. I just try to make people into better singers, and enjoy their singing."

I think that probably shows you exactly why Fred and I got on so well. We still do.

Singing was something I'd done all my life, but I had never learned anything about it. Fred explained about the different areas of the voice—the head, the face and the chest—and how the most important thing to work on is the bridging notes between, so that the voice moves easily between the top register and the lower register without the sound seeming tight or strained. He had a very polite, respectful manner and, instead of feeling like a pupil, I felt like an adult to whom he was talking as an equal, so my attitude was a lot better than it had been with most of the teachers I'd known. I never argued with Fred, and I always tried to sing whatever he asked me, even when I thought that the notes were too high or too low for me. I trusted Fred, and that was a rare experience for me.

On top of that, Fred has a great sense of humour, and as I relaxed in his company, so did he in mine, and his manner became more gossipy and a wee bit less formal.

After I'd been going to him for a week or two, I said, "O'Neil. That sounds like an Irish name."

"Well, I'm originally from Dublin," he told me.

"You haven't got the accent."

"But I *can* have!" To my delight, Fred suddenly stopped speaking in an upper-class Edinburgh accent and changed to an Irish one. "I was a choirboy in Dublin before my family came to live over here."

"I have Irish roots myself," I told him. "My mother's family comes from Donegal and the Derry area."

"I used to go to the North for my holidays," Fred said, "because I had a granny who lived between Ballycastle and Portrush—"

"I was on holiday in Portrush when I was six!" I interrupted.

"Well, Susan, I bet you and I were the biggest two screamers on the beach!" said Fred.

I remembered that first holiday so well, how I'd loved playing in the sand, and how all the other children had jumped into the paddling pool my brothers had dug out for me. Perhaps Fred had been among them. It was a nice connection between us.

Whenever I'm enthusiastic about somebody, I tend to talk about them all the time. I was like that about Terry Wogan, and Donny Osmond, and Michael Barrymore. Now that my singing lessons were the highlight of my week, I talked about Fred so much that my mother decided to come along and see for herself. She used to sit on the sofa while Fred explained what we were doing, and she took it all in because she knew a bit about music and could play the piano herself.

"If you read about the very great singers, Mrs. Boyle," Fred told her, "you'll find that they come with humility to the music. I've had singers come to me who talk a great game, but when they open their mouths they don't have it. But people who are interested in what the song has to give approach it with more modesty. If you listen to Maria Callas talking about singing, she doesn't come across as a big head. And this is what I like about Susan. She comes with a good attitude, so she can absorb what I'm trying to give her. She's very good at taking in the finer points. Not like some people, who only want to talk about how great they are . . ."

That was certainly music to my mother's ears!

Fred was very close to his own mother and that was another nice bond between us. If my mother wasn't on that sofa listening to my singing, his mother often would be, and she was a very pleasant, encouraging lady.

Occasionally Fred used to organize musical evenings for his pupils in the Massey Hall, just beside West Lothian College, where I'd had my first and only job. He'd get a couple of musician friends to come along to accompany us, and the idea was to try to give some of the pupils who were nervous an opportunity to sing with a sympathetic audience. Although I could be nervous before singing, as soon as I filled my lungs the nerves disappeared, as if I'd bloomed into a different person.

With Fred's guidance, I developed a new and more challenging repertoire, including "The Music of the Night" from *Phantom of the Opera*, which has some very high notes. Fred is a great one for jazz and he was the person who suggested that songs like "Summertime" and "Cry Me a River" might suit my voice. The emotion of "Cry Me a River" is quite powerful, and I always think of my ex-boyfriend John when I am singing it. I sang it once at one of Fred's musical evenings, accompanied simply by a bass guitar. When I sat down, Fred told me, "That was the best rendition of the song I've ever heard. When you sing, your whole persona is like a jigsaw becoming complete."

Fred is always careful to call himself a singing teacher rather than a voice coach. He thinks the description "voice coach" concentrates too much on the physical rather than the emotional side of singing. The way he puts it is, "The diaphragm is the engine room, but the heart is where the magic is."

Fred doesn't really approve of reality television shows, but he got caught up in the fall-out from *Britain's Got Talent* and he was inundated with emails from all round the world, as well as requests from television stations. He has always been very supportive of me when people have interviewed him over the last year. Recently he told me, "When people ask me what do you think of this ordinary woman who's become a superstar, I tell them, look, she's not an ordinary woman, she's an extraordinary person who'd got a different kind of voice and a different personality. There's a whole lot of things which are different about you, Susan, but that's what makes you unlike anyone else. You've had long enough to mature, like wine in a cask, so you're not a watered-down version of a famous singer, as so many of these reality television stars are. You are your own version of Susan. You're not like another person in the world!"

"Well, thank God for that!" I replied. "If there were two of me, you'd be worried!"

It was only after going to Fred and learning more about the art of singing that I found confidence in my own unique voice rather than simply trying to do a good imitation of another artist. I set about increasing my repertoire and trying out new songs on my friendly audiences at The Happy Valley and the Bowling Club. Some of my favourites were "Save the Best till Last," "I Only Want to Be with You," and "Tell Me It's Not True" from *Blood Brothers*. After the film *Titanic* came out in the UK in 1998, people were always asking me for "My Heart Must Go On." The first time I sang it was at the Bowling Club. There was a howling gale outside, and when I reached the top of the song, all the windows suddenly blew open. I'd love to say it was the force of my voice, but I think it was just the wind. A power cut made the room go black and the mic I was holding was dead.

"Now I know how it felt on the bloody *Titanic*!" I exclaimed in the darkness.

When I wasn't singing in competitions, there were always the karaoke nights that had become very popular in local pubs, like The Turf in Blackburn. The standard of singing wasn't as high as it was in the competitions, but it was great fun with all the different levels taking part. One of the songs I most liked to sing solo was "Killing Me Softly," and sometimes I was asked to sing in a duet. On one occasion I sang "I Know Him So Well" with a local woman I'd not sung with before down at The Turf. I took the Elaine Paige part and she took Barbara Dixon's tune. We brought the house down.

It was around this time that I was reading the local newspaper and saw an advertisement for an Edinburgh studio called Heartbeat, where you could make your own recording. I thought that would be a great experience. It cost a lot of money, so I saved until I had enough, then I rang up the studio and made an appointment.

Heartbeat Studio was large enough to hold a band, and as I stood in the middle of this big room with just me and a mic on a stand, I felt a wee bit self-conscious singing in front of a guy I didn't know. The producer's name was David and he was very good at putting me at my ease and giving me hints about which takes sounded better, talking to me through a microphone as he operated the great board of knobs and switches behind a glass wall.

By the end of the day we had laid down three tracks. "Cry Me a River" and "Killing Me Softly" sounded really good. I felt I'd made a bit of a mess of "Don't Cry for Me Argentina," but it was really exciting holding my own CD in my hand and I couldn't wait to get home and play it to my mum. We took it round to a couple of the neighbours and they were really impressed at how good I sounded. It was a strange feeling for me, because up until then I'd never heard myself singing as other people heard me. I never quite got used to the excitement of putting on the CD and hearing myself singing like a proper professional. I was still far too shy to pluck up the courage to send the demo tape off to record companies, but it was worth every penny I'd saved just for the experience of recording it.

Not long after that, I won a proper competition. Previously, whenever I'd entered a singing competition I'd come second. The competition was at Whitburn Miners' Welfare Club, where I often sang, but this time the prize was £1,000. I sang "Somewhere Over the Rainbow" again, with "I Don't Know How to Love Him" as my second song. I'm too shy to stay very long on the stage after I've performed, even when the applause is still going strong. As I made my way back to my table, I got the usual compliments and pats on the back, and, as usual, the compère read out the winners in reverse order. I wasn't second, so I assumed that I wasn't even in the top three. I was just about to take a sip of my lemonade when I heard my name. At first I couldn't believe it. I had dreamed about hearing my name read out so many times, and then woken up in bed. This time I was still sitting at my table after I'd pinched myself. The applause reverberated round the room. People were looking at me, smiling. I can't remember going back up to the stage. I think I must have floated there. I was bubbling when the compère handed over the money.

"Does this make me a professional, then?" I asked him.

"Well, what do you think?" he asked.

That was more money than I'd ever seen in my life, but it went like water. I took myself out to the shops and spent the lot—a gold necklace for me, and for my mother a wee pink twinset. On the way home I passed a jeweller's. There was a pretty gold clock with a glass dome on it and a mechanism that whirled one way, then the other. It was the kind of special gift you buy to commemorate an occasion and it was the most expensive item I'd ever considered purchasing, but I knew that my mother would like to look at it as she sat in her chair. After all she had done for me, it was a wonderful feeling to be able to give her something precious with money that I had earned myself.

There was an even more profound moment on my singing journey when I sang "Ave Maria" during a Mass for a friend of mine called Francis Whelan, who was receiving a special award from the church.

It's very daunting to sing on your own in church. I practised the song many times, but nothing prepared me for what I felt as I stood up in Our Lady of Lourdes. I was used to singing as part of the congregation, looking towards the altar. Now I was facing the congregation. Too shy to look anyone in the eye, I gazed up over their heads towards the balcony at the back of the church, where a stained-glass window depicting the story of Lourdes runs across the width of the church. Focusing my gaze on the bright azure robe of Our

Lady, I opened my mouth to sing and felt the same stillness descend on me that I had felt in the grotto at Lourdes. It was as if I was on my own, in the presence of Our Lady, and the song I was singing was my simple prayer. I sang to her with an open heart, her purity and clarity reflecting in my voice as I offered myself to her service. Even though I was singing in a public place, it was an intensely private experience.

St. Augustine said, "He who sings, prays twice."

19
Family Matters

My parents celebrated their Diamond Wedding anniversary in 1996. Even though they'd sometimes had their arguments over the years, their love for each other and their strong faith in God held them together for more than six decades. There was a big family party to celebrate, and everyone kept saying how good they were for their age.

My dad compèred the sing-song with his customary sergeant-major efficiency, and when it was his turn to sing his favourite "Scarlet Ribbons," the notes were still there, even if his voice was a wee bit coarser now, as if you could hear in it the years he'd worked down the mines. I'd heard him singing that song all my life, but watching him I felt a wee bit sad inside, and when he'd finished I clapped as hard as I could.

Our daily routine at home was simple. Until they were into their eighties, my mother and father did their own shopping. My father spent most of his days pottering about in his garage, doing endless repairs to his car. In the evenings, he watched television with Michael, the two of them often arguing vehemently with people on the screen.

Sometimes I would take my uncle Michael to the cinema in Bathgate and buy chips to eat on the walk home.

My mother still got her four books a week from the library. As she had been for her own children, she became a fount of knowledge for her grandchildren, then the great-grandchildren who followed. If anyone ever had a problem with homework, Granny Boyle was the first port of call. My mother was a great enabler, always encouraging people to find things out for themselves and showing them how to look things up in the encyclopedia. She would have made a great teacher herself.

With all of her chicks except me flown the nest, she finally found time to pursue a hobby of her own. There was an art club in Whitburn, and when she went along one evening, she discovered that she liked painting. There was a good mix of people in the group and she enjoyed the social side of it, but she also had a talent she wanted to develop. Very often, when I came in from a walk or a singing lesson, I'd call out, "I'm back!" in the empty hall, and she'd shout, "Hello!" down from my bedroom upstairs, where she had set up the card table for her paints, along with an easel, but she wouldn't come down for hours because she was so absorbed in her painting.

Often she used photographs for inspiration, like the picture of me as a baby in my pram. Some of my mother's paintings were judged good enough to go into an exhibition in Whitburn Library. Sometimes she'd copy scenes from prints, like the three rustic scenes that are now on our living-room wall and were viewed by a much larger audience when I did my first transatlantic television interview!

As if sensing a certain emptiness in the house, a series of stray cats adopted us. My mother loved cats and she took them in like wee orphans, cuddling and making a fuss of them.

It's funny how cats have different personalities. Our original cat, Twizzle, was more of a kids' cat who liked to play. Then there was Flo, who lived up to her name, leaving a trail wherever she went in the house! Betsy, whom we nicknamed Bagpuss because she was so fat, was a motherly cat. It was obvious that she'd been kicked around by her previous owners because she flinched when you went to touch her, but she had a lovely nature and soon settled into our household, eating like a horse and bringing home a friend whom we called Jake. Jake was a black tomcat and he had the nerve to set himself up as a rival to my father. One of the armchairs in the living room was my dad's chair—nobody else could sit in it. Jake was the only one who dared to challenge that rule. Dad made attempts to prise him off, but the cat was having none of it. So my dad was reduced to watching television sitting on the pouffe, with the cat in his chair. The two of them sat there side by side like characters in a newspaper cartoon!

Jake's challenge went down just about as well with my dad as Betsy Bagpuss eating a whole string of sausages my mum had bought at the butcher's shop. When Betsy passed away, it was agreed we wouldn't have any more cats.

Every family has the occasional conflict. My sisters were always complaining that I didn't do enough around the house, even though my mother used to tell them to mind their own business. Once when Mary came round she told me that I had to vacuum my own room, so I stamped upstairs, switched the vacuum cleaner on and left it whirring on the landing so she would hear it going, while I went into my room and listened to my records. Unfortunately, because I had my headphones on, I didn't hear her coming up the stairs, so I was caught out!

I realize now that my sisters could see better than I could that my parents were getting old. It never crossed my mind that there would come a time when my parents were no longer there. Being with them in the house was the only world I had ever known.

Around Easter 1999 my dad started feeling unwell. He had suffered respiratory problems for some time and he was becoming a little forgetful, but there had never been a time when he hadn't got up in the morning and come downstairs for his breakfast and his first cigarette of the day. Now he didn't seem to feel like doing anything at all.

After he'd stayed in bed for two weeks, my mother sent for the doctor. The doctor could feel an obstruction in his abdomen, so he said that they'd take him into St. John's Hospital in Livingston for investigation.

"What's wrong with you?" I asked my dad, as we waited for the ambulance to arrive. "I know there's something wrong, so tell me."

My dad said nothing. He must have known it was serious because there was blood in the bed, but he didn't tell anybody.

At the hospital he had an operation to remove a tumour in his bowel, but he still wasn't well because of his respiratory problems. My mother spent most of the days with him and I went along every evening. One evening, he was looking right at me, not saying anything, but I could see he was sad about something. I gave him a kiss and said, "See you in the morning" as I always did, then I left him with my mother and went home as normal. I had no idea at all that my dad wasn't going to get better.

The next day, I was coming back from the shops when I saw my brother John in the car. He said, "Why aren't you at the hospital?"

"What's wrong?" I asked.

"Dad's seriously ill," he told me, so I jumped in the car and went with him.

When we arrived, they'd put my dad in a side room. The rest of the family were around the bed—Kathleen, Mary, Bridie, James, John, Joe, Gerard, the whole lot. My dad looked different somehow, thinner and greyer than he had been the night before. Mary turned towards me, and when I saw her stricken face, I realized why they were all there. The whole family gathered round when someone was about to die, didn't they? That was what happened.

I began to panic. I'd never seen anybody die before and I didn't want to, so I ran outside.

I asked the nurse, "Is my dad going to die?"

She said yes.

I didn't know what to do.

I paced up and down in the empty waiting room, saying to myself, "Please don't let him die."

My body was numb with terror, like a much more dreadful version of the feeling I always had before exams. You want to run away, but you know there's no escape, and the moment keeps getting closer and closer. You don't think you can physically bear it. You want to scream but you know you mustn't.

I stared out of the window, not seeing anything. In my head there was a rushing river of thoughts colliding around that I was unable to channel in any direction.

I can't tell you if it was a minute, or several hours, that I stood there before my brother John came in and said my dad was gone.

The house was very quiet in the weeks after, but inside my head it wasn't peaceful because I kept asking myself why I hadn't spent more time with my dad when he was there, and why I hadn't been brave enough to stay with him at the end.

People said he'd had a happy life because that's what people always say, but I was never quite sure that was true. My father was a well-respected figure, and he'd worked very hard to provide us all with what we needed. He was a devout Catholic and, as a member of the Legion of Mary, had helped people in the community. He'd certainly led a good life, but I'd never seen him laugh with abandon like my mother sometimes did. I think he had probably seen too many bad things in the war to allow him real happiness. There were things he would have liked to have done with his talents, but he never got the chance because circumstances always held him back.

I knew I'd caused him a lot of worry as well, and I had never said sorry.

My mother wasn't a big person, but she was tough, like a wee diamond. There had always been a force field of energy around her that seemed to fade a little after the death of my father. She and dad had been a team for sixty-three years. They'd been through a lot together, and when he died it was as if part of her died too.

My mother had looked after us all; now it was time for all of us to look after her. That is how Pebbles came along. Not to replace my dad, but to be a comfort and companion for my mother and to cheer her up.

Pebbles' original owner had another cat who used to bully Pebbles, so she needed to find her a better home, although it broke her heart to say good-bye because Pebbles was an affectionate wee animal. When Pebbles arrived at our house she brought a toy with her, a soft wee pink duck made of furry fabric. That duck used to go everywhere with Pebbles. She used to play with it, tossing it in the air, but she also used to cuddle it in her paws, like a security blanket, because she knew that she was somewhere she shouldn't be and that was her comfort.

Pebbles was only a wee kitten when Gerard brought her in and let her out of her box. She went running round the living room like a mad thing. When she calmed down, she went to my mother and sat on her knee and my mother said, "Oh, you wee hairy baby!"

And we saw her smile for the first time in weeks.

You never get over the death of someone close to you, but gradually, with time, you get used to it. Our family were only beginning to adjust to my dad's absence when we suffered another devastating blow.

My sister Kathleen had developed asthma at the age of forty and eventually had had to stop working in the Miners' Welfare in Whitburn because of the very smoky atmosphere. She took a job working as a nursery nurse at a children's playgroup, where she found joy working with the little children, but 1999 was a very sad year for her, because as well as our dad dying, her husband, who had been working away in Norway a lot, suddenly announced he was leaving her. Kathleen was distraught and lost so much weight it almost seemed as if she was trying to make herself disappear. She was one of those rare people who could laugh even when the situation was bad for her, so it was bewildering to see her so sad. She was the last person in the world to deserve unhappiness.

Kathleen had only one child, my niece Pamela, who by that time had grown up but was still living at home. The two of them had a great relationship and supported each other through their troubles. Money was tight after Kathleen's husband left, so Pamela took on two jobs, one during the day and a part-time job on Thursday and Friday evenings so that she could help her mother out financially. Pamela used to come home on the Thursday evening from one job and Kathleen would have her dinner ready for her, then Pamela would go to her bar job, and when she came home Kathleen would be waiting up for her with a cup of tea and a slice of toast, and they'd have a good chat and a laugh about their day.

One late-summer evening Pamela went off to her evening job as usual. She remembers her mother standing at the window smiling and waving all the way down the street, as Kathleen always did when anyone left her house.

That evening Pamela got a call at work to say that her mum was in hospital with an asthma attack, so she headed off to Accident and Emergency. She wasn't overly concerned, because Kathleen had taken asthma attacks on previous occasions, but this time the nurses wouldn't let her sit with all the other people in the waiting room. Alone in a side room, Pamela began to feel apprehensive, then a doctor came in to tell her that her mother had stopped breathing.

I don't remember who told me what had happened. For ages, I couldn't register the information at all. It didn't make any sense. Kathleen was only fifty-three years old.

I wasn't able to go to Kathleen's funeral because someone had to look after my uncle Michael, who was very frail himself at that time. Missing out that important stage of grieving perhaps made it harder for me to accept.

There are times when I still find myself thinking, just for a split second, "I'll just ring Kathleen and ask her . . . ," before the thump of reality and the sharp, agonizing pain of loss hit me again.

Kathleen and I were so very close. She and my mother were the only people in the world who ever truly understood me. Kathleen was one of those rare people with the gift of making others happy. I think my mother thought that Kathleen would help me a bit after she herself died. But it wasn't to be.

God puts things in front of you to test you. We believe that Kathleen has gone to a better place where she's not sick any more and she's not unhappy any more. We know she is looking down on us, but it still is very difficult for the ones who are left behind to pick up the pieces.

Our tears still wait very near the surface, ready to be tripped at the slightest memory of Kathleen's sparkling smile and her gentle, generous nature.

We have all devised different ways of paying tribute to her. I try to visit Knock with the Whitburn Legion of Mary every year in her memory; Mary and Bridie make the trip to Fatima in Portugal, where Kathleen went just before she died. These journeys provide some comfort.

There is a gaping hole in the family.

20
Millennium

As the Millennium approached, there was a great sense of anticipation throughout the world. It was a time when people were taking stock of their lives and making resolutions, not just for the next year but for the new century. There were Millennium projects everywhere: London had its giant big wheel; an interactive natural history museum called Our Dynamic Earth was being built in Holyrood Park in Edinburgh. In West Lothian, Whitburn Community Council decided to do something for the Millennium that would celebrate the local area. A group of people who had been involved in the voluntary arts, drama and music organizations over the years thought it would be a great idea to capture the musical talent in the region by recording a Millennium CD and they were supported by the local newspaper, the *West Lothian Herald & Post*.

Anyone interested in contributing was asked to send in a tape, or to go along to the auditions that were held in the school hall of Whitburn Academy, so along I went with my CD backing track of "Cry Me a River."

All schools have a similar odour—a mixture of gym shoes, chalk dust and cooked vegetables. As I waited my turn, I was reminded of my first ever singing competition at Our Lady of Lourdes Primary School. This time there were no naughty boys jumping up and down outside to distract me, but I was just as nervous. When it was my turn, I tried to give a display of confidence by joking around and I could see that the panel of five judges were wondering what to expect. As soon as I started singing their expressions changed. Though they weren't able to tell me whether I'd passed the audition until they'd seen all the other acts, I sensed that they'd liked what they'd heard.

A week or so later I took a call at home from a man called Charles Earley, informing me that I was going to be included on the CD. I started whooping and running on the spot like a child. At the other end of the line, Charles had to wait for me to calm down before asking me a further question. The artists who had auditioned for the CD were of such a high standard, the panel had decided to organize a celebration concert in the spring of 2000. Would I like to take part? I'm sure you can imagine my response!

The Millennium Celebration Concert was held in the hall of Whitburn Academy on 28 April 2000 and the show was called *Sounds of West Lothian*, which was also the title of the CD. It was a real mixture of different styles of music, including the Bathgate Concert Orchestra playing a medley from *My Fair Lady*, conducted by Marco Marzella, and the Broxburn Public Band playing *Bohemian Rhapsody*, conducted by Michael Marzella. The Marzellas are one of West Lothian's most musical families. The programme also included the Bathgate Menzies Choir, of which my sister Mary is a member, singing two gospel songs. There were also several children, a couple of individual singers who had composed their own songs, a pipe band and a saxophonist.

We were all very nervous as we waited backstage listening to the buzz of the audience taking their seats. Some of the wee ones couldn't resist peeking out to see where their families were sitting. The hall was packed to capacity, with about three hundred people, and there were some VIPs there, including the local MP. I was the penultimate act in the second half, so mine was one of the longest waits of all, but I tried to keep my nerves under control because I knew it was important to set a good example for the kids.

The terror of stepping out on stage in front of the biggest audience I'd ever had was completely different from standing up to sing in the local pubs and clubs where nearly everyone knew me. I knew my mother was somewhere out there, but I couldn't pick her out in all the rows of people. I was wearing a long black dress with some sparkles on it, which seemed appropriate for the bluesy "Cry Me a River," but underneath its elegant drape my legs were shaking like jelly as I walked across the stage. As soon as the music started, however, I relaxed, putting everything I had into the song. When I finished singing, the hall erupted into applause and my whole body was tingling with relief, from the tips of my toes to the great beaming smile on my face. I felt as if this was the moment I had been waiting for all my life, and all I wanted was to do it again!

Luckily, I wasn't the only one who was thinking that way. The concert was such a success that it was decided there was a need for an organization to recognize and promote the wealth of talent in the West Lothian area on a regular basis. John Curran and Charles Earley, who were instrumental in putting the CD together, decided to set up the West Lothian Voluntary Arts Council as a sort of umbrella organization that would give one voice to all the different groups, choirs, bands, operatic societies, as well as individuals, in the area. The organization was enthusiastically supported by West Lothian Council's Arts and Cultural Services.

A regular newsletter called *The Box Office* was produced with information about forthcoming events, and once a year, auditions were held for the annual talent showcases. In 2001 I passed the audition and sang "What I Did for Love" at the Deans Community High School, and in 2002 I sang "Somewhere Over the Rainbow" at Howden Park Centre in Livingston. People told me it was a very moving performance. The showcase concert became the highlight of my year. I enjoyed singing on stage so much that I longed to do it more regularly.

"Why don't you join a choir, Susan?" my mother asked.

The Toccata Ladies Choir, based in Livingston, has been established for a long time and has an excellent reputation and a repertoire stretching from Bach to the Beatles. I knew that it wasn't easy to get in, so I was thrilled to be accepted after an audition. We practised regularly once a week and gave a two-night annual concert in May every year, as well as participating in other events and workshops. The Toccata Choir is an amateur choir, but when we performed we set a professional standard, all wearing black skirts and the same bright turquoise blouses. At a Christmas concert in the Howden Park Centre in Livingston, I sang a solo from my place in the second row among the first sopranos. I could see my mother and my brother John watching me in the audience, and I felt very proud.

In the world of television talent shows, the first decade of the twenty-first century belonged to a new giant of popular entertainment, Simon Cowell. First appearing regularly on our screens in October 2001, Simon was the judge everyone loved to hate on a new television series called *Pop Idol*.

My mother and I became addicted to the format as rapidly as the rest of the nation, although sometimes we thought the comments were a wee bit too harsh, because the performers were basically just kids doing their best.

The first series produced some great singers, including Will Young, Gareth Gates and Darius Danesh. A Scottish lassie called Michelle McManus won the second series. She wasn't exactly out of the usual mould of pop singer because she was a big girl, but the Scottish public fell in love with her and she had a very powerful voice.

It didn't occur to me to apply for an audition because I was way too old to be a pop star, but the following year, when *Pop Idol* was replaced by the *The X Factor*, there was a category specifically for the over-25s, and that category produced the first winner, Steve Brookstein.

In the third series, another over-25 contestant was a lady with a beautiful voice called Kerry McGregor who was paraplegic and sang from her wheelchair. Everyone in Blackburn was supporting her, not just because of her voice and her courage, but because she came from West Lothian herself.

As my mother and I settled back on the sofa to watch her performance in the first of the live heats, Mum asked me, "Why don't you try to do something with your singing, Susan?"

"You mean like this?" I said, pointing at the screen. Did she really think I was good enough to go for *The X Factor*?

"If you can," she replied.

After each programme, a number came up on the screen to ring if you were interested in auditioning for the following year. I wrote it down, but it took a couple of weeks before I plucked up the courage to call.

By the time the next *X Factor* auditions came round, my mother was in hospital for a wee spell. I knew she'd be alarmed at the idea of me going into Glasgow by myself because I wasn't familiar with the city in the way that I was with Edinburgh, so I didn't tell her what I was doing. I caught a bus to Glasgow and another one to Hampden Park, where Celtic play. I had quite a job finding where I was supposed to go, but I saw a bunch of teenagers who looked as if they were heading there, so I followed them in.

The song I had practised was "Whistle Down the Wind," but when I saw all the young people there I realized that it was a mistake. What they were looking for was a pop singer. There were so many people in the stadium, I knew they'd never get through them all before the time of the last bus back to Blackburn. I didn't stand a chance of being seen, let alone getting through. It was not my time, so I just turned round and came home again.

Funnily enough, the competition that year was

won by Leon Jackson, who was probably one of the sea of excited young faces I saw in the stadium that day. He also comes from West Lothian and we actually participated in some of the same local competitions, so there you are!

My mother recovered enough to come home from hospital, but she was becoming more and more frail, so I never bothered telling her about my wee excursion.

21
Caring

It's often pouring with rain at significant moments in my life. I don't know if that says something about me, or whether it's just the weather in this part of Scotland. In the spring of 2005 I was in the Corstophine area of Edinburgh, out near the airport where Queen Margaret University used to be situated, making my way to an interview there. As well as having to deal with the rain, there was a stray dog snapping at my heels. It must have been some entrance I made into the reception area, fighting off with my umbrella a dog who was trying to tear the pants off me.

"Will somebody come and get this damn dog out of here?" I shouted.

Eventually the staff managed to shoo it away.

There was a man sitting in the reception area laughing his head off at the scene. I glowered at him as I removed my rainhat and went up to the desk. I was in quite a mood.

"Can I help you?" the girl asked.

"I'm looking for a geezer called Frank Quinn," I informed her.

At which point, the man stood up, and said, "I'm Frank Quinn."

Oh my God!

"Never mind," he said. "Now why don't we go and see if we can get a coffee somewhere?"

He had a warm smile and a very strong Irish accent.

"OK, then," I replied.

I'd come to see whether there was a possibility of taking some modules on a Higher Education Certificate course in Caring.

My mother had never completely recovered from Kathleen's death. She was used to speaking to Kathleen all the time, and Kathleen often came to our house after work to cook supper, so there was never a day that we didn't miss her. Soon after Kathleen died, Michael had to be put into care because my mother was getting too old to look after him, and then he died as well, so she had lost a husband, a daughter and her younger brother in a very short period of time.

My mother's decline was gradual. First it was her sight that was going, then her hair, but always she retained her sharpness of mind. She used to love it when Bridie came over. Bridie had moved back from Coventry to Motherwell and the two of them used to chatter about all the families my mother had known in her youth. She still considered herself a Motherwell person even though she'd lived fifty years in Blackburn. When my father was alive, they always returned to Mass in Motherwell Cathedral on their wedding anniversary. Sometimes Bridie would bring over the bulletin from the cathedral and there would be a list of people who'd died. My mother would joke that she'd know she was dead when she saw her name there.

She never lost her sense of humour. As she grew less mobile, we had a stairlift installed and Mum always used to salute as it went up! But she was growing increasingly weak and needed specialist nursing care. There were carers who came in, but I wanted to be able to do more to help her, so I thought I'd see if there was a course that would train me to do that.

In the university canteen, Frank Quinn bought me a coffee and a scone and we found a quiet corner to sit and talk. It wasn't like any interview I'd been to before. I felt relaxed.

"I can tell you're a very kind person," I said.

"I can be," he replied, with a twinkly smile.

"I like your Irish accent," I told him.

So we talked about Ireland. I told him about my Derry and Donegal connection. He told me his family came from Longford. I thought he must be a Catholic because he mentioned that, as well as being a tutor at the University, he worked at St. Joseph's, which was a home for people with disabilities that I'd heard of because it was run under the auspices of the Daughters of Charity of St. Vincent de Paul.

"Now, what would be your reason for wanting to do a course?" he asked.

Normally I find it very difficult to talk to a stranger, but there was such a warm feeling about this man that I trusted him immediately. I told him that my mum was very elderly. There were carers who came in to help us, but my family were always saying I should do more to look after her and I was finding it very hard because I didn't really know what to do. I did the best I could for her within my own ability, but I didn't have the skills that were necessary.

"And that's the reason you want to come here?" He immediately understood.

He started telling me about the different modules on the course. One was practical, which would teach me the skills I was looking for; another was about advocacy and empowerment. I asked him to explain what that meant.

"It's really about what it means to carry a disability, and the difficulties people would have in speaking up for themselves," he told me.

"I'd be very interested in that," I told him, and then I admitted, "I have a mild disability myself."

"That's very honest of you, Susan, to share that at this point," he said.

"Is it going to be a problem?" I asked him.

"There's no such things as problems," he said.

"There are! I have loads of problems. I *am* a problem!" I told him.

"There's no such things as problems," Frank repeated. "There are only issues to be resolved."

I liked his way of thinking.

"Are you going to help me resolve them?" I asked.

"Well, I'm a great believer in the right people being on the right course for the right reason," Frank told me.

"Will you take me, then?"

He told me that he didn't have the authority to tell me that there and then, but that he would do his very best to take me on those two modules.

I was really pleased, but a little nervous as well.

"Do you think I would manage?" I asked him straight.

He said, "If we take you, I give you my word that I'll support you and help you."

I was so overwhelmed by that that I did the one thing you're not supposed to do at an interview, and that was cry.

But he still took me on the course, and he kept his word because he has supported me ever since.

I didn't get off to a very good start on the course, because the bus was late on the morning of the first lecture and it was raining again. I entered the classroom dripping all over the floor and cursing under my breath.

Frank Quinn was standing at the front.

"Excuse me," he said, "would you mind telling the class who you are?"

"I'm Susan Boyle," I announced. "Soaking wet, fed up, and very glad to be here!"

I found some of the work very difficult and sweated all night over written assignments. Sometimes I became very anxious and distracted in class, and there were times when I was sure that Frank would throw me off the course. But he always said, no, we're not even going to go there, and he tried to help me understand the cause of some of my problems. Frank genuinely believed that if you'd been accepted on the course, then it was up to the teachers to teach you, whatever difficulties you had. He taught me that my learning difficulties were to do with my anxiety not my ability, so we tried to identify the triggers for my anxiety. We worked on getting me to focus on the things I could do, rather than the things I could not. That way I learned a lot.

As part of the advocacy course we talked about inclusiveness, and the importance of everybody, irrespective of ability or disability, being allowed to achieve educational attainment and being treated with dignity and respect. I hadn't encountered that approach during my own education and I was excited by it. I think that the other students probably learned something from me, as I contributed my experience of some of the issues they were learning how to handle as carers.

I managed to pass my two modules, but then I had to give up my studies because my mother's health was deteriorating so rapidly that someone needed to be at home twenty-four hours a day.

At Christmas 2006, my mother told me that it would be her last Christmas.

"How do you work that out?" I asked her.

"I'm not going to live very long, Susan," she told me. "I want you to look after my house, look after Pebbles, and remember you're mine."

I've never known why she said that last thing. I think she was telling me to be strong like her.

"Promise me you'll try to do something with your life . . ." she said.

I was so upset, all I could say to her was, "I love you, Mum. Don't worry."

She was taken into hospital on 6 January 2007. I visited her all the time, but she kept saying to me, "Please go home, Susan. Just go home now."

It was almost as if she was trying to get me used to life without her.

She was so weak that each time I said good-bye I wondered if it was the last good-bye I would say to her, but then I'd go back the next day and she was still there. In a way, I got used to her being very ill but still surviving. I must have known it was coming, but it was a terrible shock when I went in on the Friday before she died. She looked so different, I couldn't believe it was my mum lying there. I couldn't tell if she was even aware that I was there.

I sat and held her hand, and I said, "Maybe you cannae hear me, Mum, but I'm sorry."

I sat there for another half hour, and then I left.

The next morning I got a phone call from the hospital to go back in. When I arrived, most of the family were there: my sisters Mary and Bridie, my brothers John, Joe and James. Gerard arrived later because he was stuck in traffic coming out of Edinburgh. My mother had already had the priest. A rosary was hanging above her bed.

I'd never seen anyone die before. I was very, very scared, but I knew I must stay. I held her hand and I could sense that she wasn't in pain. Any tension that was there seemed to have left her body. Just before she died, her eyes went very blue and shone with a kind of light as if she was looking at something marvellous. Whatever she saw made her very happy. Whether it was my dad coming, or Our Lady, I'll never know, but I do know that it wasn't frightening at all. It was peaceful, almost a pleasant feeling, because she was delighted, absolutely delighted.

My mother died at half past one that day.

I went home to an empty house and told Pebbles what had happened.

"Granny isn't coming back," I said.

The wee thing looked so sad, and went and hid behind my mother's chair.

• • •

I'd never lived alone, and in the months that followed I didn't cope very well. My mother had always done everything for us, not just with the house, but with the finances. I had no idea how to cope with all the bills. I didn't dare to have the heating on in case I didn't have the money to pay. Mary rang up the gas company and they said I'd paid so much I was in credit. I didn't know what to do about my benefits, but a neighbour helped me with that.

The house was a mess and I was a mess.

Bridie came over from Motherwell every week to help me with the housework. As well as making sure that I had food in the fridge, she used to buy me clothes, including a pair of Wellington boots so that my feet didn't get wet when I went out for walks. She was fantastic like that, and so was her daughter Joanne, who'd recently given birth to her own wee son. I used to go over to Joanne and her husband Kenny's flat in Bathgate once a week for a cup of tea. My brother John was also very kind to me. He often invited me round to his place to eat and walked me home after. Without him, my sisters and the social services to help me sort myself out, I don't know what would have happened to me.

But they couldn't be there all the time.

The days seemed so long without a routine and with nothing to do, not even visiting the hospital.

When I was younger I had trained how to counsel people in bereavement, but it's a bit more difficult when it comes to yourself.

At home, everything seemed to emphasize my mother's absence, even getting dressed. She had always made sure that I wore nice clothes and made me do a little twirl in front of her before I went out the door. She wasn't there to do that now, so I stopped noticing how I looked.

My mother had always liked to hear me sing, but now that she wasn't there to listen, I stopped singing.

It was so very quiet in the house with just me and Pebbles. They say animals have no feelings, but of course they have. Pebbles pined for my mother. At night she used to go into Mum's room and lie on the bed with her paws on the housecoat Mum used to wear. During the day she would lie on the floor beside the sofa, looking up longingly at the empty space where my mother used to sit.

My mother and I had always watched television together, but I couldn't even enjoy that now. Sitcoms aren't funny when you're laughing on your own, and talent shows aren't compelling when there's no one to share your comments with.

With my mother gone, there was no focus to my life. I went for long walks, often in the pouring rain. I didn't really notice where I was going. On one occasion I found myself five miles away outside the house in Whitburn where Kathleen had lived. My niece Pamela spotted me through the front window.

"I'm just out for a walk," I told her.

"You're absolutely soaked," she said, so she brought me inside, dried me off and gave me a cup of tea. Her husband, Mark, offered to drive me back to Blackburn, but I told him I was fine. There's something about the rhythm of a long walk, like the tick-tock of a metronome, that allows your thoughts to shuffle themselves into some sort of order.

Even though my mother was gone physically, I began to realize she was still with me spiritually. I started to go to Mass more frequently because I felt closer to her there. I prayed to Our Lady for guidance, asking her to be my compass and show me the way forward, just as my mother had always told me to.

I decided to join the Legion of Mary in Whitburn. I knew that my dad had been a member when he retired, and he had found the charity work very rewarding, but I didn't know much about it. I can't go into any detail about what we do here because the whole point is to help people with the right spirit, and that means you don't look for praise or acknowledgement—you do it because you want to. I found it very comforting to be with people who shared my devotion to Our Lady. Helping other people who were in need gave me purpose and perspective.

At home, sometimes I felt so sad and so lonely I just sat on the sofa and stared at the clock I had bought my mother with my only winnings, as the gold whirling mechanism ticked my life away under its glass dome. On the wall above was the picture my mother had painted from a photo of me in my pram when I was a wee bairn. One day, I found myself thinking about what she would say to me if she could see the state I was in.

The answer came back as clear as if she were in the room with me: "For God's sake, Susan, stop feeling sorry for yourself, get off your backside and try to do something with your life . . ."

The time of year was approaching when auditions were held for the annual showcase by West Lothian Voluntary Arts Council. I didn't feel much like putting myself forward, but I forced myself to get out and give it a go. I had promised my mother I would try to do something with my life and here was an opportunity.

In a previous audition, Charles Earley had suggested that I might like to sing something from *Les Misérables*. He'd been to see the show in Edinburgh and thought it might suit my voice. The musical had always been a favourite of mine. I'd seen it several times at the Edinburgh Playhouse, so when I went to the audition in 2007 I took along the backing track for "I Dreamed a Dream."

Although it's written for a different context, the words of the song and the poignant power of the melody symbolized the misery I was feeling. The song allowed me to express all my emotions at that particular time. The dream I was dreaming was to go back to a time when my mum was still alive. I was singing it for her.

I passed the audition and sang the song for the first time on stage at the Regal Theatre in Bathgate. Ironically, that was the last of the showcase concerts because after that the West Lothian Voluntary Arts Council was wound down. The arts community is now channelling its efforts into renovating the art deco Regal Theatre and making it a community theatre for the area. I'm hoping that there will be more showcases in the future to give the wealth of talent in West Lothian a chance to shine.

In April 2007 the first series of *Britain's Got Talent* came on television. In the living room in Yule Terrace, I watched it with Pebbles sitting on my lap. I couldn't help thinking about my mother, and how she would have laughed at some of those characters.

Watching Paul Potts's audition, I was as surprised as everyone else when he sang "Nessun Dorma" so beautifully. I was even more astonished when he won the first series, because he didn't look anything like an opera singer was meant to look.

Somewhere in the back of my mind, a seed was sown.

My beloved mother with me, 1961.

My christening photo. My sister Mary is my godmother and she is standing next to our dad.

This is me with my teddy bear, Boo Boo. He went everywhere with me.

I've always loved the beach. This was taken on one of our Sunday afternoon trips out to Gullane in 1966.

My sister Bridie and me, 1966.

My brother Joe with his guitar.

The Austin Cambridge 1968. We went everywhere in that car.

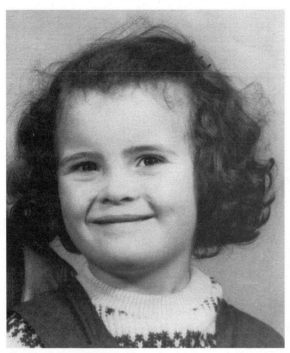

My school photo when I was in
Primary 2.

Subjects	Class Teacher's Notes (1)	Class Teacher's Notes (2)	Head Teacher's Re
English (a) Oral	Very Good.	Marked progress in all subjects. Very Good	(1) Commendable effort.
(b) Written	Good.		
Mathematics (a) Basic	Good.	Good.	
(b) Practical Skills	Good.	Very Good	
Environmental Studies (a) History-Geography Natural History	Very Good	Very Good.	(2) Good progress made class work during session. Very good
(b) Science			
Arts and Crafts	Good.	Good	
Other School Activities (a).................			
(b).................			
(c).................			
Attendances / Actual Possible	161 / 164 Class Teacher L. M. Byrne Head Teacher S Parent Bridget Boyle	Class Teacher L. M. Byrne Head Teacher S. Parent	
Conduct			

My school report for the year 1969/70, when I
was in Primary 4.

This is me in 1972 with some of my wee nieces and nephews.

Clockwise from top left: Kathleen, me, my uncle Michael, my mother holding baby Pamela, and my dad, in 1972.

School mug shot with my new short haircut for St. Kentigern's, 1973.

With my niece Frances, Mary's oldest daughter, and Pamela on the day of Pamela's First Holy Communion, 1979.

My dad with me
pulling a daft
face for the
camera at a
family wedding,
1985.

Mum, me and Michael at a family wedding, 1988.

With Kathleen at her house, 1993.

Kathleen's
sparkling smile.

My wonderful mother, Bridie Boyle, taken at Knock.

My parents: happy together for more than six decades.

My parents at home.

With my beloved mother at a family birthday party, 2001.

Singing on the *Britain's Got Talent* tour, I wore the same dress as I did for the final.

Getting used to receiving visitors at my door, with Frankie, who came up from London to help me.

My mother painted this portrait of me in my pram from a photo.

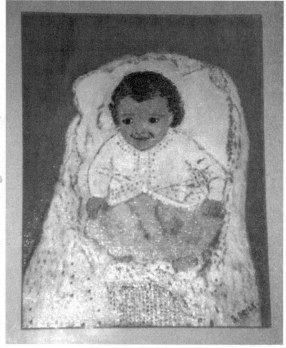

The clock I bought for my mother
with my prize money from the
only singing competition I have
ever won!

Piers Morgan was the perfect presenter for my television special.

Above and right: The nerve-racking semi-final of *Britain's Got Talent.*

I've been lucky enough to travel all over Europe.
Here I am singing at the Sanremo Festival in Italy.

A cold November morning in Rockefeller Plaza,
when I launched my debut album.

Who I was born to be!

Singing with Elaine Paige on my television special.

The unique and amazing handmade quilt my fans presented to me in New York.

Arriving at Los Angeles airport before my first solo performance.

The badge my dedicated fans made for my Tokyo concert.

The legendary Budokan in Tokyo.

Shibuya crossing in Tokyo. Even in sunglasses
I was recognized wherever I went!

Right:
Reading my birthday cards, 1 April 2010.

Below: The beautiful birthday cake with a sugar replica of my album that I shared with my fans in Tokyo.

A very proud moment with conductor Masahiko
Enkoji and members of the Yomiuri Nippon
Symphony Orchestra after performing at the
Budokan.

Another great honour was meeting Cardinal
Keith O'Brien.

Part Three

Britain's Got Talent

22
Bloody Fantastic!

21 January 2009
There were thousands of people, row upon row banked up behind the judges, and they were all watching me in anticipation. I knew what they were thinking. "Just look at her! She's got a bum like a garage, a head like a mop, I'm not too sure if her teeth are her own, and she's claiming to be a singer! She cannae sing! She cannae! Well, come on, let's hear you, then . . ."

So I opened my mouth.

I dreamed a dream in time gone by . . .

I could tell by the end of my first phrase that the wall of hostility had opened up. All the muscles in my body, taut and braced against ridicule, relaxed like a happy sigh, allowing my voice to soar.

I dreamed that love would never die . . .

As my voice went out to the audience, their energy came back to me and seemed to flow straight into the song.

But the tigers come at night
With their voices soft as thunder
As they tear your hope apart
And they turn your dream to shame . . .

At the top of the crescendo, I was suddenly aware that the buzz I could hear was applause. I was going down well! With spirit uplifted, I had to make myself focus very hard on the quieter, more dramatic finale and put in all the meaning those words contained for me.

I had a dream my life would be
So different from this hell I'm living
So different now from what it seemed
Now life has killed the dream I dreamed.

I didn't hear the final few instrumental notes of my CD backing track because of all the stamping and applause. The audience were on their feet! Row upon row of strangers cheering me.

I thought, "Holy baloney!" Nothing like that had ever happened to me before. It was the most amazing moment of my life.

With no idea how to return the compliment and express my thanks to them, spontaneously I did something I had never done before that just felt right. I blew all these people I didn't know a kiss, before walking off stage.

In my delight and astonishment, I'd completely

forgotten about the judges. I heard someone calling, "Come back!"

I was suddenly aware of Ant and Dec gesticulating at me from the wings.

Feeling a fool for doing the wrong thing, I did an about-turn. Then I saw the judges were standing up as well. I thought, Wait a minute, there's something wrong here, I mean, come on! It was bewildering.

Piers was the first to speak. What he said was, "Without doubt that was the biggest surprise I have had in three years of this show. When you stood there with that cheeky grin and said I want to be like Elaine Paige, everyone was laughing at you. No one is laughing now . . ."

What I heard was "everyone was laughing at you."

I was back down on earth with a thump.

With that phrase still ringing in my head, my brain couldn't compute his next words.

"That was stunning, an incredible performance. Amazing. I'm reeling from shock, I don't know about you two?"

Then Amanda Holden said, "I am so thrilled because I know that everybody was against you. I honestly think that we were all being very cynical, and I think that's the biggest wake-up call ever . . ."

What I heard was "everybody was against you."

And that was another blow.

But she went on. "And I just want to say that it was a complete privilege listening to that."

My emotions were see-sawing. My eyes and ears were telling me one thing, but I didn't want to be heading for a fall.

The judge you're not looking forward to hearing from is Simon, because he always tells the truth, with no frills. He said, "Susan, I knew the minute you walked out on the stage that we were going to hear something extraordinary, and I was right!"

"Oh Simon!" I said, relieved that he had decided to be funny and not critical.

"You're a little tiger, aren't you?" he said.

"I don't know about that," I replied, unsurely. I hoped I hadn't given the wrong impression with that daft wiggle.

"OK, moment of truth. Yes or no?" Simon asked the panel.

I'm being totally honest when I say that I had no idea what their verdict was going to be.

Piers started. "The biggest yes I have ever given anybody!"

I couldn't believe it. I found myself blowing him another kiss.

My sister Bridie told me after she watched the audition on television that once she'd got past the shock of what I was wearing, the only thing that surprised her about my performance was the blowing of kisses. What was all that about?

Then Amanda said, "Yes, definitely!"

Somewhere at the back of my mind I knew that, according to the rules of the competition, two yeses meant I'd got through to the next round.

"You too, Amanda?" I asked in disbelief.

Then Simon said, "Susan Boyle, you can go back to the village with your head held high. It's three yeses!"

But I didn't really hear what he was saying because the whole theatre erupted again, and buoyed on the great wave of triumph, I started running on the spot like a child. Then I remembered where I was and thought I should probably be more ladylike, so I attempted a curtsey instead.

My attempt at composure didn't last very long because when I left the stage I grabbed both Ant and Dec and gave them a cuddle, and when they repeated the judges' comments, I went completely berserk! I was up and down like a yo-yo! I don't think they'd ever seen anything like it because they were saying, "Come on, now, you're fine."

They had to cut an awful lot of my screeching and running around when they edited the audition tape. But they left in my instant reaction, which has now become a kind of catchphrase, and it sums up exactly how I felt at that moment.

"Bloody fantastic!"

I eventually started making sense again and was taken off to do interviews to include in the later programmes. I must have talked a lot of rubbish, because I was still high as a kite on the adrenalin of success. One of the jokes I made was, "If you're thinking of getting me a straitjacket, I'd like one with pink spots!"

When they finally told me I could go home, I asked, "What time is it?"

I'd been in the building since early that morning, and I hadn't been near a window for hours. The producer who was interviewing me looked at her watch.

"Just after twelve," she said.

"Midnight? You've got to be kidding!"

"What is it?" she asked, concerned.

"I've missed the last bus!" I wailed.

None of my family knew where I was, and I didn't fancy ringing my brother John and asking for a lift in the middle of the night any more than I fancied the idea of wandering round Glasgow on my own until the first bus.

"Don't worry, I'll get one of the runners to arrange a cab," the producer assured me.

"But it's over twenty miles!" I didn't have that sort of money.

"It's all right, we'll pay for it," she reassured me.

The city streets were dark and quiet, and there were few other cars as the taxi purred along the motorway towards Blackburn. I kept going over everything that had happened in my mind, but as the sodium glow of Glasgow receded into the distance, it began to feel unreal. I was dying to tell someone, anyone, what had happened, just to try to fix it by saying it out loud. However, I had just promised to keep the information confidential and I didn't know whether the taxi driver was somebody I could trust.

As the car turned off the M8 and into the familiar streets of Blackburn, I was beginning to wonder whether any of it had really happened at all. The clunk of me closing the taxi door reverberated down Yule Terrace, but there were no lights on in my neighbours' houses. For a moment, I was tempted to shout out in the silence, "Hey, listen! You'll never guess what! I just got three yeses!"

Some people would probably throw things at me for waking them up; others already thought I was a bit odd. They'd never believe me. Shivering in the chill of the early morning, I opened my front door and switched on the light in the hall. There was the telephone where I'd received the call telling me to come to the audition. I'd raced around hollering and shrieking then as well. What I'd just done seemed as distant and unlikely a memory as that.

Pebbles came and nuzzled round my legs and we went into the kitchen to get her some long overdue supper.

I turned on the gas fire in the living room at the back of the house to warm the place up a bit. Then

I sank into the sofa, finally able to take off my high-heeled shoes and wriggle my sore toes. I felt completely exhausted, but I didn't want to go to bed just yet. I was afraid of shutting my eyes and waking up to find I'd dreamed the whole day.

After she'd eaten, Pebbles came in and jumped on my lap.

"You'll never guess what I've been doing," I began, stroking her back, and, as she fell asleep, I told her all about my day.

23
Reveal Day

"What happens now?" Bridie finally managed to control her surprise when I rang her the next morning.

"I have to go down to London," I told her. "That's when they select the semi-finalists."

"Oh, no, no, no, you're not going down to London on your own!" Bridie warned.

The Christmas just past, Bridie had invited me over for Christmas dinner, along with my brothers Joe, James and John and a friend of hers. I'd worn a black dress with silver glitter on it, and apparently I'd left a trail of it all over the soft furnishings. When I'd mentioned, after a wee glass of wine, that I'd got an audition for *Britain's Got Talent*, all of them as one had tried to put me off going along. I know they were only trying to protect me, but if I'd taken any notice then, I would never have gone to the audition. Now those protective instincts were surfacing again. I knew as well as my sister did that it was an outside chance, but if you don't give yourself that chance, you'll never know what might have happened. There are enough people in the world who are going to write you off. You don't need to do that to yourself.

"I am going," I told Bridie. "They can't choose me if I'm not there, can they?"

"You can't go to London on your own," Bridie insisted. "I'm going to ring Gerard."

By the time my family had sorted out who would be going with me, I'd already been down to London on my own and was back up in Scotland.

I got myself dressed up in my gold dress, black tights and white shoes, because we had to wear the same clothes as we had at the audition for continuity. I was beginning to wish that I'd chosen some other outfit, because it was the middle of February and there was biting wind that went straight through the gold lace to my skin.

A cab came to take me to Glasgow airport and I'd been told that I would be met at Heathrow. The only bit I needed to do was get myself on the plane.

It was the second time I'd flown. The first time had been on a second visit we'd made to Lourdes when I was in my thirties. Unfortunately I'd been so frightened then that I'd fainted. Not a pleasant experience. There was no way I was going to mention that to the people from *Britain's Got Talent*, so when they said they'd send me a ticket I said fine, as if I were a seasoned traveller.

If it took a lot of courage to get out on stage and sing, it was nothing compared to what it took to get me on to that plane.

I said to myself, "Susan, are you going to give up this chance because you're not brave enough to get on a plane? That's not going to impress anyone."

So I said a prayer, took a deep breath and handed my boarding card to the stewardess.

The part I hate most is when the plane leaves the ground and you're suddenly aware there's nothing underneath you. It gets better after that because, when you're in the air, you know there's nothing you can do about it. I sat gripping the arms of my seat, and when we touched down, I exhaled such a sigh of relief, it felt as if I'd been holding my breath all the way.

The selection of the semi-finalists—the "reveal day"—is probably the longest and most nerve-wracking day of the whole process. I was taken from the airport to a studio where they did some further interviews. I was asked about how much it meant to me to get through, and I didn't know whether there was a right thing to say. I'm never my best when I'm put on the spot, so I found the interview process quite stressful. The only way to handle it is just to be yourself; my problem was that being myself had never impressed anyone else very much.

After the interviews, they took some of the acts on double-decker buses around London. I was about to climb on a bus when one of the runners said, no, you're on a different bus. I said OK. I only realized when I saw the programme on television that I'd tried to get on the bus that had the unsuccessful ones on it. But none of us knew that then. The only other time I'd been in London, I'd seen the inside of a modern hotel room and the Underground to Victoria Station, so it was quite exciting being on a big red bus, seeing all the landmarks like the monument outside Buckingham Palace, the Houses of Parliament and the London Eye, but none of us could really enjoy the experience.

I didn't recognize many faces from the audition day in Glasgow, and the atmosphere wasn't the same jolly camaraderie I remembered from the SECC. Everyone had been nervous there too, but there'd been a good buzz about the place because people weren't taking themselves too seriously. On that day, we'd all known we had a chance of proving ourselves once we got on to the stage. On the reveal day, there was no performance, no audience, no buzzers. All we were doing was waiting for the judges' verdict. You can't help running through what you did in your performance and, of course, you only remember the things you could have done better. My memory had wiped out the standing ovation and the nice comments. All I could think about was the nerves in my voice. I knew I'd sung the song better on other occasions. On top of that, there was this horrendous flashback. I'd told the judges I wanted to be a professional singer. I wanted them to take me seriously, so what on earth had possessed me to do that wiggle?

They took us to a grand hotel where we sat in groups and they filmed us looking anxious. It was a very, very long wait. After a few hours you get to thinking, I don't care what the verdict is, I just want to know one way or the other. But then, when you're finally called, you wish you could just stay in that room a little longer.

I was in a group with two lads in white suits who did disco dancing, a ten-year-old singer called Natalie, a wee break-dancer with a flat cap called Aidan, and a strong man wearing nothing at all except a cape and pair of Union Jack shorts. A bit of a mixed bunch, you might say! We were taken to one of the biggest rooms I have ever seen in my life. It was like a palace, all gold, and red velvet, with two massive, ornate staircases you'd half-expect to see Cinderella walking down. At the bottom of the staircase, behind a table, sat the three judges, and they were surrounded by a semi-circle of about twenty television cameras all trained on the rectangle of carpet where we were supposed to stand awaiting our fate. No look, no smile, no tear, no shriek was going to be missed.

None of us had any idea what the judges were going to say.

When Simon finally said, "It's good news . . ." I kept holding my breath because I'd seen the format of the programme. Sometimes expectations get twisted.

When he said we were through to the semi-finals, it still didn't sink in. One of the disco-dancing boys picked up wee Natalie, and I was aware of a lot of hugging around me. I stood transfixed. I'd never been this close to the judges before, and it still didn't feel real.

"Can I shake your hand, Simon?" I asked.

He stood up and offered his hand, so I walked across to him and it was only when my palm was touching his that I began to believe what I had heard.

I was in the last forty! I was going to be on television!

I barely needed a plane to take me back up to Scotland because I was already flying.

The reveal day was in February, but the first programme didn't go out until Saturday, 11 April. That's a long wait. The only people I told were my family, and it's fair to say that they were amazed enough that my audition was going to be shown on television, let alone that I was also going to be singing live in the semi-finals. I don't think any of us really dared to believe that bit, because it was such a long time ahead it felt as if anything might happen in between.

In fact, nothing much happened at all. The production crew came up to Scotland to film me sitting on a hill looking wistful, and I was interviewed about my dreams. In between, my life went back to exactly the same as it always was. I got the bus to Tesco in Bathgate; I did my shopping. On the way home, the same gang of teenagers on the same street corner laughed at me just as they always did. I practised a few songs. I went to church. I sang the hymns, just as I usually did.

It was my forty-eighth birthday on 1 April, and that was just like any other day too. There was nothing special about it, not even a meal out with friends. I didn't have the money for that.

I spent more time telling myself not to get my hopes up than I did getting excited, but just occasionally a secret shiver of happiness would go down my spine as I allowed myself to think about what was coming up.

As the first show of *Britain's Got Talent* 2009 drew nearer, I couldn't resist bringing it into conversations I had with my neighbours.

"I can't wait for *Britain's Got Talent*, can you? Are you going to be watching? You never know, you might see someone familiar!"

I got a few odd looks. Anyone who guessed what I was hinting at probably thought I was delusional. That's just Susan carrying on!

On Friday, 10 April, a journalist from the local newspaper appeared at my door and told me that my name was in the papers. Apparently the *Sun* was calling me Paula Potts. What did I have to say about that?

I wasn't sure what to do because I'd been told to

speak to no one about it, so I thought I'd just stick to what they'd told me on the reveal day. Don't talk to the press. So I gave him one-word answers.

"Yes . . . no . . . maybe . . . I cannae tell you . . ."

More journalists started to turn up. Some of them were very persistent. They kept knocking on my door, knocking on my front window. Some of them even went round the back and knocked on the window of the living room, where I was sitting.

My brother John called to say that there were several articles in the papers about the programme that mentioned me.

"Where are you going to watch the show?" he asked.

"Here," I told him.

"You can't watch it on your own," he said. "I'm going to watch it with you."

"Fair enough," I said. "But you've got to remember, if I've made a mess of it, then I've made a mess of it. Don't come round here and give me a row, OK?"

So we sat down and watched it together.

My bit came right at the end of the programme, and I was almost beginning to wonder whether it was going to be shown after all. Then there was this comical music, a bit like you'd get with a Charlie Chaplin film, and there I was in the middle of the screen, munching my sandwich.

Oh my God! Of all the film they had of me, why they chose that I'll never know. I glanced anxiously over to my brother. He was frowning at the screen, then his expression turned to dismay as he saw the wiggle. I could almost hear him thinking, "Oh no, Susan, don't do that! Not on telly, for God's sake!"

But when I started singing his face changed. Then he was smiling, and I could tell he liked what he saw.

"Well?" I asked as the credits rolled, anxious for his opinion.

John didn't get a chance to answer because suddenly there was a knock at my front door, and as I went to open it, one knock became a battering. I was greeted by a barrage of screaming from all the kids in the neighbourhood. The whole street had come out of their houses to congratulate me. I hadn't seen anything like it since Celtic won the European Cup. The same kids who were always laughing at me were now clamouring for my autograph and taking photos of me on their mobile phones. I was glad that I had my brother there with me. If I'd been on my own, I'd have been suspicious that it was some sort of elaborate joke. When I'd posed and signed for what seemed like hours, the crowd finally began to disperse. I closed my door and went to make us a cup of tea.

"Peace at last!" I said to John.

And then the phone started to ring.

24
Interviews

My brother Gerard, from his experience of performing in pubs and clubs, used to say there's no such thing as an overnight success. In a way he was right. I believe that it was all the things that had happened, or hadn't happened, in my life that had taken me to the moment where I dared to risk putting myself up on stage for the *Britain's Got Talent* audition. But if you look at it from an outsider's perspective, I went from being nobody on Saturday evening to national fame on Sunday morning.

When my phone started ringing, it was brilliant. My sisters and nieces sounded so excited about my performance. Bridie said she'd smash me for wearing those black tights, but she also told me how proud our mother would have been. Lots of people have said that since, but it only really counts when it's someone who knew my mum.

"If you become rich and famous, will you please remember that I was the one who bought you Wellington boots," Bridie joked before she rang off.

"If I become rich and famous, you can have the boots back," I shot back.

As soon as I put down the phone, it rang again.

Patrons of The Happy Valley and The Turf called to say they'd known I was going to shock the judges because they'd heard me singing all these years. I was getting calls from people at church, calls from members of the Toccata choir. Lorraine rang to congratulate me and told me how it had reminded her of hearing me sing nearly forty years before at school. People I hadn't seen or spoken to for years were ringing me up. I never realized I knew so many people. It was a really nice feeling.

Then the first journalist got hold of my number and after that, as soon as one call ended, it would ring again, and it was always another journalist on the line. I didn't want to be rude and put the phone down, but I'd been instructed to be careful not to say anything. I'd had no media training at the time, I didn't know how to bat the questions away or politely decline. I had no idea how to handle it, and to make matters worse, I was worried that if I said the wrong thing I'd be kicked off the programme.

In the end, I just took the phone off the hook on Sunday night and went up to bed.

I live in a quiet street. In the mornings, men and women go off to work, kids walk to school. During the day, a neighbour might be out repairing his car; a plumber might draw up in his van to fix a broken washing machine; an aerial-fitter might put a ladder up the side of a house to install a satellite dish. That's the sort of activity that goes on. From time to time a police car will speed up to the flats down the road. Drug arrests have been made, but I've never seen one. On summer weekends you might hear the distant jingle of an ice cream van. When there's a siren, you look out of your front window to see who the ambulance has come for. The closest any of us inhabitants of Yule Terrace had ever been to the media was when the paper boy delivered the local free sheet. Nobody was prepared for the invasion of the world's newspapers and television stations, least of all me.

There was an awful lot of noise early on Monday morning, as if several dustbin lorries were coming along all at once. I peeked out under the curtains of my bedroom window to see what was happening. There was a van outside in the street with a satellite dish on the roof. At first I thought it was a TV detector van. Help! Had I paid my licence? I quickly let the curtain drop. My heart was racing. What was happening? There was banging on my door. I looked out again. The street was filling up with photographers with flashbulbs and television cameras. The banging on the door was so persistent I thought they'd batter it down if I didn't do something, but I had no idea what to do. Further down the road, more vans were parking up with satellite dishes on the roof. Some of my neighbours came out in protest, telling them not to block the highways.

There were paparazzi fighting to get the best photograph of my window. I couldn't go out of my house. I was scared to go to the loo in case there was a journalist sitting inside the pan!

I did what I had been told to do if there were any problems and rang the producer at the programme.

"Things are getting out of control here," I told her. "I need help!"

"We've never had anything like this in our lives," she said. "It's because of YouTube."

"What's YouTube?" I asked.

The only tube I'd ever heard of was a tube of Smarties.

"It's on the Internet," she said.

I knew the Internet was something to do with computers, but I'd never used a computer. I had no idea what she was talking about.

The producer said she would send one of the runners up to help me. In the meantime, I must only talk to the people that she had authorized.

The problem was that just about everyone who banged on the door said they had been authorized. They barged in with all their equipment, plugging things in, setting up microphones. It wasn't just British television, but people from all over the place—Dutch television, a lassie from Croatia. I kept asking them, "Do London know you're here?"

"Well . . ."

"You shouldn't really be here because I'm not supposed to give interviews . . ."

Did they take any notice? Did they heck!

I was getting into a panic, not knowing who to trust, and I couldn't actually escape because of the mob outside. My friend Lorraine came round to be with me for a while. Lorraine is the proprietor of the Balbairdie Hotel in Bathgate, but she is also trained as a social worker and so she's usually quite good at saying the right things to calm someone down. Just as she was leaving, there was another knock at the door, and who should be standing there but my teacher Frank Quinn. He had seen the melee on television, and knowing my tendency to anxiety, he'd imagined me in the middle of it and decided I might need some support. I've never been so happy to see someone in all my life! We had a nice reassuring chat together and he left just before my first television interview with GMTV.

The lassie who interviewed me for that asked me at the end whether she could have my autograph.

"What do you want my autograph for?" I asked, roaring with laughter.

By the end of the day, Frankie, a very nice lad from Talkback Thames, had arrived to help me and the programme had organized a PR in Edinburgh to answer the phone calls. But the crowd outside was growing. The attention I was getting had become a news story in itself, so there were people who were filming the people who were filming.

The house where I had spent my whole life

feeling safe suddenly felt like a cage where I was trapped, with all the media trying to shove their cameras through the bars.

In that first week, I gave over a hundred and fifty interviews. It's difficult enough remembering what you've said when you've said it so many times, let alone when you're trying not to say the wrong thing. Journalists sometimes try to trick you and you have to tread carefully. When I was first asked who my favourite judge was, my immediate answer was Piers Morgan, because that was the truth. I thought he was good-looking and I've never made any secret of that. But as soon as I'd said his name, I thought, Oh my God, I've probably just offended Simon, which is not a sensible thing to do, so I said Simon Cowell as well.

Sometimes journalists ask the daftest questions. They wanted me to tell them how I was coping with all the attention, when I thought it was pretty obvious that I was overwhelmed. I mean, come on! Having the world's media outside my house was hardly what I was used to.

But when one of the first television interviewers asked, "How's Pebbles taking it?" I couldn't believe he was serious. Pebbles is a cat, for God's sake!

"In a normal cat way," I told him.

In fact, Pebbles had very sensibly retreated

upstairs away from the mob. It must have been terrifying for her with all the noise and all these strangers in the house, and she refused all inducements to come down. There were times when I wished I could go upstairs and hide under the bed with her.

For the first few days, I read the articles in the newspapers that Lorraine and my family brought in for me. They were calling me the Hairy Angel. The fascination seemed to be as much about my bushy eyebrows as it was about my voice. I wasn't hurt, because I've been called worse than that in my life and I've learned to be resilient. Beauty is only skin deep, and I've always said you should never judge a book by its cover.

To be honest, it had been a wake-up call for me when I saw how I looked at that audition. They say that television makes you fatter, but I wasn't aware that my backside was as wide as that! I like to look my best, just like anyone else does, but in the period of bereavement I must have let myself go. It upset me to think that my mother would have hated to see me looking so dishevelled.

What was more distressing was the distorted picture of my family that was coming across. People love a Cinderella story, so the media looked at my life and assumed that I'd been kept at home to look after my ailing parents, but, as you'll have gathered by now, my history was a wee bit more complex than that. My mother was ninety-one when she died, but until the last year of her life she'd always been a strong and feisty presence. We'd looked after each other. And she'd never tried to stop me doing what I wanted to do. My family thought it was a shame she was being portrayed like that, so there was a wee bit of tension to deal with there, as well as all the madness that was happening outside my front door.

The more YouTube hits there were, the more the statistics became the news story and the more hits I got. One thing built on another and by the Wednesday morning I was being interviewed over a satellite link to *Good Morning America*.

You can't see the person who's talking to you, but you have to look into the camera as if it's a face you're having a conversation with. The presenter, Diane Sawyer, asked the questions slowly, so that made the process a wee bit easier. They filmed me standing in front of the glass ornament cabinet in our living room beneath the pictures painted by my mother. Diane asked me if I was going to get a makeover. Having seen my audition on television at the same time as everyone else, I was aware that I was definitely in need of attention from a hairdresser, but I'd been so busy and hemmed in I hadn't really had a chance to do anything more than tidy myself up and put on clean clothes in the morning. I was unemployed, so money was a consideration, but I was planning to get an appointment at Miss Toner in Whitburn as soon as I could get out of my house. I told Diane Sawyer that yes, I thought a makeover might be nice, assuming that was what she meant. Without realizing it, I'd unleashed a global debate. People started writing newspaper columns about whether I should change my looks or remain the same; opinions were sought from leading hairdressers and cosmetic surgeons; photos of me were doctored to show what I might look like after work had been done. My nieces heard strangers debating the issue at the check-out in Tesco.

What I didn't know then, because I didn't have a computer at the time, was that every time there was a mean comment about me in the press, a dozen messages of support would appear in response. On the Internet there was a growing community of fans. I had no idea how many people out there in the world felt moved to stick up for me, and I want to thank everybody for that.

Cards, gifts and messages of encouragement from people I didn't know kept arriving at my house, which was very pleasant, very humbling and, on occasion, downright hilarious, like the good luck card I received from the local bunch of toughs that said, "Be Good . . . Or Else . . . !"

In my interviews, the one subject I did feel confident in talking about was my faith. It has always been the backbone of my life, my foundation of certainty in this insecure world. I've always believed that if you put God first in your life, he won't forget you. I was deeply moved to receive a message of support from His Eminence Keith Patrick O'Brien, the Catholic Cardinal of Scotland. The card had a photo of him with Pope John Paul II, and inside His Eminence expressed his delight that I was managing to continue practising my faith. He had seen in the papers that on Easter Monday, in an effort to avoid the photographers, I had gone to chapel in Whitburn, rather than to Our Lady of Lourdes, where I'd been mobbed on Easter Sunday. As it happened, the paparazzi followed me to Whitburn too. There was nowhere they wouldn't go to get a photograph. It was great to feel that the Cardinal was supporting me in this extraordinary time, and I picked up that card and read it more than any other. It helped me to stay grounded.

Church had always been a peaceful place for me, and during those first few weeks it became a sanctuary. In church, my suddenly complicated life became simple again and I could focus on the one fundamentally important thing in my life, my love of God. I've always known that God loves me and sees me as a unique and worthwhile individual. That is the reason I've managed to keep going through the difficult times in my life.

I wasn't aware of all the religious blogs on the Internet then, but I knew from the cards I was getting that people claimed to be inspired by me.

As I've struggled to understand what was happening at that time, I have wondered whether God was using me as an instrument to show that every person, however unlikely, is worthwhile. Unmarried women in their forties, with false teeth and tousled hair, aren't usually held in the highest esteem by our society. The feeling seemed to be that if I could be a success, then anyone could!

With all the interest in me, other material started going up on the Internet. Someone unearthed a copy of the Millennium CD so the world could hear me singing "Cry Me a River"; another person found a video of me auditioning with Michael Barrymore. I couldn't have been more surprised when, in the middle of *News at Ten* one evening, I saw myself singing "I Don't Know How to Love Him" on a grainy home movie taken twenty years before at my parents' Golden Wedding anniversary.

I said, "What the hell is going on here?"

I got on the phone to Gerard.

"Where on earth did they get that?" I asked him.

"It must have been a pal put it up on YouTube," he replied.

Columnists and academics who'd never met me started writing their theories about me. Even the posh, intellectual papers were getting in on the act, like the *Times*, which called me an avenging force for the ordinary and careworn, and the *Guardian*, which asked, "Is Susan Boyle ugly, or are we?"

Some newspapers managed to get even the trivial details of my life wrong. There was a cartoon with me in my gold dress and Pebbles, and they'd drawn Pebbles as a tortoiseshell cat, when in fact she's black and white!

That's when I thought, I'm not going to pay attention to any of this any more, because all the inaccuracies were getting me a wee bit annoyed. In the midst of such a surreal situation, it was difficult enough to remember who I was. But it's more difficult to remain yourself if you're trying to shake off a label that's been stuck on you, and I had more labels stuck on me than raspberry jam!

I think that a lot of shy people dream of being famous because they think it would mean that they wouldn't have to go up and start talking to people, because people would come up and talk to them. That's what I meant when I said in one interview that I wouldn't be lonely any more. I didn't know then that fame brings a different kind of loneliness, but I'll go into that a wee bit later.

It was a chaotic time, but it was extremely enjoyable too and there were some funny moments.

My audition had aired on the evening of 11 April. Less than a week later, I was appearing on *Larry King Live*, which is one of the most influential shows on American television. With me, at the other end of the link, was none other than Piers Morgan himself.

On most "live" radio and television shows there is a thirty-second delay in case something untoward happens. I didn't know that at the time. I was wired up with a microphone on my chest and my tummy was rumbling. That normally means one of two things. Either you've got indigestion, or you're about to let one go. I couldn't shift around in my armchair because the battery pack for the mic was wired behind me. We were just counting down till the moment when we went on air when, suddenly, I knew I couldn't hold it back.

Was it a quiet one? Was it heck! It sounded like the rumble of a concrete-mixer.

I heard Larry King say, "What the hell was that?"

And then Piers's familiar voice, "Congratulations, Susan—the first transatlantic fart! Lucky you have a thirty-second delay!"

They cut that bit out of the interview, of course, but when I came on camera my face was as pink as a beetroot from trying not to laugh.

That was the occasion on which Piers issued an invitation to dinner.

"I accept!" I said immediately.

25
Makeover

"Does everyone know what they're doing?"

Three of us were standing in the hall. My two blonde nieces, Joanne and Pamela, and myself. We all had our jackets on ready to go out.

"Let's run through it one more time," Joanne was whispering, in case there were microphones on the other side of the letter box.

"Susan will come in my car with me, OK? We'll be the first car."

We were formulating an escape plan. Joanne was so organized, I half expected her to produce a flip-chart with a diagram and arrows showing the route.

"You're right behind me in your car, OK?"

Pamela nodded.

Both my nieces are in their mid-thirties, but I think we all had butterflies in our tummy as if we were conspiring to sneak off from school.

"Your job is to keep really close, so no one can get in between us, OK?" Joanne added, taking her mobile phone out of her handbag. "I'm ringing you now, so that the line is open, right?"

There was a moment of silence, then Pamela's mobile started ringing and we all jumped. It broke the tension for a moment, making us giggle at the ludicrous situation.

"I'll have the mobile on the front seat. When I'm ready to go, I'll shout 'Go!' I'll pull out and you pull out behind me, blocking them off, OK?"

"Got it," said Pamela.

"Are we ready?"

Joanne looked from one to the other. We nodded. She put her hand on the latch.

"On a count of three . . ." she said.

"It's like being in *Ocean's Eleven*," Pamela observed.

"It's like being in *Prison Break*," I added.

"Are you ready, Susan?" Joanne wanted to know. I nodded.

"Remember, we're not saying anything to anyone. The cars are round the corner. We're heading straight to them, OK? One, two, three!"

She opened the door.

If you've never experienced it, you can't imagine what it's like to step out in front of the world's media. For a start, the noise is very loud as the camera drives go off like very fast machine guns. Then there are flashbulbs and arc lights so blindingly bright you can't really see where you're going, and even if you can, you think you can't move because everyone is pressing against you. When you first see this wall of people, you think, I'll never get through that, so your instinct is to retreat back to safety, but you learn to understand that they don't actually want to block you because they've got enough photos of your front door.

They're actually longing for you to do something different, so if you look as if you're on the move they'll let you go. Once you take the first step, the crowd moves backwards as if it is one entity with a life of its own and not a collection of individuals. Then the shouting starts.

"Over here, Susan!"

"Where are you off to, Susan?"

"How are you feeling, Susan?"

I don't know how long it took us to get to those cars, and we didn't feel very safe even when the doors were closed and we were inside because the photographers were all leaning over the bonnet with their cameras.

If it takes determination to step out of your door, it takes even more steel to turn the ignition and put your foot on the accelerator so that the car moves forward into a crowd of people like that. I don't think I could ever do it. But I've never learned to drive, which is probably just as well.

"Go go go!" shouted Joanne at her mobile phone as the photographers scattered.

Looking in her rear-view mirror, she could see that Pamela was the next car behind us, but close behind her, car doors were slamming and tyres screeching as the media raced to catch us up. There are sleeping policemen across the roads in our estate, so it was a rather sedate car chase. Fortunately, there were so many parked cars that it made it impossible for anyone to overtake us. At the edge of the estate we turned right and accelerated towards another bottleneck, the little bridge over the ditch. Then we waited to turn right into the main road. There had to be enough of a gap in the traffic to let both our car and Pamela's out, because otherwise the plan would be ruined, but it was a tense moment before Joanne pushed out decisively.

Turning in my seat and looking out of the back window, I could see Pamela behind, with the cars following her swerving out to try to overtake.

"It's no good! I can't hold them!" she shouted down the phone.

Up ahead of us were traffic lights, but we weren't quick enough to make it through green.

"Shall I jump them?" Joanne called.

"No!" I shouted. "It's not worth us all getting killed."

We slowed down. The convoy of cars came to a standstill behind us. Pamela had managed to keep her place.

"When the lights go green, you go and I'll not move," said her disembodied voice from the phone. "Hopefully you'll have enough time to get clear."

It was a great idea, although I did worry about the press cars slamming into the back of her. I could hear their engines revving like bulls about to charge.

Miraculously, the second phase of the plan

worked brilliantly. As soon as the lights went green, Joanne put her foot down and we were off, racing down the road into Whitburn. Pamela didn't move and so the press cars were stuck behind her. When we stopped outside the hairdresser and got out of the car, it felt like just a normal day.

We squinted back down the High Street, almost unable to believe that we'd managed to lose them.

"Quick! Get inside!" said Joanne, hurrying me in to Miss Toner's.

"It's lovely to see you, Susan!" said Hazel, the proprietor. "Did you have any trouble getting here?"

Suddenly, all the adrenalin and nerves burst out in laughter. The other customers looked at us as if I was mad.

"Where are you?" Joanne was asking Pamela on her phone.

"I've taken them round the back way," Pamela replied.

"They're all following you?"

"Looks like it!" said Pamela.

"Well done!"

"That's all right for you," Pamela said. "But what am I supposed to do with them now?"

My poor niece found herself with a tail of press cars driving round and round the streets of Whitburn, and she couldn't go home because then they'd see where she lived and start camping out there. After a while, the pack who were following her realized that they were going round and round in circles and left her alone.

Now that I was safely delivered to my destination, there was no point in Joanne hanging around, so she went off and they arranged for Pamela to come along and pick me up later. I was left to have a nice relaxing afternoon, getting some colour put through my hair and having my eyebrows plucked. Actually, that bit wasn't so relaxing because I'm a bit of a baby when it comes to pain.

I don't know how they do it, but it wasn't long before one of the newspapers tracked down where I was. It was a young woman who came in. From the clothes she was wearing and the way the other customers looked at her, it was obvious straight away that she wasn't a local girl. I was sitting in my chair with foil on my hair. She sat in the chair next to mine.

"Where are you from?" I asked. I was a wee bit wiser by then.

"I'm from the *Sun*," she told me.

"Does London know you're here?" I asked her.

"No," she admitted.

"Well, you know I can't give you an interview, then," I told her.

To give her credit, she went away, and nobody else came in. I spent the rest of the afternoon having a nice chat with Hazel. It felt really good to be out of the house after being cooped up like a battery chicken.

When I was done, Hazel called Pamela, who came down in the car and pulled up outside, but as soon as I walked out of the salon, with a nice red colour through my hair, bang!, the flashbulbs started going off again and the chase was back on. I ran towards the car.

Luckily Pamela had her son with her, and for some reason the press don't photograph babies—perhaps they're not allowed to—so away we were again.

You'll never guess the headline in the newspaper the next morning.

"Dye Me a River!"

26
Yvie

While one wee Scottish woman in Blackburn was learning to cope with all these shenanigans, on the other side of the world another Scottish lassie was watching developments with interest.

Up to this point, Yvie Burnett and I had led very different lives, but we are both Scottish, we both come from humble backgrounds and Yvie has a mezzo-soprano voice with a very similar range to mine. However, all the time I was singing in the smoky pubs and clubs of West Lothian, Yvie was strutting her stuff on the stages of the world's great opera houses. She was singing *Carmen* when I was singing "Killing Me Softly." In normal circumstances, our paths were never destined to cross, but we were brought together by the curious phenomenon that is *Britain's Got Talent*.

Performing and travelling with an opera company is an extremely taxing schedule and when Yvie had children she didn't want to be away for three months at a time, so she decided to take up teaching instead. Now she works with several of Simon Cowell's singers and you probably know her as the voice coach on *The X Factor*, who does a piece to camera about the singer before the person performs. She is also the voice coach on *Britain's Got Talent.*

Yvie was on holiday in America when the whole Susan Boyle volcano began to erupt. Suddenly you couldn't switch on the television without seeing that footage of me in my gold dress. I was interviewed by Oprah Winfrey, the biggest television star in the world; I was name-checked by Homer Simpson. You couldn't get away from me. That's when Yvie remembered that in her suitcase she had packed her homework from *Britain's Got Talent*—a DVD with all the singers she was going to be coaching for the forthcoming live shows. So she got out the DVD and found my unedited audition amongst all the rest of the contestants who were going to sing in the semifinal. She was quite excited at the thought of meeting this woman that everyone was talking about.

Meanwhile, up in Scotland, I was getting nervous again. The day was fast approaching when I was scheduled to go down to London for my voice coaching. The thought of another flight was scary enough, but even if I managed to survive that, I was about to meet the woman I'd seen so many times on television saying things like, "It's a very big song . . . I know she has the voice to sing it, but will she be able to control her nerves?"

As she waited to meet me in the offices of Talkback Thames in Stephen Street in central

London, Yvie was expecting a big, cheeky personality. What she got was an awkward, shy woman with no idea what had hit her. I thought I was the one who was meeting a famous person. It didn't occur to me that Yvie might be feeling that as well.

I was anxious to tell her straight away that I was quite slow at learning things.

"I hope I won't let you down," I said.

Yvie was surprised by that. She promised me we'd start with the very first basics and take it at a pace I felt comfortable with.

First of all, she explained the importance of mastering the really technical elements of singing.

"If you've got a basic vocal technique, you can hide the nerves," she said. "If you haven't, you can't."

"OK, then," I said. "Let's have a go!"

Ten years before, Fred O'Neil had taught me breathing exercises, but I had stopped having lessons a few years ago and in the intervening time I had slipped into bad habits. When Yvie asked me to sing some scales, the way I was taking a breath was by lifting my shoulders just as everyone does. If you want to be a professional singer, you have to learn to breathe with the diaphragm. That way you can take much deeper breaths.

The analogy Yvie used was to get me to imagine a jet of water with a ping-pong ball on top. That ping-pong ball is your voice. If you've got a fantastically strong jet of water, the ping-pong ball bounces happily on top of it and doesn't have to do any work at all. If you've got a little trickle sometimes and a big whoosh at other times, the ping-pong ball doesn't know what it's supposed to do, so it stutters about up and down. I found the visualization very helpful, and when we started doing the exercises I could immediately feel in my lungs what Yvie was talking about.

The first thing we did together was let the tummy muscles go all relaxed and make the sound "Vvvvvvv," just for a few seconds to begin with, then trying a little longer. I could feel the difference immediately.

"This is really good!" I told her in surprise.

I'd been prepared to work hard, but I hadn't expected to enjoy it as much. I went home and practised just as she told me to, and the next week when I came back for my lesson Yvie seemed excited at my improvement, and that made me excited too. I was hitting notes that I didn't know I could hit.

Yvie said my progress was incredible because some singers take weeks to understand, but I just got it.

"You told me you were slow at learning!" she said. "What is this? You're not slow at learning singing."

"No," I admitted. "When it's singing, I seem to just understand what I'm supposed to do."

Once you have the breathing controlled then you can add colour and emotion to your voice. Yvie explained about the different breaks in the voice, and how you can use various parts of the voice for particular types of songs, but the breaks should be smooth so everything blends together.

To help with that, we practised an exercise we call "the kitten." You take your voice up and down the scale like a siren, but very, very quietly. The more you do an exercise, the more the muscles in your voice remember it, and after a while your voice just does what you want without you thinking about it. I would never have been able to sing a song like "Wild Horses," because for that you need your voice to float to the high notes, not belt them out. I can do that now.

It wasn't only the singing that made me look forward to our sessions. Yvie and I have a great professional chemistry, but she was also the first person I'd met in the world of television who felt anything like a friend. Piers Morgan had been friendly over the satellite, but I hadn't yet met him. Frankie, the runner who had stayed with me those first weeks in Scotland, was a great guy and the production people from the programme were efficient, but we lived in different worlds. They had no idea where I was coming from, and I had no idea about their busy metropolitan lives.

Now Yvie is very attractive, and expensively dressed, with a passion for high-heeled shoes with red soles, which she informed me were by Christian Louboutin, as if I would have any idea what that meant. She moves in exalted circles, mixing with people like Sarah Brightman and Andrew Lloyd Webber, but her roots are very much in her humble Scottish background and she empathized with how difficult it must be to have the world descend on your doorstep. Yvie was an only child, and my upbringing was very much like that of an only child even though I am part of a large family. For both of us, our mums had been the most important people in our lives. That immediately gave us something in common.

The very first time I met Yvie, I arrived just before midday. We were introduced and were just starting our exploratory conversation when I noticed her glancing at her watch.

"Would you mind very much if I just called my mum?" she asked, apologetically.

"Go ahead," I told her. "Mothers come first."

Yvie's serious professional face relaxed into a smile.

"It's just that she's disabled and she's in a home," she explained, as she pressed buttons on her mobile phone. "They put her in a wheelchair to have her lunch, you see, and that's when she can come to the phone."

I wasn't sure whether Yvie wanted me to go outside or stay, so I sort of compromised and looked out of the window at the narrow street below, pretending I wasn't listening to the conversation. I could immediately tell from the warmth in her voice that she and her mum had a great relationship.

When she finished talking, I asked her where her mum was and she told me that she lived in a nursing home a mile away from Yvie's house. I mentioned how my own mum had been an invalid at the end of her life, and how I'd wanted to look after her myself and had taken a course in caring. It was a very personal conversation to have so early on in a professional relationship and it created a special bond between us.

After that, Yvie often rang her mum during our lessons, and sometimes she put me on the line to have a word with her myself because Molly was a fan of my singing.

"Now, back to the lesson," Yvie would say, with teacherly strictness, when we got off the phone.

"Mothers come first," I'd always reply.

It became one of those private catchphrases that are the foundations on which friendships are built.

27
Semi-final

The waiting was finally coming to an end. It had been five weeks since my audition aired for the first time on television and in that time my life had changed. The only way I can describe what it felt like was a demolition ball smashing through everything I knew.

I've never been a good sleeper, but each time I found the brief oblivion of unconsciousness, I would wake up in my childhood bedroom with a shudder of relief. Of course! It had all been a dream! Then a noise like the click of the gate as the postman walked to my front door, the electric whirr of paparazzi motordrives anticipating a shot of me in my dressing gown, the flutter and thump of hundreds of letters on the mat, the phone ringing with a persistence it never had before (nobody had previously rung me before six in the evening, when the rate's cheaper). It wasn't a dream.

I had never before lain in bed wondering how I was supposed to feel, but for the past few weeks my mind had been full of contradictions. As newspapers speculated on how many millions I was about to earn, I was still struggling to cope on my benefits. Whenever I ventured out, there were people wearing T-shirts with my face printed on. My clothes were scrutinized as if I were a candidate for marrying into the Royal Family, but my idea of luxury shopping was Dorothy Perkins. I'd spent all my life failing to find anything I could be good at. Now people were talking about me going to America to sing for recently elected President Obama. I was enjoying myself, of course, but it was all so unreal I couldn't trust it.

All I had done was sing one song. Now thousands of people said they loved me. But was I the person they thought they knew? Was I a talented person who had never been given a chance? Or was this all just a piece of astonishing luck that could turn at any moment, especially if I started believing in it?

Being a straightforward person, I found it very hard to keep up the pretence of not knowing whether or not I was going to be in the semi-finals, even though the whole world seemed to have decided that I'd already won the competition.

"Baby steps, baby steps!" was my response whenever I was asked about the future.

It was a great relief when the reveal programme was finally aired on television, and at least I could admit that I had made the semi-finals. If I'd thought that the furore would die down, I was wrong again.

I have always struggled under pressure. My

276

brain doesn't seem to have the same filtering system as other people's when it has too much information to deal with, so I find it very difficult to sort out for myself what I should be concerned about and what doesn't really matter. It's as if everything has the same weight, and it's all stacking up inside my head until there's no room any more.

In a world that was suddenly strange to me, the only thing that was familiar was my religion. I've always believed that if you put your life in God's hands, he will look after you. In my prayers to Our Lady, the simple truth of my devotion was revealed, the assertion of my faith like pure, cool, holy water rinsing through my mind.

My former teacher, Frank Quinn, who had volunteered his support at the beginning, was becoming a great friend. He is a devout Catholic himself and in my conversations with him about spirituality, I felt reunited with what really matters. He encouraged me to believe in myself, as he always had done in class.

Apart from church, the only place I could find peace of mind was when I was singing. From the earliest moments at primary school, singing has always been a calm space for me. On the way into my coaching once a week in London, I was chased by a whirlwind of paparazzi, and I was chased on the way out again. The hours spent inside with Yvie were the eye of the hurricane.

• • •

A few months later Andy Stephens, the man who was to become my manager, said something to me that made a great deal of sense, and I wish he'd been looking after me at the time.

"You can be as determined as you like not to change who you are, Susan, but you have no control whatsoever on how people behave towards you."

That was one of the things I was finding very confusing. People who'd never taken much notice of me before were suddenly my best friends. My family didn't change their way of thinking about me—I was still the baby sister—but that was causing problems too. My brothers John and Gerard decided to express their opinion that I was getting too big for the show. I know that they were trying to look after me and to make sure that I benefited from my moment in the spotlight. None of us knew how long it was going to last. But they shouldn't have made those comments in the press because nobody likes a bighead, and it gave the press just the sniff of controversy they needed once they'd exhausted every angle of the makeover debate. There was no way I was ever going to drop out of the show. I knew it was the chance of my life. I didn't want to annoy Simon Cowell. But the last thing I wanted to do was to cause any conflict within my family.

My acting training came in useful as I tried to

disguise my inner turmoil, but some friends and members of my family could see what was happening and were worried about me. They knew from previous experience that when I go quiet it's often an indication that there's a storm brewing. It was suggested that I take someone with me when it came to the semi-finals, but nobody could agree who would be best, and since none of them had any experience of London themselves, it would have been the blind leading the blind. I thanked everybody for their concern and made the decision to go on my own.

When I finally arrived in my room at the Wembley Plaza Hotel and closed the door behind me, I had the definite sense that I was at the beginning of a new phase of my life. Here I was, in London, on my own, doing something that I'd achieved all by myself. It's probably how students feel when they first arrive at university. As I hung my clothes up in the cupboard, bounced up and down on the bed to test how comfortable it was, then checked out the freebies of shampoo and conditioner in the bathroom, the great rush of independence felt fantastic. I had finally left home, and here I was, in the big smoke. Yes, it was scary, but every time I got a frisson of fear I tried to remember what Frank Quinn was always telling me.

"Susan, believe in yourself. You are the person writing your story."

• • •

My niece Kirsty came up to the hotel for a drink that first evening. The bar was quiet and we were able to have a good chat together. I was aware out of the corner of my eye of a couple of people recognizing me. One man eventually plucked up the courage to come over. He told me that he and his wife were rooting for me, and that was great to hear. I thanked him for that. Otherwise we were left undisturbed; in fact, that first night, the hotel was a lot quieter than my home in Blackburn had been in recent weeks. The anonymity made a pleasant change. I slept fairly well and woke up to a fine morning. It was the first day of my new life of independence and summer had come early. I went downstairs for my breakfast and ate in peace. A car picked me up to take me to the studios nearby.

As somebody who likes walking, I didn't much appreciate constantly travelling around in cars. Walking is a good way of getting to know a place. Even though I'd been down to London many times now, the city didn't feel any more familiar to me than it had on that first trip on our way to Lourdes. When we drove into the centre of town from the airport, I could see beautiful parks, and since the reveal day in February, the wintry black skeletons of trees had exploded with vibrant green foliage and pillowy pink blossoms. I would have liked to explore those gravel avenues fringed with brilliant flower beds and to throw bread to the ducks on the lakes.

There's not a lot of green space in Wembley. The hotel was very near Wembley Stadium, and the area around is geared to match days and gigs at Wembley Arena. When there's nothing on, it's a deserted urban landscape. In the air-conditioned car, I craned my neck to look up at the silver arch towering over the huge grey stadium and gazed at the acres of empty concrete that sparkled in the blistering sunshine.

The song "Memory" was the obvious choice for me to sing in the semi-final because it is so closely associated with Elaine Paige and she was the singer I had declared I wanted to emulate. It is not just her voice that I admire, but the force of character she brings to a song. There was also the small matter of the song coming from *Cats*, and the world had gone mad for Pebbles, so that added an extra dimension.

Singing the song for the first time in the television studio, I noticed some people arriving at the back and thought to myself, "Calm down, Susan!"

All the excitement must be making me hallucinate, because the man looked exactly like Andrew Lloyd Webber. But I wasn't seeing things. Lord Andrew Lloyd Webber had come to hear me sing his song. I was shaking when I was introduced to him. He's been part of my life since the early seventies when I first heard *Jesus Christ Superstar*. Whatever else happened, I thought excitedly, I had met one of my heroes and nobody could take that away from me.

Back at the hotel, the other contestants in my semi-final, who hadn't had so far to travel, had begun to arrive and the paparazzi had got wind of us all turning up, so the lobby was a much busier place.

We were a mixed bunch: Nick Hell, a horror-movie of a man on the stage, but a surprisingly ordinary guy in person; a lissom belly dancer called Julia Naidenko; the two dancing lads called Faces of Disco, who'd been in my group on the reveal day; Darth Jackson, who was a cross between Darth Vader and Michael Jackson (only on *Britain's Got Talent!*); Sue Son, the classical violinist who had been persuaded to drop her friend and perform solo; the wee lassie, Natalie Okri, who had also been in my group when we were told we were through to the semi-final; and, of course, Diversity. Because we were going to be the first to go to the public vote, the spirit among us all was not competitive so much as we're-all-in-this-together. A live show is very different from something that's pre-recorded, because you have only one chance—you can't do it again, so it is essential to make sure it is right.

When you first see your own dressing room, it's

amazing because you really do have your name on the door and there really are lights round the mirror, like in *A Star Is Born*. As soon as the runner closed the door and left me there on my own, I couldn't stop myself doing my little running-on-the-spot dance of joy, which always happens when I'm thrilled to bits. When the designer arrived with the gown that had been specially made for me, I felt like a wee lassie with a dressing-up box. I was a larger lady then than I am now, and there was a wee tiny bra inside the dress. I didn't know how I was going to fit into it, but it was made to measure, so it went on snugly. When I looked at myself in the mirror, I hardly recognized the sophisticated lady grinning back at me in bronze brocade, with bronze shoes to match.

Getting dressed wasn't just about putting on beautiful clothes, it was like putting on a new persona. As I waited for the screens to part on the first dress rehearsal, I no longer felt like Susan Boyle, the wee wifey with a wiggle, I felt like Susan Boyle, the performer. Unfortunately, the elegant effect was somewhat marred when I put my best bronze-slippered foot forward and slid all the way down the runway. I just about managed to stay on my feet, but let's say it wasn't the most graceful entrance, but it was only the rehearsal, so we all had a good laugh about that.

I was last in the running order, so I spent a lot of time during the rehearsal days waiting in my dressing room for my call. Dressing rooms are usually soundproofed so you can practise singing without disturbing anyone, and there's normally no window, for the obvious reason that you don't want people, or cameras, looking in. After a while it can start to feel a wee bit airless and claustrophobic. Sometimes I went for a walk up and down the backstage corridors to see if there was anyone to have a chat to, but the production team all have their earphones on so that they can hear the director's instructions. The other competitors were friendly enough when our paths crossed, but people had their own preparations to make, their own nerves to keep under control, and they generally had their families with them.

There wasn't the opportunity to get out of the studio for a walk and a breath of fresh air because you never knew when you were going to be needed. Besides, I was wary in case there were photographers outside. It's not that I object to having my photograph taken. I recognize it's part of the job. But going for a stroll to clear your head is not the same as walking up the street with a swarm of photographers buzzing round you.

In the evenings, when we'd finished at the studios and were taken back to the hotel, there were bigger crowds of fans and paparazzi to negotiate each night. The acts from the other semi-finals had begun to arrive to rehearse too and the lobby began to resemble a scrum. I was interrupted so much in the restaurant that I was barely able to eat my food, and there wasn't any privacy in my room either, because by this time the photographers had found out where I was and were staying in the hotel opposite with their telephoto lenses trained on my bedroom, hoping to get a shot of me in my nightie! I had to have the curtains drawn all the time.

The days were very long because I was going from one windowless room to another. My throat was beginning to feel a wee bit dry and scratchy, as if I had a cold coming on.

Be careful what you wish for, Susan!

All the times in my life when I wished that people would take some notice of me, and now there were dozens of people photographing me and clamouring for my autograph, but I'd never felt more lonely in my life. I'd always been happy enough in my own company, or when it was just me and Pebbles, but, away from the comforts of home, I had to admit that I wasn't really coping very well by myself.

I told myself that I'd elected not to have anyone from my family with me. Some of them were going to come down to be in the audience on Sunday. I wanted them to see me perform and be proud. In the meantime, for once in my life I was going to do something by myself and show everybody that I was capable. I was a grown woman of forty-eight. I'd achieved this opportunity without anyone else's help and I was going to go as far as I could without anyone's help. I didn't want everyone else telling me what I should and shouldn't do as if I were a child. More than that, I didn't want anyone telling Simon Cowell what to do, because he's got a lot of good singers and he didn't need anyone bothering him.

Frankie, the lad who'd come up to help me in Blackburn when it all blew up at the beginning, suggested I might like to ask a friend to come down.

"What about Lorraine?" he said.

"Lorraine's got her hotel to run," I reminded him.

Lorraine would hardly be able to drop everything just to keep me company. But on the Thursday evening, when I was leaving the studios after spending the whole day rehearsing, another car drew up and out stepped Lorraine, dressed to the nines, as usual, and, even though I'd promised myself I'd cope on my own, I have to say I was very pleased to see her!

It's amazing how quickly human beings adjust to changed circumstances, and when you're in the middle of it, you soon get used to a different routine. It takes someone coming in from outside to show you just how weird your life has become. Lorraine couldn't believe the crowds in the hotel lobby, or the chase to the lifts that had become a way of life for me. When we finally reached my room and shut the door behind us, she went over to open the curtains because it was a fine sunny evening.

"You can't do that!" I stopped her. "Not unless you want to be snapped by the paparazzi!"

"I can't believe you're living like this!" Lorraine exclaimed.

"I haven't been out since Monday," I told her. "Except to the studio."

"That's not right," said Lorraine, checking her make-up in the mirror. "We're in London, so you and I are going to go and have ourselves a wee girls' night out!"

It was one of those summer evenings we don't get enough of in our cold, wet country, where the air remains warm even after the sun has gone down. Tables and chairs appear on the pavement outside pubs and coffee shops, and the whole world seems to be out on the streets making the most of it.

"Look, it's Susan Boyle!"

Everyone we passed stopped us to say hello, and I posed with them so their mate could take a picture on their mobile phone. As cars went past, they were slowing down and tooting their horns. One almost smashed into a taxi cab because he was looking at me, not the road.

Lorraine stood with her mouth open.

"You've had one showing on telly, Susan," she said, "but they've never forgot you!"

It took quite a while to walk a couple of hundred yards, and when we finally got up to Wembley High Street, we were trying to find somewhere quiet to eat, but it was mainly McDonald's and Nando's-type places, which are nice, but very public. Then Lorraine spotted a little Greek restaurant. I'd never eaten Greek food before but Lorraine said it was good, so we went in. As soon as we were inside, I noticed two familiar figures sitting at the back of the restaurant—Yvie and Nigel, the musical director. I didn't think they'd want to be seen with us, so I said to Lorraine, "We cannae sit in here."

Lorraine said, "Well, we cannae go outside now."

I turned round to see a bank of eager faces smiling at me through the door. It was going to be the same anywhere we went. By that time, Yvie and Nigel had spotted us and they asked us to join them, which was very nice of them, but I didn't feel comfortable because I was very aware that some of the other competitors' families already thought I was getting special treatment.

All the bookies had me down as the winner, and it was me the photographers went after, even though I always suggested they take pictures of the other contestants too. I knew better than anybody else not to believe what everyone said. I had a semi-final to get through before I even got to the final. I also had a long track record of coming second in almost every singing competition I'd ever entered in my life.

Lorraine was right. Greek food is delicious, and I had quite an appetite. Yvie and Nigel finished and left before we did, and over coffee Lorraine said she'd noticed an Irish pub with live music just down the road, so why didn't we go there for a wee drink? However, when we came out of the restaurant, everyone I'd spoken to on the way up to the High Street seemed to have texted their friends and now there were hundreds of people waiting for us. Everyone, whether they were young or old, wanted a piece of me. Don't get me wrong—I am always pleased to meet fans, but it took a very long time to get back to the hotel.

I needed to get a passport photo done, so the next morning Lorraine suggested we try the Asda up the road. We decided not to risk walking and ordered a cab. Dashing from the car into the store, I went into the booth and pulled the curtain across so my face couldn't be seen.

"Don't you move till I get back," Lorraine whispered. She went off to get a few toiletries that we needed while we waited for the photo to develop.

But when she returned, less than ten minutes later, I'd been surrounded by about thirty lads, all ringing their mates, saying, "You'll never guess who I'm with!"

We had to order another cab to get back to the hotel, although it wasn't more than a couple of hundred yards. That's when Lorraine said, "Right. We'll have to stay in the hotel."

The problem with that was that the weekend of the semi-finals of *Britain's Got Talent* coincided with three Wembley play-offs for promotion from football League Two, League One and Championship. Where were the fans staying? The Wembley Plaza Hotel. So on top of the contestants, their families, the fans and the press, the hotel lobby and bar were now filled with football supporters. If you've ever seen the Marx Brothers' film *A Night at the Opera*, where Groucho is in a cabin on a liner and he keeps ordering more room service, and the tiny space fills up with dozens of waiters and maids and technicians all on top of each other, you'll know how it felt in the lobby of the hotel. Sheer pandemonium!

On the Friday night there were just a few fans who'd made the journey to see Shrewsbury Town play Gillingham. On Saturday the noise increased as the supporters of League One's Scunthorpe came down to face London club Millwall. But on Sunday the place was packed with fans in claret and blue for Burnley, and red and white for Sheffield United, who were lined up against each other in one of football's biggest games, with the winners getting into the Premiership. It didn't bother them that I was a Celtic supporter;

they all wanted my autograph just the same.

Breakfast was hectic, and lunch was hectic, so Lorraine said to me, "Susan, this isn't enjoyable. I think what we should do is go down at half past seven rather than nine o'clock to get our breakfast."

But half seven was hectic too, so we decided to get our meals in our room.

"I knew I was coming down to help on a famous television programme," Lorraine joked, as we sat on our twin beds with the curtains drawn. "But I didn't realize it was going to be *Prisoner Cell Block H*!"

Instead of sleeping, I was lying in bed most of the night with my heart palpitating and my eyes wide open, trying to block out endless choruses of "We are going up, we are going up!" floating up from the bar. My mood was all over the place. One minute I was cresting along on a wave of giddy excitement, the next I was sinking down into the cold depths of fear. Sunday was the night when I had to show that I wasn't just good for one song, but had a real future as a professional singer. If I made a mess of it, all the interest in me would disappear as instantly as it had arrived. I'd watched enough reality television to know that. Simon Cowell had called it "the most important performance of my life." No pressure there, then.

My friends Sadie and Patricia from church came down from Scotland for the weekend to see the semi-final, along with my niece Joanne and her husband, Kenny. Kirsty was also there and they all tried to help me relax by offering to take me out for a few hours, but that wasn't possible because I never knew when I was going to be needed for rehearsals. It would have been nice to have a bit of a break in different surroundings, but I didn't want to cause any problems, so again I felt caught in the middle.

The only place I was able to focus on what really mattered was in the rehearsal room. Yvie understands about nerves because she's worked with so many singers, but she doesn't take kindly to crying because it's bad for your voice. We established a routine where Yvie would start singing the exercise and I'd sing it back. As soon as I was singing, none of the stuff that was going on outside mattered. I was exhausted from lack of sleep, but when it came to singing I possessed incredible reserves of stamina.

You could taste the tension in the air, and not just among the performers. The production team, who always appeared so professional with their headphones and head mics, were a wee bit brittle. Delivering a live television programme was almost as scary for them as it was for us.

Finally, there was no more preparation to be done. The producer of the show had let me get ready in Piers Morgan's dressing room as a special treat. (He wasn't there, of course!) Frock on, hair tamed, face painted, I kept glancing at the mirror, as if to catch it unawares. Wandering up and down the corridor before the show was about to begin, I bumped into Piers on his way to his seat. I had a big crush on him and I thought, Oh my God, this is my chance to talk to him in person, so I said, "Hi Piers!"

And he said, "Whoa! It's you!"

"Yes!"

"People in the States are always asking me, how is Susan Boyle?"

"I'm fine, no problems," I told him.

"Well, I'll see you later," he said.

I'd finally met another one of my heroes. I was buzzing.

The opening credits of the programme are designed to stoke up the excitement for the audience at home, so you can imagine how thrilling it feels to be backstage. Adrenalin starts coursing through your veins, but that boost is difficult to hang on to, and I was last in the running order, not due to go on for another hour.

It was the longest and the shortest hour of my life. I didn't want to get in anyone's way, so I stayed in my dressing room, but I could hear the applause from the audience after each act. It sounded like a good, supportive audience, and I knew that Lorraine, Patricia and Sadie were out there, as well as Joanne and Kenny, and Kirsty and her husband, Shaun. I wanted them to be proud of me. I thought of Bridie tuning in to the show in her flat in Motherwell. At least she'd have no quarrel with the way I looked tonight. Each time I glimpsed myself in the mirror, there was a split second when I thought, Who's that?

Walking to my starting position behind the screens was like wading through treacle. My mind had gone blank. I'd rehearsed my song, practised it in my hotel room and warmed up with Yvie, but now I couldn't remember what note I was supposed to come in on. My mouth was so dry, it was likely no sound would emerge at all. What were the words? I told myself, "For God's sake, Susan, whatever you do, don't slide down that runway."

As I waited there, listening to the video-tape introduction, I heard myself on tape saying, "All my life I've wanted to prove that I'm a worthwhile person . . ."

The stage manager was frowning at me, and I realized that I was pulling funny faces, like you do when you hear yourself talking on tape.

"Susan Boyle!"

The screens parted. I could hear cheering, but I couldn't see the audience because the lights were very bright. I tried not to look at the judges in front of me. I didn't even think about the millions of people out there watching me. All I was thinking about was getting to that microphone in my high bronze shoes without falling over.

The first arpeggios of the backing track started slightly sooner than I expected, I opened my mouth to sing and was suddenly trapped in my worst nightmare. The cold that had been coming on all week made my voice croaky, and the wrong notes came out.

You don't stop, you keep going!

It had been drilled into us at Edinburgh Acting School all those years ago. Through the mist of dry ice swirling round my feet, I spotted Yvie sitting in her position just next to Piers.

"You can't control your nerves, but you can control your breathing."

I placed my hand on my diaphragm and, thank God, it worked.

The judges were very generous with their comments. Piers told me that I'd cheered the world up; Amanda said I'd nailed the song, which wasn't true because the first note was bad. Then Simon started apologizing for laughing at the audition and that was embarrassing, so I put on a funny voice and tried to make a joke of it.

"I know nothing, I am from Barcelona."

It was a reference to the hapless character Manuel in the classic sitcom *Fawlty Towers*, and I was doing my classic thing of being a wee bit off the wall. I realized when Simon looked askance.

"She's not from Barcelona, by the way!" said Dec.

Backstage, the more I looked at the other contestants, the more I wondered how I had ever thought I stood a chance. I'd seen all their acts time and again at rehearsals. Diversity were fantastic dancers and a great bunch of lads. That little Perri, what a character! Ashley Banjo was one of the tallest guys I'd ever encountered, and one of the politest too. Little Natalie had a great voice and she was a cute wee dancer. I was sure the audience at home would like her. Then there was Sue Son, who had a great story and people liked a modern take on a classical instrument. You just had to think of how well Escala did on the previous series. Faces of Disco had a very entertaining act, something different. To be honest, I wasn't too bothered about Darth Jackson or Nick Hell, but you never knew what the audience would go for.

I was the only one who had messed up.

For the first time, I thought about all the millions of people picking up their phones to vote. I couldn't imagine anybody wanting to vote for me.

It is terrifying standing waiting for the results. You're hoping that they'll call out your name and at the same time you're telling yourself it's not going to happen and you're trying to set your face into a suitably dignified mask that won't show how disappointed you are.

"Susan Boyle!"

Oh my God!

I was so gobsmacked, I literally didn't know which way to turn and started walking the wrong way, until I was called to the other side of the stage by Dec.

I was walking on air, I was dancing on the spot, and then I did what I'd promised myself I would never do again because it's just not what professional singers are supposed to do. The wiggle. Not once, but twice, and another one specially for Piers.

Oh my God!

28
Final

The backlash began almost immediately. People started writing and tweeting their reviews of the semi-final, and some of them weren't exactly complimentary. To be honest, they had a point. I knew better than anyone else that it hadn't been my best performance, but the public had had the opportunity to vote me out and they had kept me in, so there wasn't anything I could do about it.

I tried to avoid the newspapers, but that was no longer possible with everyone asking me for my comments as soon as I stepped out of my room. There were undercover journalists staying in the hotel now. Lorraine and I started to recognize them lurking in the corridors. I tried not to take the criticism personally, but my high spirits came crashing down to earth with a bang.

It was a week since I'd arrived in the Wembley Plaza Hotel, and I was running out of clean clothes to wear because I hadn't expected to stay for the final. Lorraine had also been planning to return to Scotland, but now the producers of the programme asked her if she would continue to keep me company. It was difficult for her because she had things to arrange at her hotel, but she agreed because she feared for me being on my own. The producers of *Britain's Got Talent* were very sensitive about me being seen to be treated differently from the other contestants, so a secret plan was drawn up whereby Lorraine and I would fly to Scotland, spend Monday night at her partner Benny's house, pick up what we needed, then return the following morning. We made our escape in cars with tinted windows and managed to get through the airport unnoticed. We can laugh about it now, but when you're in the middle of the subterfuge, you feel as if you've done something wrong, like a criminal on the run.

Benny met us at the other end and drove us to his house. Once we had checked that there were no paparazzi lurking, I managed to nip into Yule Terrace to get some clothes and things I needed. The house sounded a wee bit echoey with nobody there, but it was fantastic to feel the familiar texture of the banister, the carpet, the sofa in the back room, and to see all the pictures and ornaments, each with its own memory, that made it my home. I knew I had to be quick, because if anyone spotted me news would travel fast, but as I stood in the back room, gazing at the little figure of Our Lady in the corner, I paused for a moment. What if I just stayed behind? Lorraine would be able to return to her work and I could get my old life with Pebbles back.

I thought about my mum sitting in her chair.

What would she say if she were here in the room with me now?

"You're not going to let a couple of bad reviews stop you, are you, Susan? Thousands of people have spent good money voting for you. You can't let them down!"

My fighting mood returned. I'd show everyone I could do better. I would! I'd show them!

Burnley had been promoted to the Premiership and their supporters had left to celebrate back at home. The hotel lobby was quieter.

"Do you fancy a cup of tea?" Lorraine suggested, walking ahead of me towards the bar.

When I failed to answer, she turned round and saw that I'd been swallowed into the middle of a Japanese television crew. They were all smiling expectantly, bowing and speaking to me in Japanese, but I had no idea what they were asking. It sounded like

"Blaa blaa blaa, Susan Boyle, blaa blaa blaa, Susan Boyle . . ."

One of the men was filming my face with a hand-held camera, another was wielding a great big furry mic on a pole, another was holding a mic to my face, and there were about twenty others bobbing around me.

Lorraine said, "Susan, let's forget about the tea and go up to the room."

I was trying to be polite, bowing back to them as

they bowed to me, which only made them bow and smile even more.

"Blaa blaa, Susan Boyle, blaa blaa, Susan Boyle!"

"Thank you, thank you!"

I felt like the Queen, but what else was I supposed to say?

Lorraine started frantically pushing the buttons to try to call the lifts, while the Japanese were grabbing at me, urgently, as if they were trying to tell me something important.

The lifts weren't arriving.

"Quick, let's go up the stairs!" Lorraine suggested, flying towards the fire exit and straight into the furry mic, which is actually not as soft as it looks.

"Blaa blaa, Susan Boyle, blaa blaa, Susan Boyle!"

"Are you all right, Lorraine?" I called over the crowd.

"I'm fine, Susan," called Lorraine, but she was rubbing her head. "What are we going to do?"

The Japanese woman who was holding the mic in front of my face finally mustered the language to say, "Future husband!"

A ancient Japanese man I hadn't noticed was thrust in front of me.

"You kiss future husband!"

The old guy went to put his arms around me to give me a kiss. He must have been at least eighty years old!

"Hell, no way!" I said.

Of all the stupid things I've said, the one that's caused me most bother is my remark about never having been kissed. As I made clear at the time, it was not an advert, but nobody ever remembers that bit.

When we finally made it back to our darkened room, Lorraine and I both fell on to our beds laughing, but it was the last time we'd do that for a while, because if the pressure had been difficult to handle until then, it was nothing compared to the week that was to come.

That evening, along with some of the other contestants, we watched the third live semi-final on the big screen in the hotel bar. I was constantly being pestered by journalists, so I left before the end of the programme.

The following morning, the front pages of the tabloids had the story that I had sworn at the television in the bar downstairs and flicked a V sign at the screen following Piers's comments about Shaheen's performance. All I can tell you is that if I did make such a gesture, it was only as a kind of "Go on with you! I thought you said you liked me!" kind of joke. I would never, ever criticize a fellow singer.

Reading the reports was like free-falling into a dark chasm. I'd never believed in the fairy story. I'd always half expected a note saying, "Ha ha, only kidding!" But nothing had prepared me for being turned into an ugly monster.

I didn't feel safe any more. I was terrified to leave my room until we got a call that the car was outside the hotel, and then Lorraine and I would make a dash for it. On one occasion I made the mistake of waiting while Lorraine went to get a bottle of water for me. A woman approached and asked if I would have my photo taken with a girl in a wheelchair, so of course I agreed. But when Lorraine returned she noticed the girl was very agitated, then the girl's mother came up and pushed the wheelchair away. I'd assumed that the first woman who'd asked for the photo was the mother, but she wasn't, she was a journalist.

Lorraine said, "How dare you? I can't believe you've just done that!"

The journalist asked me, cool as you like, "Is it true you were shouting at Piers Morgan on the television?"

I just snapped. I went ballistic.

And the journalist said, "Well, you've just proved my point!" and walked out smirking.

I know the press have their job to do, but when they start trying to create stories using a disabled person as a prop, I think that oversteps the line of decency.

"That's it!" said Lorraine. "I want the police involved here. I'm sick and tired of people trying to set you up!"

And so the police got involved, and that led to more stories in the papers about me losing the plot.

"Boyling Point!" screamed the headlines above reports about me shouting. Nobody reported what had happened just before.

I'd entered a television talent show, so I'd put myself in the arena, but I never claimed to be perfect. All I wanted to do was sing. I couldn't understand how I'd suddenly become Public Enemy Number One. People try to tell you that today's newsprint is tomorrow's litter-tray liner, but they don't know what it's like when you're the one portrayed, and if you complain, you only make things worse. I felt the same humiliating powerlessness as I had in the playground at school when people were saying nasty things about me. I couldn't stop crying.

My dream of success and independence was crashing down around my head. I thought my only hope was to go back home, shut my door and try to pick up the pieces of my life, so I packed my case and phoned the producer to tell her I was quitting. She suggested that I have a chat to Piers Morgan, so he came on the phone and I tried to explain through my tears what had been happening.

He was very honest, actually, because he said he had been a journalist himself once, and he had chased people. If I gave up now, I'd be doing exactly what the press wanted me to do. He advised me to go back and prove my point. I should say to myself, and to them, non-verbally, obviously, I'm going to go through with this, and to hell with you!

"Should I leave my cases where they are, then?" I sniffed.

"Yes," he said.

The next day, there was a torrent of stories and speculation about whether I was staying or going. It all added to the strain of rehearsing all day, sometimes until late at night. All the fuss around me wasn't really helping the other finalists, who were all under a lot of stress themselves. But some of them, particularly Stavros Flatley, Diversity, Flawless and wee Aidan's mum, are very grounded people and they were very supportive to me.

After a great deal of debate, Lorraine and I were finally allowed to leave the Wembley hotel to go to stay in a house in Chelsea with a lovely woman who is a cousin of Benny's. A secret location, it said in the papers.

Still I couldn't sleep. I was awake throughout the night, listening to the rumble of the teeming city that's never perfectly quiet even in the small hours of the morning. I must have drifted off around dawn, waking up again only a couple of hours later in unfamiliar surroundings and taking a moment to remember where I was. Chelsea. It wasn't an area I knew at all, but I was so desperate to get outside in the air that I decided to go out for a walk.

Closing the heavy front door behind me carefully so as not to disturb anyone, I stepped out into the street. The house was on a busy through road, and there was a strong smell of exhaust as cars and buses thundered past, but it was great to be outside. I hadn't seen the sky for so long, it was exhilarating to look up at the sheer expanse of blue dotted with just a few cotton-wool clouds.

Glancing left and right along the tree-lined street, I didn't know what I was going to do or where I was going. I decided to head off towards the junction I could see in the distance where the street I was on crossed a main road. I thought I might find a newsagent and buy a paper to see what they were saying about me today. As I started walking, I felt very happy to be outside, and a wee bit naughty, almost like I was sneaking off early from school.

At the crossroads, I turned left and headed towards a Tesco Express sign a hundred yards or so along.

Back at the house, the housekeeper had seen me leave, and she rushed up to Lorraine, who had only just got up and was in the shower.

"Madam! Madam! Susan's left!"

"What?" Lorraine came out of the shower, pulled on her jeans and T-shirt and ran out in her slippers. She could just see me at the end of the street, about to turn into the main road. She raced after me, calling, "Susan!"

I turned round impatiently but I didn't stop walking.

"I just want to walk down the street. OK?" I said, irritated, when Lorraine caught me up.

"Well, you cannae!" she protested, panting from her run. "You're too big now just to walk down the street!"

"I just want to get a newspaper!" I said, shrugging her off, and marching into the Tesco Express.

Sure enough, my face was all over the *Sun* and the *Mirror*. I bought a copy of each and scanned the stories.

"Come on, Susan!" Lorraine was hissing at me, aware that I was beginning to attract attention. People in the shop had obviously recognized me, and as we went back out on the street, cars were slowing to have a look at me.

"Let's go back, then," I said.

"We cannae go back now," Lorraine cried, exasperated. "They'll follow us and it's meant to be a secret location!"

She looked around desperately, trying to work out what to do. I noticed that she was still wearing her slippers.

The crowd was growing now. The traffic on the main road was very loud and getting louder because, as people saw it was me, they were beeping their horns and winding down their windows to shout out "Good luck!"

We were standing outside a funeral director's. Next door was an estate agent's. There wasn't even a café we could duck into. Further up the road there was a big hospital, but I didn't want to go in there and cause a commotion. We were trapped.

I don't know what made us both look up at that moment and find ourselves staring at a statue of Jesus above the words "Servite Catholic Church." A church entrance seemed completely incongruous right in the middle of an ordinary terrace of shops. It didn't look like any other church I'd ever seen, but it appeared that we were standing outside Our Lady of Dolours Catholic Church. You could walk past it a hundred times without noticing.

The iron gates to the small, arched vestibule were open, but the glass door into the church was firmly closed. We read the Mass times. Morning Mass was at ten o'clock and there wasn't another until 6:30 in the evening. With so little sleep, I was finding it difficult to keep track of time, but I think it must have been around midday.

Lorraine spotted an entry-phone on the side wall. It looked so old, I doubted it would work, but Lorraine pressed the buzzer anyway.

"Can I help you?"

It was difficult to hear the voice because of the traffic noise outside.

"Can you let us in, please?" said Lorraine.

"I'm sorry, the church is closed, I'm afraid," said the woman's voice.

"But I'm desperate," said Lorraine. "I've got Susan Boyle here."

"You're having me on," said the voice.

"No, I'm not joking!"

In fact, Lorraine was on the brink of tears.

"Wait, I'll come down," said the voice.

A moment or two later, a very pretty lady appeared.

"Oh my goodness," she said. "It *is* Susan Boyle!"

And she opened the door into the colonnade inside that leads to the door of the church. There were a few tables and chairs there, and all the parish notices pinned up on noticeboards.

"Would you believe all the things they're saying about me in the press," I thrust the papers at the nice lady. "It's not true, you know!"

"You don't have to pay to read that and give yourself pain," she replied soothingly. "You don't need to explain to me. Those are just gossip-mongers. There are millions of people out there who love you. I can tell you that."

She told us she was the parish secretary, then sat us down on the chairs and went to get the parish priest, who was having his lunch.

"I've got Susan Boyle here," she said.

"You're joking!" he said.

"I'm not," she told him. "And I'd really appreciate it if you could have a word, because she's very upset."

So Father Dermot came down to meet us.

"Would you like to see inside the church?" he asked.

"I would," I told him.

Father Dermot and I went on a tour of the church, while Lorraine went upstairs with the lady for a cup of tea.

It is the sort of old church that you would expect to find standing alone in some prominent position in a town, surrounded by a churchyard, so it felt very strange that instead it was almost hidden on a busy London street. As Father Dermot opened the glass door and we stepped inside the cool, dim interior with its dark stone columns and high vaulted ceiling, it felt as surprising and magical as finding Narnia at the back of a wardrobe.

The priest told me a little about the history of the place and pointed out the stone pietà, with Our Lady cradling Christ's body. In front of it, there was a special prayer in a frame, hand-written and decorated like a manuscript. Some of the words seemed particularly resonant for me at that time: "Take and offer on the Cross our labours, weariness and low spirits and struggles and faint-heartedness . . ."

Murmuring those words before a representation of such courage, I was able to put my own struggles into perspective. As often happens in church, I came away feeling much lighter and refreshed.

Upstairs in the Founders Room, the lady, whose name was Dupe, had made a cup of tea and offered me one of my favourite ginger biscuits. Lorraine had cheered herself up and we were all feeling much better.

"Dupe—that's not a name I've heard before," I said.

"I come from Nigeria," Dupe told me. "All African names have meaning. My full name is much longer, and it means 'Thank God,' but Dupe is the short version."

"Are you going to give us a song now, Susan?" asked Father Dermot.

His Irish accent made me feel completely at home. So I sang "The Fields of Athenry," which is an old Irish ballad that dates from the famine, but is probably better known as the anthem of the Celtic supporters. Father Dermot and Lorraine joined in the chorus.

By the time we left an hour or so later, we were feeling much more relaxed. As we said good-bye, I left the newspapers behind with Dupe.

"We are one hundred per cent behind you," she said. "And I can assure you of the prayers of this parish."

"I'm sure there's a reason for this, Susan," Lorraine said, in the cab back to the house. "I don't know the reason, but there is a reason and it will make you survive this, because you give the world something good."

It was a nice thought to take back with me to the studios for the final rehearsals that carried on all that day, until after midnight.

The stories in the newspapers I had read that morning had turned to criticism of the programme. That had made everyone jumpy and upped the tension all around me. The producers were getting nervous. My family were worried. Simon Cowell spoke to me himself and told me that if I didn't want to do the show, then I didn't have to. But I did want to do the show. It was the opportunity I'd been waiting for all my life. So that was that, but still I couldn't seem to stop all the noise and arguments and images flashing around my head.

Lorraine had been hanging around Wembley all day waiting for me, and when we finally got into the car to go back to Chelsea, we were both exhausted.

It didn't help that the paparazzi saw me get into the car and started to give chase.

The driver said, "I'll see if I can get away from them."

So he put his foot down and we were thrown back in our seats. I was looking through the front windscreen at how close he was getting to the cars in front, my knuckles gripping the seat as he swerved out to overtake. We were jumping red lights, and in the end I was so scared I just closed my eyes and prayed. Next to me, Lorraine was looking out of the back window, doing a running commentary in my ear. We weren't losing them, and she was panicking because she had done her best to get me to a place where I could be myself and relax, but now there were guys on motorbikes chasing us with cameras.

"I don't know what I'm going to do," the driver said. "They're determined."

Lorraine got out her phone and rang the people we were staying with, and she was saying, "They're going to cause an accident! It's like Princess Diana here!"

That didn't exactly help me calm down, so I shouted at her, "For God's sake, Lorraine!"

And she screamed back, "It's not my fault, Susan! It's out of my control!"

When we finally arrived outside the house in Chelsea, Lorraine said, "We can't get out of the car. We'll have to get the police."

She was seeing them as a physical threat, as if it were guns not cameras they were pointing. I was all for getting out and giving them what they wanted, but she wouldn't let me. So now the two of us were going at each other like a couple of headless chickens.

The driver told Lorraine that there was nothing the police could do if the paparazzi didn't touch us, so we had to get out and run the gauntlet.

"I've taken a lot of celebrities," he said, "but I've never had anything like this. You're big, Susan!"

"I'm only five foot three," I told him.

In those sort of circumstances, you have to keep your sense of humour.

That night, I sat on the chaise longue staring at nothing. My brain was whirling inside my head like a waltzer at a fairground.

In less than twenty hours I was going to have to get out there and sing live on television to an estimated audience of twenty million people and the car was coming for me at seven o'clock in the morning. I didn't get one single second of sleep.

I'd never seen so many flowers. There were more flowers than in a florist's shop, at least a hundred bouquets, and that was first thing in the morning. Flowers kept arriving all day and the scent was heavenly. I was so overwhelmed I burst into tears. People from all over the world were wishing me well—film stars, politicians, football teams, as well as names I didn't recognize. There were presents too, scarves and lucky charms. Lorraine and I started reading each of the labels and we should have written down a list, but I was so busy there wasn't time. I'll take this opportunity to say a long overdue thank you to everyone who was so generous.

To say that I was wobbly on the day of the final would be an understatement. I tried to eat a wee bit of breakfast, and a bed was put in my dressing room, but I still couldn't rest, and the nerves were beginning to build again.

I'd assumed that nerves would be something you'd get used to. After the semi-final I'd thought nothing could be worse than that. I'd sung on live television and I hadn't done as well as I could have, but I'd survived. Weren't nerves all about fear of the unknown? But since then I'd had virtually no sleep, I hadn't eaten properly for days, and the world had turned against me. The stakes seemed higher than ever.

I was called in with Lorraine to see Simon Cowell.

He asked me if I could remember what I said at my first audition.

"I'm going to go out there and make that audience rock!" I told him, through my tears.

"Well, get out there and do it!" he said.

I came out of his office feeling resolved. There was no going back. But that still didn't make the nerves go away.

The song I was singing was "I Dreamed a Dream." I started thinking that if I messed up, the clip would fly round the world just like last time and that would be it for me. The newspapers were probably writing the headlines already: "Fallen Angel!" I didn't want to let my family down, nor all the people in Blackburn and the rest of the world who had supported me.

Lorraine had an idea.

"Let's ring Frank Quinn," she said. "If anyone can calm you down, it's him."

Poor Frank was on a weekend away with his wife and some friends of theirs in Lytham St. Annes, and I expect the last thing he wanted was me weeping down the phone. But as usual, his calm reassurance helped me see through all my worries.

"Susan," he said, "the result of this thing does not matter. What matters is that you are given the opportunity to stand up there and sing."

I could tell that the production team were losing patience with me. My outbursts were becoming a nuisance. Lorraine was doing her best to soothe me, but as you do with the people you know best, I was kicking off at her as well. The programme-makers decided that her presence wasn't helping, so Lorraine was sent off to the canteen to get some lunch. The way things turned out, I didn't see her again for several weeks.

In my dressing room, I was climbing the walls. Every time I calmed down enough for hair and make-up to come in, they'd put the make-up on my face and I'd wash it all off with my tears. There was mascara pouring down my cheeks, and when I looked in the mirror, the face that looked back was ragged and miserable, as if I had turned into the ugly character the papers were writing about.

In my warm-up with Yvie we went through the

Vvvvvvvs, the kitten, the lot. Yvie started singing and I sang back, just as we always did in our lessons. The regular breathing and the familiar rhythms grabbed hold of my racing heart and my whirling brain and slowed them down.

Yvie was conscious that I was tired, but when she asked me, "Would you like to go over the song again?" I said yes please. I didn't seem to be tired when I was singing.

"It really is a natural thing for you," Yvie told me. "When you're singing, you're fine. You'll be fine once you get out there and sing."

So there I was, sitting in my long, shimmery gown. My make-up had been done for the final time. The show was on air, but I was way down the running order, eighth in a list of ten. I wasn't aware of what was happening with the other acts. I wasn't aware of anything except that time was running out for me.

I can't do it! I can't do it!

In desperation, I rang Frank Quinn again. We said a prayer together, and just before stepping out in front of an audience of millions, I found the quiet place that is my faith.

"Now, Susan," he told me, "when you go out there, on your right hand will be Our Lady and on your left hand will be your mother. You are in the middle, and you've got the job of singing."

317

29
Aftermath

Somehow I got myself out on that stage. Somehow I sang. Somehow I remembered to thank everyone who had supported me.

"That's where you really feel at home, isn't it, on stage?" Ant asked me.

"I really feel at home on stage," I told him, truthfully. "I am among friends, am I not?" I wasn't so sure about that last bit.

In the audience, my family were shocked at how I looked. Knowing me so well, they could see the build-up of stress written across my face. Those of them who had been at the semi-final the previous week sensed a colder atmosphere in the audience and that brought out all their protective instincts. You know how families are. They know all your faults, but they'll defend you till the last.

Piers Morgan was the judge who went first and he was very supportive, but when he said that I should win the competition I heard something I'd never had before after a performance. Booing. It was only a few people, but once you've heard the boos, you don't hear the applause any more. It's like being punched. It knocks you off balance. When I looked at a video tape of the final, weeks afterwards, I saw Simon Cowell say that he adored me, but I wasn't aware of that at the time.

Then there was the wait. To be honest, I was so ragged I didn't even know what I felt any more. I forgot what I was supposed to do when my name was called as being in the final three and wandered down to the front of the stage. When Julian the saxophonist was called, he gently guided me to where I was supposed to be. Then it was his turn to leave.

So I was down to the last two.

"And the winner of *Britain's Got Talent* is . . ."

The wait was seventeen seconds.

"Diversity!"

My immediate response was relief. It was over!

My second feeling was genuine pleasure for Diversity, because it was really touching to see great big lads like that crying with happiness. You couldn't wish for a nicer bunch of people. They were fantastic dancers who'd put a lot of work into their act and a bit of humour as well. They deserved to win and I'm glad that I managed to say so, because you really don't know what you're saying out there.

I ended my *Britain's Got Talent* journey as I'd started it. With a wiggle.

So that was that, then, I thought as I came off stage. I'd come second. The story of my life. It had been since the very first competition I'd entered, when I'd sung "Ye Banks and Braes," and the whole school had heard me over the tannoy. Well, it was better than being last, wasn't it?

It was only when I got back to my dressing room that the reality hit me. All those flowers. For nothing! All the humiliation. For nothing! I pulled off my slate-grey shimmery dress and threw it over a chair. The fabric winked at me like a tawdry glitter ball. It wasn't fair!

All the stress that had built up inside me suddenly blew.

"Are you OK?"

"Of course I'm not OK!"

My family were there trying to console me, people from Syco, Simon Cowell's record label—were trying to reassure me. They were all saying it didn't matter. But it did bloody matter. It mattered missing the chance to perform for the Queen. It mattered a hundred thousand pounds, for God's sake! All my expenses had been paid while I was in London, but I'd spent more money than my usual budget over the past weeks. I'd needed new clothes, a haircut, a mobile phone. On top of everything else, I was now going to be in debt.

Everybody was saying different things about what would happen and what should happen. My family were suggesting that I should go back home and get some rest. The people from Syco were trying to tell me that I could still have a recording contract, but I was exhausted and I needed to get myself well enough. All around me different voices were firing off. Everybody was just diving into the pool, and all the water was going out, and there I was left in the empty shell in my bathing suit.

I wanted so badly to become a professional singer, and now it was all slipping out of my grasp.

My family knew me well enough to realize that the best thing for them to do at this stage was to go and leave my disappointment to burn itself out. It was agreed that I would be taken to a different hotel. Everybody knew that there were press waiting outside the building, and I wasn't looking my best, so one of my nieces picked up one of the bouquets and tried to hide my stricken face behind it. Flowers whose purpose had been to celebrate and wish me well were now being used to hide me.

30
Priory

I regret now that I said that I'd needed to be in the Priory "for a rest." I did need a rest, but that wasn't the right place for me.

I was very upset and exhausted the day after the final of *Britain's Got Talent*. I'd had little sleep for a week, but all the adrenalin and emotion after the show still seemed to be pumping round my body, keeping me awake all night. I don't think it helped that I was in a different hotel room, surrounded by strangers. When it was suggested to me that I should go to the Priory, I went along with it because I didn't know what else to do.

I didn't know what the Priory was, but when I arrived I was immediately aware that it was some kind of mental hospital. I found that very frightening because I knew what happened in mental institutions. They locked you up. My uncle Michael had been locked away for years. All the potential he had in life had been taken away from him because by the time he came out to live with us, he was too old and too traumatized to lead a full life.

I wasn't mental. I tried to explain that to the doctors, but they didn't seem to want to know.

I wanted to phone out, but they wouldn't let me.

I wasn't allowed to see a television either, so I didn't know that my story was being followed in the news. I didn't even know if anyone knew I was there. I thought I was locked up and they were going to keep me indefinitely. It was the most terrifying thing that has ever happened to me in my entire life.

I was still trying to accept that my dream was over, but this was truly a nightmare, on a completely different level from being chased by the paparazzi or vilified in the newspapers. I felt as if I was having to fight for my survival as a person, literally to fight for my sanity.

I have never felt more alone, because I couldn't get in touch with anyone who could help me. I wished my mother was there. I knew what she would say was, "This is not right. This is not the place for Susan."

But she wasn't there.

When I was finally allowed to use the phone, I called the first telephone number in my memory, which was my sister Kathleen's house.

My niece Pamela answered the phone.

"They've put me in here and it's a mental home," I told her.

"Susan, it's the Priory," said Pamela. "All the stars go there. Have you not seen anybody famous yet?"

"It's not funny," I told her.

I think she thought, as other people do, that the

Priory is like a kind of spa for celebrities to relax in. But it's not.

When nurses came into my room, I was saying, "Get away! I don't need you!" but it was starting to dawn on me that the angrier I was, the more they thought there was something wrong with me. The best thing to do was to keep quiet.

On the third day, I left.

As the car pulled out of the Priory, with a Chinese driver wearing dark glasses in the front and me in the back with a bodyguard, the paparazzi followed, so we went into an underground garage and I changed cars. The paps followed an empty car. If I'd felt as if I was the central character in a psychological thriller, now I was in a James Bond movie.

We drove to a place on the outskirts of London which had once been a convent but had been converted into luxury houses. I was finally able to get some rest.

After a couple of days, a glamorous doctor came to take me out to a boutique for "shopping therapy." The press were there to witness my recovery. At least that proved that I was right and there was nothing wrong with me apart from exhaustion.

So there you are.

Part Four

Who I Was Born to Be

31
Ave Maria

August 2009

There were golden, late-summer roses in the front garden of St. Bennet's, a large Victorian house in the Morningside district of Edinburgh, where His Eminence Cardinal Keith Patrick O'Brien resides. In the corner of the garden facing the entrance, as if welcoming us there, stood a statue of Our Lady. The car tyres swished to a standstill on the gravel drive. As soon as I got out, I immediately sensed the tranquillity of the place. I walked along the path of flagstones that led to the statue and said a prayer, as I always have done since I was a wee girl and my mother taught me how.

The inscription over the front door of the house reads "SALVA ME BONA CRUX," meaning "Save me, good Cross."

Frank and his wife, Maureen, were there, along with Mario Marzella of the musical West Lothian family, Lorraine, Benny and Sadie. Frank and Mario already knew the Cardinal well from their work at St. Joseph's, but for the rest of us it was very exciting to be there and some of us were a wee bit nervous as we waited for the bell to be answered. As devout Catholics, an invitation to lunch with a Cardinal of the Catholic Church was an honour and a privilege none of us had ever dreamed of.

The door was opened by Norah, the Cardinal's assistant. A lovely, Irish-looking lady with red hair and a sparkling smile, she immediately put us at ease as she showed us into the reception hall where His Eminence was waiting below the statue of St. Andrew, the patron saint of Scotland. His Eminence greeted us all individually and said that it was wonderful to welcome me and my friends to his home. We then followed him along the corridor to the private oratory.

St. Bennet's was originally owned by a solicitor and was bought from him by the Catholic Church in 1878, so the corridor is fairly dark, just like any other big Victorian dwelling, with carpet underfoot and closed doors leading off. The oratory was added to the building about a hundred years ago and nothing prepared us for the beauty that was revealed when the door to it was opened. Those of us who had not been there before gasped as we walked in. It is a perfect miniature jewel of a chapel, with rose pink walls, white stucco columns and bright stained-glass windows that flood the interior with intense light. On the left of the altar is a statue of St. Joseph, and on the right is a very delicate statue of Our Lady looking young and ethereal, with her robes floating around her. It was an incredibly beautiful and uplifting place in which to celebrate the Mass of the Assumption together.

The Cardinal in his robes is a figure of immense power and authority. After Mass, he asked me if I would like to sing in the chapel, but I felt far too awed, and overcome with shyness.

A photographer had arrived to record our visit and I was allowed to sit on a chair made specially for Pope John Paul II when he visited Scotland all those years ago. I remembered so clearly bowing to him as he passed by me on the Mound in his white Popemobile. Sitting in his chair, in a chapel he had prayed in, it almost felt as if my life had come full circle.

We all went to the dining room for our lunch. I was seated opposite the Cardinal and I felt tongue-tied at first, but he soon put me at my ease because he's a very approachable man with a twinkly smile and a great sense of humour.

After the final of *Britain's Got Talent*, His Eminence had sent me a second card congratulating me on my achievement, and he'd obviously kept up to date with the reports in the press since then. As we ate, he told me that wherever he went in the world, when he said he was from Scotland people always asked, "Do you know Susan Boyle? How is Susan Boyle?"

When he'd been in Ireland recently, President Mary McAleese had told him that all the generations of her whole family had come together to watch me in the final. She'd made a meal, and it was the first time they'd had an evening together for a long time. My singing brought people together.

"Saturday-night entertainment's always done that," I said, not wanting to take the credit.

The Cardinal asked me about the journey that I'd been on over the past few months. I told him that I'd had my ups and downs, but that things seemed to be falling into place now. I was recording an album and I wasn't allowed to say anything about it, but I wanted him to know that there would be hymns included. He was pleased about that and said he hoped I'd give him a copy when it was released. I said I certainly would. I couldn't believe how easy it was to talk to him.

Afterwards, we went back to his comfortable sitting room for coffee. In our living room at home there are all sorts of religious statues and souvenirs from shrines we've visited, so I was surprised to see there was no religious imagery at all in the Cardinal's sitting room, although clearly visible through the large windows there was another stone statue of Our Lady in the leafy back garden. On the mantelpiece there were lots of photos, just like you'd get in any ordinary person's house, except that instead of being of weddings or First Communions and occasions like that, these were mementoes of significant moments in the Cardinal's life, like when he was created a cardinal by Pope John Paul II, or one taken in the Sistine Chapel when he was a member of the convocation of cardinals that elected Pope Benedict XVI.

I was relaxed enough to ask him questions about all the photographs, as well as the very large oil painting above the mantelpiece. It is a picture of four French peasant women, one with a baby in her arms, all waiting for their fishermen husbands to return from the sea. To me, it seemed a very human picture rather than the more traditional Christian art you might expect in a Cardinal's home. His Eminence told me that it had been given to his predecessor by a friend who was dying, because it was so big he didn't know anyone else who would be able to display it.

"Do you like it?" he asked me.

"I find the expressions on their faces very moving," I said.

I could tell the women were anxious, not knowing what the future held for them.

The Cardinal smiled at me. I may not be much of an art critic, but I think he knew what I meant.

Before leaving, we all returned to the beautiful little chapel to say prayers together. Now that our nerves had vanished and we were all very comfortable in the Cardinal's company, a profound sense of peace settled over our contemplation. I felt so privileged and so very blessed, I was filled with an unquenchable urge to express my gratitude. While the others remained kneeling, I rose to my feet, and standing in front of the statue of Our Lady, I sang "Ave Maria."

My voice sounded as pure and true as sunlight filling the chapel.

Afterwards, there were a few seconds of stillness as the notes remained in the air like the memory of an echo.

The Cardinal thanked me and said that it had been a beautiful and moving moment.

On the way home I was very quiet in the back of the car as I reflected on the day. Of all the amazing times I have enjoyed, this was the one where I most wished my beloved mother could have been present. I know she would have liked the Cardinal. He is such a down-to-earth kind of guy. You can have a laugh with him, and that would have delighted her.

My mother was there spiritually. I'd come to believe that very strongly over recent weeks. In moments of greatest difficulty, I could almost feel her watchful concern, as if she were trying to guide me as she always had. Because she couldn't be there, she was putting the right people in my path. Whenever I had problems, the right person seemed to come along to help me. I was sure she was the reason I had managed to come through the difficult times, and she was with me, too, on wonderful days like today.

32
Andy

After a few days' rest in June, I had been able to rehearse again and join the *Britain's Got Talent* Tour. It was great singing live without the pressure of three buzzers over your head and the atmosphere was completely different from the shows in the television studios. Some of the stadiums we played were huge, like Wembley Arena, which holds six thousand people, and everybody who'd bought tickets to see the tour was out for a good time, not to judge or to criticize, but to enjoy. The noise and excitement rising from the audience was incredible, like waves of energy that you could channel into your performance. It buoyed me up and I got a real buzz from it.

Behind the scenes, though, there was still a lot of confusion about what sort of career I was going to be able to have, and a couple of times the stress built up again so much that I was too tired to perform. I was proud that I managed to sing most nights of the tour, especially in Scotland, where we performed in Glasgow and Edinburgh, and in Northern Ireland, where my mother's family came from, where we did a show in Belfast. The response from those audiences was fantastic.

Backstage, there was a good atmosphere now

that the pressure was off and each of the talented finalists was taking their place in the spotlight. I think my favourite act was Hollie Steel. She's such a wee lassie, with a huge, grown-up voice, and I really enjoyed listening to her singing. But the rest of them were great too.

There was a very sad day halfway through the tour when we learned of the death of Michael Jackson. We were in Bournemouth that evening, in the conference centre that looks out over sea. It was lovely sunny weather, but inside the mood was dark and very flat. Michael Jackson had been the inspiration for many of the lads, and they were young enough for him to be the first person they'd felt close to who had died. They were wandering around in shock, like zombies. It was extraordinary realizing how much of the show was due to the legendary performer, from the eccentric semi-finalist Darth Jackson to the dance crews Diversity and Flawless, as well as wee Aidan the break dancer. It was a Michael Jackson song that Shaheen sang in the show, and it was rumoured that Michael Jackson had asked him to be in his upcoming tour, This Is It. Tragically, he only got to sing for Michael Jackson at his funeral.

I don't suppose any of those street-dancing boys thought that, behind the dressing-room door with "Susan Boyle" written on it, a middle-aged woman who couldn't moonwalk to save her life was weeping too. One of my favourite songs of all time had been Michael Jackson's "Ben," and I remembered so clearly singing it into my hairbrush with all the heartfelt emotion of a teenager.

That evening we dedicated the show to Michael Jackson, who had given us all so much inspiration.

The *Britain's Got Talent* Tour was very cleverly designed to allow all the finalists a chance to shine in front of their fans, and there were also one or two surprises for the audience. One hilarious moment was the appearance of Darth Jackson, followed on stage by a group of very fit-looking *Star Wars* stormtroopers—the dance crew Flawless dressed up in the white uniforms of the Empire's army. Behind them stomped a couple of shorter, bulkier stormtroopers. It took the audience only a second to realize that the two tagging on at the end were Demi and Lagi, aka Stavros Flatley. That number invariably brought the house down.

Back in London, in my temporary home, my niece Kirsty introduced me to a tall, middle-aged man with something of the look of Harrison Ford himself. To continue with the *Star Wars* theme, his character turned out to be less Han Solo and more Obi-Wan Kenobi, because he has the patience of a Jedi Master! The man's name was Andy Stephens.

After a lot of discussion, I had decided that my career would be best managed by a team that included Ossie Kilkenny, a management supremo with a great deal of experience, and Kirsty, who is a media lawyer. Between them they could help me navigate through the maze of business relationships and contracts that go on in the background of a music career. It's a complex world and I was very relieved to have people I could trust involved so that I could get on with the singing. A third member of the team, a manager who would look after me on a day-to-day basis, was probably the most important piece of the jigsaw, and that's where Andy Stephens came in. Ossie asked him if he would like to meet me to see if we had the right chemistry.

At the time, I'd only recently been through the very traumatic experience of the Priory and I was in no mood to trust anyone. When Kirsty introduced Andy to me, I was so shy I couldn't look him in the eye.

"I'm not going to hurt you," he said. "I just want to have a conversation with you."

I found him very pleasant and very nice.

A few days later, he took us out to dinner. He talked about his own management experience and how he saw my career progressing, and everything he said seemed to make sense. He didn't want me to rush about doing live concerts all over the place to capitalize on my immediate fame; he wanted to concentrate on getting an album made and then take everything gradually from there, building up in increments to allow me to cope with each different stage. Baby steps, in other words. I found this approach very reassuring.

In an attempt to give me some rest away from the constant intrusion of the press, I had been living in the secluded convent house in North London with a personal assistant, Julia, who had been appointed by the record company. She was staying with me, and I also had a security guy called Ciaran. It was a very luxurious new conversion, but there were no home comforts or things I was familiar with, so it felt a bit like living in a show home. Whenever I went out for a walk in the grounds, I was accompanied. Sometimes you just want to be on your own! I think that the record company must have felt some responsibility to protect me from the press and that's the way they decided to do it, but for someone down to earth like me it was impossible to understand why I couldn't have the same life as before. I missed being with people who knew me in Blackburn. At times, it felt more like being in prison than in a luxury house.

When I met Andy, I instinctively felt that he would be able to help me find a bit of balance, that he would be at my side and, more importantly, on my side. I'm very glad to say that those instincts were to prove correct.

33
Album

If you'd told me when I auditioned in January that six months later I would be recording an album for Simon Cowell's record label, Syco, I would have laughed my head off. Nothing that had happened in the meantime had truly convinced me that the prospect was anything more than another dream. The foundations on which success might be built seemed constantly to be shifting and I never felt as if I was standing on firm ground. Then when Yvie Burnett got back in touch and said that she'd been asked to help me learn the songs for an album, I allowed myself to start believing that it might really be going to happen.

Yvie invited me to come and stay at her house for the time that we were working together. Over breakfast each morning we would decide what songs we were doing that day. We learned one in the morning from ten until twelve, took a wee break for lunch, then went straight back to work on another song from one until five. In the evening we might go over the first song again. Each song required a different placement of the voice, and it was exciting to learn new techniques. I felt as if I was constantly stretching myself. It was difficult stuff, but I just seemed to get it. When you're learning the songs, you're not just learning to sing the notes, but thinking about the underlying emotions and how to feel them in the song. This is what singers called the dynamics. It's not a matter of singing loudly because you can, it's a matter of SINGING LOUDLY BECAUSE YOU'RE PASSIONATE at this point, or singing softly because you're sad.

We kept to a strict timetable, but there was still plenty of time to relax and chat over our meals together. Yvie has a nice husband and two great teenage children who made it very easy for me to fit into the family. In the evenings, Yvie always went to visit her mother, Molly, and I asked if I could go with her. I'd spoken to Molly on the phone once or twice during my first lessons with Yvie in London. I liked her sense of humour. She had been a teacher in the village primary school in Methlick, Aberdeenshire, where Yvie grew up. As soon as I met her, I could tell that the children who had been educated by her had been very fortunate. Molly was a vibrant character with such a beaming smile that when you walked into the room you felt as if she were coming over to greet you, even though she couldn't get out of bed. Although she was paralysed due to an illness, Molly's mind was not affected and she retained her intellect and her sense of humour. When we met, she showed me a poem she liked. I think it illustrates perfectly the special person she was. The title is "I'm Fine Thank You."

There is nothing the matter with me,
I'm as healthy as I can be.
I have arthritis in both my knees
And when I talk, I talk with a wheeze,
My pulse is weak and my blood is thin,
But I'm awfully well for the shape I'm in.

Sleep is denied me night after night
But every morning I find I'm all right,
My memory is failing, my head's in a spin
But I'm awfully well for the shape I'm in.

How do I know my youth is all spent?
Well my "get up and go" has got up and went.
But I really don't mind when I think with a grin,
Of all the grand places my "get up" has bin.

"Old age is golden," I've heard it said,
But sometimes I wonder as I get into bed,
With my ears in the drawer, my teeth in a cup
My eyes on the table until I wake up.
'Ere sleep overtakes me, I say to myself,
"Is there anything else I could lay on the shelf?"

When I was young, my slippers were red,
I could kick my heels over my head.
When I was older, my slippers were blue,
But still I could dance the whole night through.
Now I am old, my slippers are black,
I walk to the store and puff my way back.

I get up each day and dust off my wits,
And pick up the paper and read the "obits."
If my name is still missing, I know I'm not dead,
So I have a good breakfast,—and face what's
    ahead.

An enormous amount of care and thought had gone into choosing what I would sing on my album. Nick Raymonde, who is my A and R guy at Syco, had been through hundreds of possibilities to come up with a very different repertoire from the songs from musicals that I was used to singing, and that, perhaps, people expected from me. Syco's intention was to surprise the world with a unique and interesting combination, and I was very happy with the selection. Some songs were personal favourites of mine, others I liked but might not have thought of singing myself, and a couple were completely new to me, but quickly became favourites.

I'd heard the name Steve Mac many times over recent months. Everybody who spoke about him was unanimous in their opinion: he was a great guy and he would be a fantastic producer for me to work with. So, you can imagine that I was fairly nervous when I first went to the studio to meet him.

The studio itself was situated down a mews street in southwest London. It's a functional-looking building that could easily be the back of any old office in any old town, but when you go inside it's minimalist, modern and full of state-of-the-art equipment.

For someone who has such a great reputation, and has worked with top artists and bands like Leona Lewis and Westlife, Steve Mac was much younger than I was expecting. He has very intense, dark eyes, but a friendly, open smile and the confidence of someone who knows what he's doing. He was a little apprehensive himself because he'd been warned that I could be a wee bit moody, but we clicked straight away.

The studio is a normal-size room with a fairly low ceiling. There are no windows, except the one into Steve's room, where he sits with an engineer who organizes the backing track and records the takes. The studio is air conditioned, so it always feels cool, and there's the facility to change the lighting to suit the mood of the song.

It was all new to me, so I was quite nervous as the door clicked shut behind me and I was all by myself in this dimly lit room standing in front of the mic. I put on the headphones. Steve asked me if I was ready. I gave him the thumbs-up, feeling a wee bit more tentative than I was letting on.

The first track we laid down was "Cry Me a River." We decided to try that one first because it was the only song that was going to be on the album that I had recorded before, so I'd probably feel more comfortable with it.

The plangent opening strings transported me immediately into the mood of the song. I closed my eyes.

Now, you say you love me . . .

A lot of water had flowed under the bridge since I first recorded at Heartbeat Studio on the outskirts of Edinburgh, but singing in these sophisticated surroundings in the middle of London, I could summon the same emotions: the sadness of love denied, the hollow triumph of revenge.

The notes came as naturally as breathing. Alone with just the music, I felt a rush of satisfaction, as if I had finally found what I'd been looking for all my life.

The studio became my sanctuary. In order to be nearer, I moved out of the convent and into a very nice flat in West London. Each morning, a car would pick me up and take me to the studio and we would work from about eleven until four o'clock in the afternoon. I still longed to go for walks on my own, especially since the new flat I was in was situated near the Royal Botanic Gardens at Kew. I'd like to have seen the colourful flower borders and the exotic tropical plants in the Palm House, but now the recording studio was my escape from the rest of the world.

For me, the studio is like being inside a precious rainbow bubble floating above all the swirling clutter and worry of life. In the studio, it's just me and the music, and I love that pure connection with the song. As soon as I put on the cans, I feel that I have come home to a place where I know I am safe. I become a calm person, a person who knows her value, a person who has been given the great privilege of doing what she does best without any distractions. My only conversation is with the song.

Next, we recorded "I Dreamed a Dream." The song had come to symbolize my dream of success, but when I had sung it at my audition I'd been singing about longing to go back to the security of the life I'd enjoyed before losing my mother. Now I was on a new path, and one that I had no doubt that she wanted me to follow, so the song had taken on a subtly different meaning for me.

Steve is a clever guy and knows exactly how to get what he wants from me. Sometimes he'll ask to hear the songs sung in slightly different ways so that he has a range of options when he is mixing the album. I found it really interesting and exciting to stretch to that kind of challenge. I've always enjoyed acting, so when Steve says something like "Have a go at singing it as if you were ten years younger" I relish the opportunity to get into character. I was open to trying anything and Steve found that refreshing. He is a natural enabler—positive and encouraging when you're doing well, but perfectly straightforward when you muck up—and that clarity and honesty meant I trusted him right from the start. When he says, "That's exactly what I wanted," I know he's telling the truth, and it gives me a fillip to have pleased him. In turn, I think my growing confidence feeds back to him, creating a special alchemy from our individual talents. It's a great professional chemistry and respect that we have developed. Steve works at a fast pace. It's hard work, but I found I could keep up, and I found the recording process uplifting and exhilarating.

It's a funny feeling singing a hymn with earphones on in a studio instead of openly in church as a member of the congregation, but wherever I am singing I feel closer to God, because he gave me this gift in the first place. I was keen to include the hymn "How Great Thou Art" because it is the favourite of my friend and teacher Frank Quinn, who has been such a support to me. I think the words of praise sound particularly pure, the message simple and true.

"Amazing Grace" is another very powerful hymn for me because it expresses so beautifully how God is always there, especially when I am scared.

I once was lost but now am found,
Was blind, but now I see.

It is a hymn that was to take on a special meaning for me later on in my journey.

"Who I Was Born to Be" is a song that was written specially for me and the lyrics encapsulate so much about my life. This seems to be the favourite song of many of my fans, and whenever I sing it, it feels almost like a rallying cry.

The anger in my voice during the Madonna song "You'll See" is a strong and productive anger, rather than a frustrated anger that brings bitterness and tears. When I recorded this track, I felt I was singing not only to those bullies at school, but also, to a certain extent, to the media for all the pressure I'd been subjected to. I'm not scared of the media. It's part of the job, part of the territory, and I recognize that artists need the press. But I am only human. I'd been built up, then smashed down, but I wasn't going to buckle. When I was singing "You'll See," I felt I was rebuilding myself, giving myself the push I needed to carry on.

"Up to the Mountain" is a Kelly Clarkson number. This is a song that was chosen for me and I really enjoyed singing it, and "Daydream Believer" brought back great memories of watching the Monkees on television when I was little. The version on the album is a slow version, so you can really hear the words—I'd never really noticed them before, but now they had meaning for me. Soon, I hoped, I'd be able to go back to

Blackburn. A homecoming queen? We'd have to see about that!

One day when I came into the studio Steve said he had a song he'd like to play to me. It's called "Proud," and Steve had co-written it. I found it very moving because it's about a conflict between a father and a son.

We've all had conflict with our parents at some stage, and I was no exception. I had a lot of difficulties when I was growing up, and even though I was loved, I always slightly felt as if I was in the way. My parents hadn't intended to have another child at their time of life. I just came along, and then I wasn't an easy child to cope with.

As I grew up, I'd continued to rely on my parents as well as trying to please them. I hadn't given myself much room to be my own person. At the same time, I'd known that if I didn't devote myself to my mum and dad, that would be wrong and I would feel guilty afterwards. So there was a sort of conflict within myself.

The other side of it was that I had always sought my mum and dad's approval for everything, and now that I didn't have their guidance, life could be very scary.

There's a line in the song that's about being your own boss, your own individual person. That was something I had been struggling with since my mother died.

For me, the song is also about regret. I'd tried my best, but I didn't honestly feel I'd given my parents anything to be proud of while they were alive. My mother always had faith in my abilities, but she must have been anxious about what I would do after she died. If she could have known what was going to happen, she wouldn't have had all that worry. She would have been so amazed and so proud of me.

The first few times I tried to sing "Proud," I couldn't do it for crying.

The biggest surprise of the album was probably "Wild Horses," and that was one of the last songs we recorded. This particular version was picked for me by Simon Cowell and I thought it was a great choice. I knew the song from my youth because my brothers were great Rolling Stones fans, and there was something about the lyrics of the first verse that reminded me of the council estate where I lived and conjured poignant memories of my early upbringing.

When I'm singing the song, I always feel I'm singing from my mother's point of view, as if she's talking to me and I'm the one who's listening, so it is quite an emotional experience.

For the singer I used to be, the inclination would have been to give the first big crescendo a lot of power, but I learned that it is so much more effective if you sing it gently. For that you need a great deal of control, so it's technically difficult to achieve, but once you have the control, you can sing quietly, then go loud and come back to quiet again. I think when people first heard me singing "Wild Horses," they started to take me more seriously as a singer. The record company in the States were certainly very excited about it, and "Wild Horses" was the song that was chosen for me to sing on my first public performance as a singer in my own right.

34
The Home of the Brave

For most people, a first-class flight and the prospect of five days in a luxury five-star hotel in Los Angeles, with a trip to Disneyland included, would be a once-in-a-lifetime holiday they'd look forward to all of their lives. But holidays are for relaxation, and I'd already had mine in the wee Scottish resort of Blackburn, West Lothian.

Steve Mac and I worked so well together that the album was made in six weeks, with just a few additional sessions to come later, so I'd been able to have some time off, happily swapping the luxury London flat for my pebble-dash council house, my entourage of assistants and bodyguards for neighbours, family and friends. I'd been able to go to Mass in Our Lady of Lourdes and visit the Whitburn Legion of Mary. I'd dined out on my favourite holiday supper of fish and chips.

In Blackburn, with familiar people and things around me, I knew who I was and what I was doing. During this whole process, I've never for one minute wished I could return to how things were before, but I've never seen why I should become a different person in order to pursue the path that I'm on. The way I see it is that I am the same person, but I am growing, exploring a potential that has always been there but that I wasn't able to fulfil at an earlier stage in my life. I'm fully aware that I am very lucky to have this opportunity, and I'm very grateful for all the gifts and luxuries that seem to accompany fame, but I just don't care very much about material things. As long as I have clothes I can wear, food to eat and I can sing, I'm quite happy. My parents worked hard so that us kids didn't want for anything, but they also taught us that the greatest gifts are not in this world.

"Can we open the window?" I asked, as the plane bound for Los Angeles began to taxi towards the runway.

Ciaran, my bodyguard, looked at me in alarm, but when he saw my face he realized I was joking. People never know quite what to expect with me.

Laughing was the only way I could disguise the sheer and utter panic that was throbbing through my whole body. We were in first class on a British Airways flight. The space and service in the upstairs lounge takes away some of the strain of flying, but nothing could alter the fact that we were about to spend nine hours in the air, the longest I'd ever flown, and I was terrified.

The purpose of the trip was my first appearance as a professional singer in my own right, and all sorts of questions were looming that could not be answered until the moment I stood up and sang in front of the audience on the biggest television programme in America, the final of *America's Got Talent*. The main question was, could I do it?

There were two days before that, I kept telling myself, so there wasn't any point in panicking yet. I might as well enjoy myself until then. When that tactic didn't work, I tried to think about all the times that I'd got up in front of an audience and managed to deliver a song against the odds. Thoughts like that should help, but they don't, because nerves aren't rational. You can be as logical as you like, but it doesn't stop your heart racing and your brain overloading. The logic should be that the more performances you give, the less nervous you become, but it doesn't seem to work like that. I know that I'm not unique in this because people keep telling me that lots of performers with years of experience still get paralysed by stage fright. It doesn't really help when everyone around you is saying it's going to be fine. They're not the ones who have to get up there! Anyway, on this occasion I knew that, whatever they said, they were really thinking that it was a very big deal indeed.

One of the great pleasures of my new life is the fact that I seem to make people happy. I haven't worked out quite why this is, but it's a very nice and surprising feeling, so I've decided that it's probably best not to over-analyse, but just enjoy. When we disembarked at Los Angeles airport, there must have been two thousand fans waiting to greet me. When I was a kid, I used to watch newsreel of the Beatles arriving at airports. There were crowds of fans, screaming and stretching out their hands to try to touch them, and I can remember wondering at the time, how did all those people know the Beatles were arriving then? How come their parents allowed them to go to the airport? My fans are generally a wee bit older than those teenage girls, but I still didn't understand how they knew when I was arriving, or how they'd managed to take time off work to come to see me. It took us ages to get to the car, and then we had a police escort to the hotel. I felt more like a visiting head of state than a singer. I do appreciate all the effort people made to welcome me, but it was also rather bewildering.

I was staying at the Hotel Bel-Air, one of the most iconic hotels in the world. I was there just before it closed for a major refurbishment, but I cannot really imagine how they're going to make it any better because it was absolutely beautiful, with all the little Spanish-style houses, painted pink with red tiles on the roof, amid luscious gardens and pools. It was a blisteringly hot, sunny day and the cool blue oval pool looked very inviting, even to someone who has never learned to swim. As I walked past the sun-loungers to my suite, it was almost like having déjà vu, because I'd seen the setting so many times in films. I kept expecting one of the slim, tanned women on the sun-loungers to take off her sunglasses and reveal herself as the young Elizabeth Taylor, or for Cary Grant to put down his newspaper and wink at me. My name would now join a list of guests that included Grace Kelly and Marilyn Monroe. I hope it doesn't sound ungrateful when I say that that knowledge didn't make it any easier to relax in my plushly furnished living room.

Disneyland is a place I'd always wanted to visit and it was as magical as I'd expected it to be, but really to enjoy a place like that you need to be with family or friends you know well so you can let yourself go back to childhood glee and excitement. It's just not the same flying up in the air on a pastel elephant accompanied by professional colleagues and a bodyguard. You're aware that every yelp and silly face you make is being photographed, so even though the visit was arranged to take my mind off things, I couldn't really relax. Inevitably that led to some clever headlines back home about Glumbo on Dumbo!

The dress I was wearing for *America's Got Talent* was designed by Suzanne Neville. I'd been to the final fitting in London a couple of days before our trip to Los Angeles. It was a plain, full-length black satin evening gown with just a few crystals to catch the light, but it was cut beautifully to give me the best possible shape. When I travel, the dress I'm wearing has to travel with me. It doesn't quite get its own seat, but we don't put it in cargo just in case it doesn't come out at the other end. On this occasion, my manager Andy carried it on board.

"That'll look smashing on you!" I joked as we were getting on to the plane.

Andy's OK. It would take a lot more than that to get him embarrassed. That first trip to the States was where I really got to know him, because when you're travelling you spend so much time together. On a long flight you see each other bored, you see each other tired, you hear each other snoring. There's nowhere to hide. Andy's a great one for banter, and we can amuse ourselves for hours playing "Name That Tune," or "Name the Artist." All those years of listening to the radio have given me a practically encyclopaedic knowledge of pop from the sixties, seventies and eighties, but Andy gives me a run for my money because he's been in the music business since the sixties himself.

Andy's presence is very reassuring. He's managed acts as famous as George Michael and Geri Halliwell, so he's seen it all before and there's nobody he doesn't know. When we arrived at the studios for *America's Got Talent*, I knew that at least one of us knew what he was doing.

You'd think putting on that dress would be the easy bit. Was it heck! With a tight-fitting garment like that, it's like trying to get a cork back into a champagne bottle, so you have to wear your

Spanx underneath to smooth you out. I never knew my body had so much flesh. I'm not kidding. Those Spanx are murder to get on. You need two people pulling them up, so that's professional distance gone for a start, then you have to try to do the dress up, and that required a foot on my backside to hold it all together in order to get the zip up. As far as adopting a sophisticated persona was concerned, it felt more like I was in a pantomime of Cinderella. I didn't know whether I'd be able to breathe, let alone sing, and when I tried to walk I felt like a penguin with constipation. That's what it takes to look elegant. At least it was a distraction!

The great thing about making my debut on *America's Got Talent* was that, although I was in a foreign country, I was surrounded by people I knew. Yvie is the voice coach on the show, so she was there already, and we were able to do a warm-up together before the rehearsals. On the day, with the audience in, there was also Piers Morgan, who is one of the three judges on the programme.

I was extremely nervous about going on stage. Piers and Sharon Osbourne came backstage to see me and were very encouraging. Everyone was reassuring me that it wouldn't matter if I mucked up because it was only a pre-record. I would be singing in front of an audience of hundreds, but if I made a mistake then it wouldn't go out to an audience of millions. To me, that sounded like it was going to be a disaster, if not a catastrophe. It took me quite a while to pluck up the courage to go on, but eventually I was brave enough to step up. As soon as the music starts, it's like a switch with me. I start singing, and all the other stuff goes away.

We did two takes, then someone took a DVD up to Simon Cowell's house to see which one he wanted to have shown. It was as simple as that! Suddenly, all the worry had gone because I'd done it! I'd sung a song nobody had heard me sing before. Now the largest television audience of the year in America would see me singing "Wild Horses" for the first time. Only then did it dawn on me what a debut this was. It felt pretty good. In fact, it felt so good I wanted to do it again!

The second time I went to the States I was no less nervous, but things were a lot easier, because in the meantime I'd been lucky enough to persuade my niece Joanne to come and work as my personal assistant. Joanne lives in Bathgate, just down the road from Blackburn, and she'd been very supportive to me after my mother died as well as during the time when I was holed up in Yule Terrace surrounded by the press. Joanne's an efficient, no-nonsense sort of person, with a great sense of humour like her mother, Bridie. Because I've known her since she was born, there's no barrier when it comes to personal moments like

357

getting my dress on, and because she's family I trust her implicitly and don't have to watch what I say all the time. Joanne's very stylish herself, so she helps me pick out suitable casual clothes to wear when I'm not on stage. There's only one problem: I have asked her to stop calling me Auntie Susan, because I don't think it sounds very professional.

On the second trip to Los Angeles, we were staying in the Peninsula hotel. My day of "relaxation" on this occasion was a tour of Universal Studios, which I really enjoyed because Joanne and Andy came along too. We toured round the sets of several films I had seen, such as *War of the Worlds* and *The Da Vinci Code*, as well as *Jaws*. That was a laugh, because as we passed the pool where some of the action shots were staged, this huge shark suddenly reared up out of the water, soaking us all. I screamed and jumped so high I almost landed in Andy's lap!

When we arrived at the studios for *Dancing with the Stars*, there was another slightly surreal experience as the lift doors opened and standing there was the head judge, Len Goodman, whom I'd seen so many times on *Strictly Come Dancing*, the British version of the show.

"Oh hello!" I greeted him as if he were an old friend.

It's funny when you see famous people, because sometimes you feel you know them so well you forget you've never actually met them. It turned out that Len was a fan of mine too and liked my singing.

On the programme I sang "I Dreamed a Dream," which was slightly less stressful than singing "Wild Horses" because it's a song I've sung quite a lot in public now. The only complication was when this dancing couple appeared writhing in front of me, doing a very dangerous-looking routine involving some impossible lifts. I knew that if I looked at them I'd be tempted to say, "Don't drop her, for God's sake!" It took an extra bit of concentration to focus on my own performance.

To be honest, the first part of that trip is a bit of a blur now, because of what happened next.

It wasn't a total surprise, because I was told in advance that he would be paying me a visit, but I couldn't believe it until I opened the door of my suite and saw Donny Osmond standing there with a big bunch of flowers for me. Actually, I still didn't believe it then. Oh my God! Donny Osmond was giving me a kiss on the cheek! I touched my face to check that it was real.

Thirty-five years after I first fell for him, Donny is just as handsome, with those big smashing eyes and that sparkling smile, and he has a really good sense of humour to go with it. He needed it, I can tell you, because I was so flustered and excited I wasn't making any sense at all at the beginning. At first, I could do nothing but giggle. I was actually trying discreetly to pinch myself to see if I was awake.

Donny was everything I wanted him to be. Very good looking, very charming, but a normal kind of guy. When I'd calmed down, we were able to talk a little about how you deal with fame. For both of us it's very important to have close contact with our families, and he understood my need to feel grounded, which is why I am at home in Scotland. He could relate to that.

Some of our encounter was being filmed for a television special about me that was going to be shown at Christmas. People have asked me what the heck Donny and I were laughing at so much, so I'll tell you.

We sat down together on the sofa and one of the crew gave me a mic to position on my chest. My hand was shaking so much, it got stuck in the zip.

"Would you like a hand with that?" Donny asked, with a twinkle in his beautiful eyes.

"You're not going down my blouse!" I responded, quick as a flash.

All those nights I'd stared at the picture of Donny Osmond on my wall at home! I'd never have believed that I'd one day be sitting on a sofa joking with him.

We just doubled up.

When I look back over this amazing year I've had, meeting Donny Osmond has to be the personal high point for me and it's a memory that I will treasure for ever.

My next trip to America was for yet another "most important performance" of my life. As soon as you've accomplished one thing, there's always another marker to hit. I think maybe that's why I can never quite trust the success I've had. Maybe one day there'll come a time when I'll know what I'm doing and it will hold no fear for me, but that hasn't happened yet because the pressure's ratcheted up with each challenge. It doesn't get much bigger than launching your debut album live on coast-to-coast American television. Does it?

November had already been a very hectic month. I'd been to Los Angeles, met Donny Osmond, had only two days back in Scotland to wallow in the afterglow of that experience, before travelling to London again and then on Eurostar to Paris to sing on a television programme there. On that occasion, I managed to put my heel through my dress as I stepped out on stage, and heard a worrying rip, but I kept on going, because that's what you do. Back in London, I'd had dress fittings, and voice coaching with Yvie, who was back in London herself because the *The X Factor* was on television. I then recorded a performance of "Wild Horses" for the *The X Factor*, before flying the next day to New York. The following morning I was due to perform live on the *Today* show, singing three songs in the open air of Rockefeller Plaza.

Usually, in the build-up to a performance, I might get that funny butterfly feeling in my stomach a couple of weeks before and say to myself, "Come on, now, Susan! It's not for a while yet." And as long as I've got something else to think about, then I can keep the wobbles at bay. But the nearer the event, the worse it gets, and even though I try to kid myself and the people around me that I'm fine by making jokes and laughing a lot, the nerves are building up inside me like a pressure cooker. The weird thing is that as the time runs down to the performance, it doesn't feel like nerves any more. A kind of dread overwhelms my whole personality, as if all the insecurities I've ever had in my life and all the unsolved problems that I've still got to deal with are swallowing me up. I don't know why this happens, but I'm hoping that it's something I can learn to control, because it's not a nice feeling for me or for anyone around me.

In New York, I'd barely had a chance to feel the usual build-up, because I'd been so busy and I was already tired before I started, so it all seemed to come, whoosh, like a mud slide engulfing me. I didn't sleep a wink in the hotel the night before. All night, the wall of fear towered mountainously above me and by the morning I had convinced myself that I would never climb it. Unable to face the world, I decided to hide. When Joanne came to give me my wake-up call at five o'clock, the door was locked and I wouldn't let her in. Alarmed, Joanne called Andy, but even his calm, reassuring voice through the door wouldn't make me open it. Andy is a resourceful chap, so he managed to get a pass key from one of the chambermaids. He found me still in the shirt and jeans I had been wearing when he said goodnight the evening before, my face all red from crying.

Andy is very gentle and calm, but time was ticking on, so he had to set out the choice for me. At 8:30 I was due to go live across America. It was now approaching seven.

"No one is putting a gun to your head, Susan. You can do whatever you want. But all your life you've waited for this moment, and it's up to you. We can walk. We can go back to the airport now and fly straight home and forget all about this, or we can go out there and show them what you're made of."

The real decider was when he added, "Just so you know, there's lots of ladies who have flown from all over the States to be there and support you today. They've been there since half past four in the morning, and what a shame to let them down as well . . ."

I didn't want to let all those ladies down, nor Andy, nor any of the people around me who had put in a lot of effort to try to help me. This was the launch of my album and they were depending on me. If I didn't do my bit, it would all fall apart.

That's when I thought of another voice—my mother's. She would have put it a different way.

"Now look, Susan, stop giving these guys a hard time. So come on, pull yourself together, or I'll skelp your arse!"

I went out into that ice-cold New York morning shivering with fear. It felt very strange to be outside in the grey light of early morning when I was used to studios and artificial lights. Surrounded by Manhattan skyscrapers, standing in Rockefeller Plaza feels like being at the bottom of a well, almost too scary to look up. It's a setting I'd seen often in the movies, but I'd never imagined I'd ever be there myself. The air was so chilly that my breath puffed out frosty clouds. In front of me were hundreds of people cheering and waving red scarves. Never in my life had I felt so exposed. It was all I could do to stop myself rushing off stage to hide again. But when the musical director pressed play, I magically switched from a terrified wee lassie to Susan Boyle, performer. People who have seen the way I am backstage say that it is astonishing to witness the transformation. Suddenly, the love coming from that crowd warmed me right through to my bones. I was doing what I was born to do.

Afterwards, a group of my fans presented me with a quilt they had made specially for me.

Bordered with fifty-two mostly red squares, all embroidered with moving and supportive messages, there are forty-nine original appliquéd designs sewn on to squares of blue, green, white and red fabric, each one decorated with a thoughtful message from individual quilters all over the world. Each image is different, from an angel to a penguin. There are too many to describe here, but every one is unique and represents something significant about my life. On the central square is a simple message embroidered on a white background: "Susan, We love you."

I'd never had anything created for me before, let alone a beautiful object like this, which really is a work of art. So much imagination and effort had gone into that quilt, so much kindness and care, it was like a symbol of the faith people had in me. I knew I didn't deserve anything so marvellous, and it was all I could do to keep control of my emotions, but when the quilters presented me with a wee miniature quilt for Pebbles too, my overwhelming gratitude swelled up inside me and flooded out in unstoppable tears. This time, they were tears of joy.

35
Europe

One of the things I had no knowledge of before becoming a professional singer was the sheer number of people who have to be involved to create one moment on stage or on television. As part of the promotion for the album, I have been asked to appear on shows all over Europe. I have travelled to France, Germany, Italy, Denmark, Spain and Holland. Each time, a phenomenal amount of organization goes into making the two minutes I'm on stage happen.

Andy and Joanne always travel with me. There are also usually at least a couple of people from Sony and Syco, like Melissa and Alex, who have one eye on what's going on and the other firmly glued to their BlackBerry. Sometimes I have a bodyguard, and there are always several technical people, like Jonathan, the sound guy, who gets to the venue before me and sets up the musical side correctly. Sometimes there's a producer as well, and that's just the personnel on the record company side. In addition, there are all the staff from the television studio to meet and greet and fuss around me. Sometimes the head of Sony in the country we're visiting will put in an appearance. It can get a wee bit overwhelming, and generally I like to be in the dressing room with just Joanne and Michelle, my hair and make-up lady.

I first met Michelle when she came up to Scotland when we were filming the television special at a hotel on Loch Lomond. She'd had quite a journey to get there. Michelle always travels with a suitcase full of make-up and hairdressing equipment. On the Heathrow Express, she had been texting and hadn't noticed when an old lady mistook her case for her own and got off at Terminal 3 with it. So when Michelle came to get off at Terminal 5, there was only a case with a Thai airlines sticker on it. Trying to think logically, she rushed back to Terminal 3, to the Thai Airlines desk, but they couldn't help her, except to suggest she report the incident to the police, which she did, but now time was running out for her flight. It was the first time she'd worked with me and she desperately didn't want to turn up late, so Michelle took the decision to go back to Terminal 5 without the case and buy as many of the things she needed in duty-free. But just as she arrived there, her phone rang and it was the police saying they'd got her bag at Terminal 3, so she decided to race back again. She only just caught her flight.

I only heard this story much later, after Michelle had accompanied me on several trips, and I'd never have guessed what she'd just been through when I first met her, because then, and ever since, she has always appeared fresh as a daisy and totally unflappable. Michelle says it's amazing what you can do with a bit of make-up!

You need nice people around you, because there is so much waiting around in dressing rooms that you'd start climbing the walls if you didn't have friends to keep you calm. I find the process of having my hair washed and styled and my make-up put on very relaxing. We go for as natural a look as possible, a kind of polished version of me. The only bit I can't get used to is the acrylic nails. Michelle and I call them Britain's Got Talons. I'm always nervously trying to pick them off even before I get to the stage.

Half an hour before my call, we start to get me into the dress I'm wearing, but first of all it's squeezing into my wee Spanx with Joanne at the front and Michelle at the back struggling to pull them up and all three of us trying not to topple over laughing. Then it's into one of three dresses. They're all by Suzanne Neville. There's a beautiful burgundy silk one with tiers all the way down, a midnight-blue one that is diamante from top to bottom, and the black satin one with diamante that I wore for *America's Got Talent*. We have to remember to put on my jewellery, and it's round about this time that I have my warm-up with Yvie.

When I'm travelling round Europe, it would be impossible for Yvie to accompany me everywhere, but we do always manage to get a warm-up by telephone. From my end in the dressing room, that's quite straightforward. We do the Vvvvvvvs, and all the other breathing exercises, with her singing them and me singing them back. I'm often trying to put my shoes on at the same time, or Joanne's trying to fasten a necklace for me, but at least I'm in one place. Down the line for Yvie, it's not quite so simple. Because Europe is an hour ahead, very often when I'm about to go on stage, Yvie's on her way home from work. She'll frequently find herself at the station trying to hide behind a coffee kiosk, with all the train announcements going on in the background. Sometimes she is actually on the train in between the carriages, singing the exercises to me, and when she goes to sit down after we've finished, all the other commuters look at her a wee bit strangely. Yvie has warmed me up in shop doorways, on garage forecourts, through a speaker phone in her car, and at the nursing home when she's been visiting Molly. A lot of the ladies there really enjoyed it!

One of the unexpected pleasures about travelling and performing is all the people you bump into. Being famous yourself is like a passport to speaking to people you'd never have dared talk to before, like Anne Robinson, whom I met in the first-class lounge at Heathrow airport. In real life she's a very nice person, not at all strict like she is on *The Weakest Link*. La Toya Jackson was appearing on the same show as me during one of my trips to Germany. Then when I was in Amsterdam in March, there was a knock on my dressing-room door and who should poke his familiar tattooed torso round the door but Demi, the father in Stavros Flatley. We had a great old chat about what we'd been doing since the tour. He and his son Lagi had been all over the world and written a book themselves.

One of the drawbacks of celebrity is that I don't really get a chance to appreciate all the wonderful places I'm visiting. The best way to see a city is by wandering around on your own, taking in all the sights, sounds and smells, and watching the little everyday dramas unfolding in shops, cafés and parks. The trouble with my face being so recognizable now is that I *am* the drama. I'm no longer somebody on the outside looking in; I'm the centre of attention. Sometimes I wish that I had an invisibility cloak like Harry Potter so I could wander around unnoticed again.

Often, if I have a few hours' waiting before a performance, the thing I most want to do is go for a walk to relieve some of the tension building up in my body, but wherever I go my face is recognized and I can't make much progress, because I'm constantly being stopped for photographs. The only alternative is to sit in a hotel room looking out of the window. I'm always lucky enough to stay in gorgeous hotels, with fantastic views, but sometimes it can feel as if I'm vacuum-packed in a sterile environment.

There was one wonderful exception to this, arranged by my friend Frank on one of my trips to Paris. A car drove me and Andy to the rue du Bac, where the headquarters of the Daughters of Charity of St. Vincent de Paul are situated. Although there were paparazzi following the car and all the motordrives were going off as I stepped out on the street, they weren't allowed into the convent. Sister Loreto, a lovely Irish nun, took us inside, shielding me from the attention, and for a moment, with all the paparazzi poking their cameras through the iron gates, I was reminded of the family in *The Sound of Music* finding shelter from the chase.

The convent is built of the pale gold stone typical of the elegant older buildings of Paris and it is set round a peaceful courtyard. Sister Loreto explained the history of the order, which was founded in 1633 for the purpose of serving the needs of the poor and sick, by St. Vincent de Paul, a French priest, and St. Louise de Marillac, who was a widow. I had always been aware of the work that the St. Vincent de Paul Society did with people of disability in Scotland. As I mentioned earlier, St. Joseph's residential home in Rosewell was the place that Pope John Paul II visited on his pastoral trip to our country in 1982 and it was there that Frank Quinn met him. Now the society's work is carried on mainly in the community, but the convent in rue du Bac is the mother house of the organization. The sisters, who wear a blueish-grey habit, live in a community there in order to develop the spiritual life.

Sister Loreto and I went into the chapel and prayed together. Kneeling in the cool silence, I was able to reconnect with everything that is really important and to find serenity in the heart of a bustling city.

36
Television Special

For someone who has watched television all her life, and was, in a sense, created by television, the idea that there was going to be a Christmas television special devoted to my story was yet another unbelievable step on my weird and wonderful journey. I was thrilled when they told me that Piers Morgan was going to present the studio part of the programme, because I've always liked Piers, but more than that, I feel that he's always given me all the support he can. When times have been tough, Piers has gone out there and stuck up for me, and he was there at the very start, so I couldn't think of a better person to host the show.

The great thing about Piers is that you can have a laugh with him, and there were some honeys of out-takes on that programme, like the moment when a member of the audience shouted out, "Can you do the wiggle?"

I turned to Piers and said, "Can you do the wiggle?"

Well, Piers may be a lot of things, but he did a pretty feeble wiggle, I have to tell you. So I decided to show him how!

Later on, when they had the smoke machine

going for one of my songs, there were clouds of the stuff wafting around the stage. I looked at Piers, and asked, "My God, what was that?"

"What?" he said.

"Did you fart?"

"No!" he said.

"Well, someone did—look at the mess it's made!"

Note to self: Try to resist the jokes and be more of a lady, Susan!

The audience seemed to like it, anyway. They were all doubled up laughing.

If the "Donny moment" was a personal favourite on my journey, then the "Elaine Paige moment" was the musical high point. We sang "I Know Him So Well" from *Chess*, the song with which Elaine Paige and Barbara Dixon had a number-one hit in 1985. I clearly remembered them singing in the video on *Top of the Pops*, both of them with big eighties hair, and Elaine Paige in a white silk shirt and black leggings on a kind of studio chessboard. Years ago I had sung the Elaine Paige part myself at a karaoke night at the The Turf in Blackburn, but this was some contrast.

Here was a woman whose voice I had admired for so many years. It had been my dream to be like her, and now I was singing with her. The atmosphere in the studio was absolutely electric and I was so excited we had to do a few takes to get it right, but it really was an indescribable feeling of delight to be singing a duet with my heroine. I am so grateful to have had that opportunity. It was one of those moments that will go into my jukebox of memories and always remain there whatever the future holds.

In the middle of the show, there was a wonderful surprise when Piers presented me with my triple platinum album. At the time of writing, I have sold nine million copies of the CD worldwide and people tell me that it's some sort of record. Sometimes I try to picture all those copies in all those living rooms all over the country, but it's just too many to think about. What I do know for sure is that I have made an album that people of all nationalities and faiths like to listen to. That is an achievement beyond my wildest dreams and something of which I'm very proud.

I've spent my whole life trying to prove to people that I could do something. It was a promise I made to my mother, but it was also a promise I made to myself. I dedicated the album, as I dedicate this book, to my beloved mother. I know that she would be proud of me. I also know that she would think it was all really funny. She would have killed herself laughing at some of the things that have happened. Even though she didn't have an easy life, my mother could laugh about anything. There was nothing she loved more.

37
Celebrity

I've come to realize over the past year that the nature of celebrity is paradoxical. It brings pleasures as well as pressures. It brings freedom, but also restriction. Sometimes one side seems to outweigh the other and the trick is to try to keep everything in balance. I'm learning all the time.

Because I'm travelling so much, Pebbles now stays in London with a very nice lady. I miss her company, but she's a wee bit old now to make the trip back up.

I can be myself in Blackburn. When I go shopping at Tesco, people say hello, but they give me space. We've all got our lives to get on with. Modern technology such as mobile phones, YouTube and Twitter, which were responsible for catapulting me to fame a year ago, now make it difficult for me to go much further afield on my own.

In January I decided to break with routine and be normal for a wee while, so I took a bus into Bathgate train station and then the train into Edinburgh. It was kind of quiet on Bathgate station, so I thought I would be OK. When I got on the train, there were a couple of people in the carriage with me who said hello. They must have texted their friends, because by the next stop it was ten, the next, twenty, and by the time I arrived in Edinburgh there was a whole platform of people waiting for me. I felt like the Pied Piper with this crowd trailing around after me. I went into a department store to get out of the way, but they all followed me in. I asked to see the manager for help, but he wanted to get his picture taken with me as well! Was I safe on the bus to Musselburgh, where my brother Gerard lives? Was I heck! It was like being on a bus with an enormous Christmas tree. I was causing havoc.

When Andy read about my excursion in the paper the next day, he said, "You went on a bus? You could have hopped in a taxi!"

"It would have cost me fifty quid to get a taxi!" I told him.

It's not just about the money. I like being outside in the air. I prefer a train journey to a journey by car. I like being normal. It's what I'm used to. But it's getting increasingly difficult and I'm reluctantly having to accept that it's no longer practical for me to do things just like everybody else.

The other side of that is it there are fantastic opportunities open to me that I wouldn't have without my fame. Andy recently got me tickets for the Spandau Ballet reunion tour concert in Glasgow. I took some friends with me and the doorman at the SECC recognized me from when I came to do my original audition, so they escorted us in and we all got five-star treatment. Afterwards we went backstage and I met Tony Hadley and the Kemp brothers, who are even better looking in real life. When I meet people who have been heroes of mine, I'm still a wee fan myself. I think that's why I'm always ready to sign autographs or have my photo taken. On the way back home, my friends and I were hungry, so we stopped at the Kentucky Fried Chicken. There were two old ladies who'd been to the pictures having a bite to eat as well. They asked if they could phone someone and tell them who they were there with. Of course I didn't mind. It goes with the territory.

Another hilarious thing happened just after Christmas when Lorraine's daughter took her kids to see a pantomime at the King's Theatre in Edinburgh. A well-known Scottish television star called Allan Stewart was starring in it and apparently he did an impersonation of me in the middle of the show. When they reported this back to me, I couldn't wait to get tickets myself, especially as I've been an admirer of Allan Stewart for years.

We arrived at the final performance and the management met me and asked if I'd like to go on stage myself to surprise him. Well, as you may have gathered, there's a bit of a devil in me, so I said, "Right, let's do it!" They said that they would come down and get me at 5:30. I watched the first part of the pantomime and it was very funny. Then, as arranged, I went backstage.

I couldn't help thinking, as I stood there in the wings, of all the plays I'd come to see in this theatre and all the effort I'd put into my acting classes to train myself to go on stage. Now it was quite peculiar to watch one of Scotland's best-known actors walking down the stage acting out the part of me. He was singing "I Dreamed a Dream of Wild Horses" dressed in a wig and a gold dress just like mine. I wouldn't have minded, but he had the better-looking legs!

I waited until the song came to the end and he was doing all his patter, then I walked on with a great big scowl on my face, as if I was very angry, and marched right up to him. I stood there for a wee second eyeballing him, then I gave him a big cuddle. It brought the house down!

I said, "You look better in that frock than I ever have, but you cannae do the wiggle, can ye?"

He said, "I can!"

And he tried it, but I said, "Naah! That's not the wiggle. This is how you do it, OK?"

And then I went off again.

It was a bit of a risk, because I didn't know how Allan Stewart would take it, but he was really good about it. It was such a laugh.

I had a couple of weeks off over Christmas, so Bridie invited me over on Christmas Day. It was the same crowd, except for my brother Joe, as the previous Christmas. Since then my circumstances had changed beyond recognition, but my siblings didn't treat me any differently. We ate our turkey dinner and drank a wee glass of wine just like any other family in the land, and I have to say, it was bloody fantastic!

The end of the year is always a time of reflection, when you review what's happened and look forward to what's to come. Christmas 2009 felt particularly Christmassy because there was so much snow around. During the first week of January, I was invited to a New Year party at the Cardinal's house in Edinburgh. There had been another fall of snow just before we arrived in the walled front garden. The lights from the house shone a warm, magical glow over the pristine white surfaces and there was that hush that sometimes follows just after the snow has stopped. My footsteps crumped across the frozen whiteness to the statue of Our Lady, where I said a prayer.

The warm, convivial atmosphere inside was such a contrast to the icy tranquillity outside, I could feel my cheeks turning pink. I recognized all sorts of distinguished people there, including the then Secretary of State for Scotland Jim Murphy, the Attorney General, the head of the Church of Scotland, and Sister Patricia Fallon from the Daughters of Charity, who had recently celebrated the seventieth anniversary of her profession. If I hadn't been with my friends Frank, Maureen,

Mario and Lorraine, I might have felt a wee bit out of my depth. However, I found a comfortable armchair in the Cardinal's living room and there was no need to worry about not knowing the other guests, because people kept coming up to shake my hand and congratulate me. Most amazing of all was when I glanced at the Cardinal's mantelpiece and saw, propped up amongst all his personal photographs, a copy of my album, with my own photograph smiling out of it.

I've been lucky enough to be given several awards, such as the Great Scot Award 2009 and Glenfiddich Spirit of Scotland Award 2009.

My name is suddenly on the invitation list for parties that previously I would only have read about in *Hello!* magazine. In March, I spent an especially memorable and enjoyable evening at the Thistle Hotel in Glasgow at a tribute to Tommy Gemmell, the legendary footballer who scored the equalizer for Celtic before the Lisbon Lions went on to win the European Cup in 1967. That was the occasion when I wished I had my father with me. I know Dad would have been delighted that I'd met the Cardinal; he would have been astonished that I'd had a number-one album; but getting to shake the hand of Tommy Gemmell, now that was really something!

I hope I'll never lose sight of how privileged I am to have all these opportunities, but the events that I enjoy most are those where I feel that I am using my celebrity to make a difference to other people. Just before Christmas, I visited a Catholic primary school where Mario's daughter Lisa Maria is head-teacher. Originally I was scheduled to see the Christmas nativity play in the local church hall, but because of the weather they'd had to cancel the performance, so the children were all disappointed. None of them had been told that I would be visiting, so when I arrived they went wild. I was immediately pulled into their games and their dancing. I think it was the most fun I've ever had at school! But there was one boy I noticed sitting sadly in the corner, so I asked Lisa Maria if there was something the matter with the wee fella. She told me that he had lost his father just a couple of months before and he was pining for him. My heart went out to the lad. I knew just how he was feeling. So I went and sat beside him and I found myself telling him, "I came here today to see all the children. But I came especially for you!"

His face lit up. I'd given him something different to think about, if only for a few minutes. It's moments like that that make you think that you're doing something worthwhile.

38
Amazing Grace

When you get to my age, you're generally not too bothered whether people remember your birthday. In some ways you'd rather they didn't! So I was surprised when Andy called to ask whether I'd like to spend the day in Japan.

I'd already been to Tokyo to appear on a New Year show and I had recorded an extra track for the Japanese edition of my album, called "Wings to Fly." Since its release, the album had gone platinum in Japan and the people from Sony were keen for me to go over again. I assumed they were talking about another promotional opportunity, where I would sing one of my songs for a television programme.

"No, it's something a bit different."

Andy explained that 1 April is a very important day in the Japanese calendar. It's the beginning of their financial year and it's also the day that students graduate from college. The song "Wings to Fly" was of particular significance because it is traditionally sung to students on that day.

"They'd like me to sing it at a graduation ceremony?" I guessed.

"Not exactly," said Andy. "They were thinking of an eighty-piece orchestra at the Budokan. Do you know what the Budokan is?"

I hadn't got past "eighty-piece orchestra."

"It's the venue where the Beatles played," Andy continued. "Seats about nine thousand—"

"You are kidding?" I interrupted.

"I'm not kidding—"

"Do you think I'm ready for that?" I eventually whispered down the phone.

"Of course I do," he said. "But it doesn't matter what I or anyone else thinks. It's how *you* feel about it. Nobody's going to have a problem if you say no. But if you're up for it, then I think you'll have a great time . . ."

Oh my God! I had never sung in front of a live orchestra before. When I put down the phone I did one of my little jigs on the spot. The idea was great, but my tummy was already bubbling with that strange, almost chemical reaction you get when you combine excitement with nerves. You're fizzing so much you think you might take off and fly, but at the same time you're frozen to the spot with terror.

Over the next few days I tried to think it through rationally. This was just another step, wasn't it? Wasn't this what being a professional was all about? Wasn't this the life I had claimed to want? When Yvie Burnett agreed to come along to support me, I began to believe that I could do it. In fact, I was really starting to look forward to it. Joanne and I made plans to go out shopping to buy some clothes for the trip.

· · ·

A week before we were due to fly, Yvie called me. I could tell straight away from the timbre of her voice that something was wrong. She told me her beloved mother, Molly, had died.

Memories of Molly's courage and fantastic sense of humour in the face of her illness flooded through my mind, washing away all other thoughts. I was so sad, not just for Molly, but because of the hollowness in Yvie's normally bright, business-like voice. I recognized that and I wanted to be able to support her, but I knew that losing your mother can be very lonely and there's nothing anyone else can do to make you feel better.

"There *is* something you can do," Yvie told me. Then she asked me to sing at Molly's funeral.

Yvie knows many singers, but I think she asked me because she knew that I understood what it was to be close to your mother and to feel as devastated as she was feeling.

Joanne and I went shopping, as planned, but what we bought was a black suit for me to wear at the funeral. On the Saturday, a car drove us on the long journey north to Aberdeenshire. It had been a hard winter and there were dirty mounds of frozen slush by the side of the country roads. The trees were still holding their leaves in tight buds to protect against the frost. Under a cold grey sky, it almost felt as if the Scottish countryside was in mourning.

On each seat in the wee stone church in the village of Methlick there was an Order of Service with Molly's vibrant face smiling from it. Printed on the back was that poem she loved so much, "I'm Fine Thank You." It was so tragic to know that we wouldn't see that smile again, nor hear her laughter.

The congregation sang Psalm 23, "The Lord's My Shepherd." The vicar spoke, but I hardly heard what he was saying because it was my turn next.

I told myself I must not crumble. This time, I was the one who had to be strong. I remembered all the times we had practised the song, but I was shaking as I rose to my feet.

Singing a first note a cappella is like making a leap of faith, but with the help of God, I sang

Amazing Grace, how sweet the sound
That saved a wretch like me.
I once was lost but now am found
Was blind, but now I see

and my voice became stronger with every word.

After the funeral, we weren't able to stay too long because it was a long journey home. As I hugged her good-bye, I promised Yvie that if she ever wanted to talk, at any time of night or day, I'd be there at the end of the phone. I wanted her to know that she had the support of someone who had experienced what she was going through.

"I know," she said, squeezing my hand. "Thank you. But I'll see you on Monday."

Surely she didn't mean she was still coming to Japan?

"It's my job," Yvie reassured me. "It might even help me if I have to focus on something else . . ."

I know how professional Yvie is, and I was so moved I started crying all over again.

Having hugged each other tight in a peaceful little country churchyard, thirty-six hours later we found ourselves hugging again in the buzzing luxury of the Virgin Upper Class departure lounge at Heathrow Airport.

There was actually a pretty good atmosphere as all the members of the team gathered. With Joanne, Michelle and the people from Syco and Sony, seven women were travelling together with Andy. He called us his netball team. Michelle was excited because it was the first time she'd "turned left" on a plane, and I'm still a bit apprehensive before I fly, so it's my natural instinct to try to mask the tension by joking around. As we walked down the tunnel to the plane, our footsteps spontaneously fell into sync and for some reason we all started humming Colonel Hathi's march from *The Jungle Book*! The air stewards must have wondered what on earth was coming on board!

We arrived at Narita at nine in the morning and drove into Tokyo with people from the Japanese end of Sony, who had come to greet us at the airport. The countryside very quickly disappears as you drive into the industrialized cityscape, with buildings as far as the eye can see and motorways on stilts winding their way through the urban jungle. Whizzing round the fast-moving freeways feels almost like being in a science-fiction movie. Occasionally a park appears like a verdant oasis, with boating lakes reflecting the sunshine and flowering trees laden with buds. The people from Sony were excited because the cherry blossom was due to flower any day, possibly even when we were there. There's something rather nice about top executives who work in concrete-and-glass towers talking proudly about their cherry-blossom trees. In the distance we could see the unmistakable outline of snowcapped Mount Fuji. They told us this was a very good omen.

The Ritz-Carlton hotel where we were staying is in the tallest building in Tokyo and the lift to reception shot up forty-five floors, making my ears pop. In the hotel corridors there was the usual densely carpeted luxury that made it feel much like any other posh hotel I've been in, but when I opened the door to my room, the view took my breath away. The entire far wall of the room was window, like a giant television screen, with city stretching as far as the eye could see.

It's very difficult to adjust to a different time zone, so I didn't manage to get much sleep. I was trying desperately to keep my nerves under control, but the next morning, when I was due to go to my rehearsal with the full orchestra, I was suddenly struck by a tornado of self-doubt.

I didn't know how to sing with an orchestra!

This wasn't just any orchestra, it was one of the best orchestras in the world!

It was crazy even to think of going to the rehearsal!

I couldn't understand how anyone could have thought that I could do it and it made me very angry when people tried to reassure me. Yvie tried to be strict with me, telling me that I would ruin my voice with all the crying, but even that made no difference. What did it matter if I ruined my voice? I wasn't going to go out there and sing.

It took endless patience for Andy to persuade me to go along to the concert hall. I didn't have to sing, he assured me. I didn't even have to talk to anyone. I could just sit there, or hide behind a pillar if I really wanted, just to hear how the orchestra sounded. What harm could it do? We'd come all this way. It would be a shame not even to listen.

We drove to the Metropolitan Art Space, a large concert hall where the Yomiuri Orchestra was rehearsing. Even backstage, they sounded brilliant and I couldn't resist having a wee peep inside the concert hall. There were just a few production people dotted about the stalls. The two tiers of seats above were empty. The acoustics made the sound of the orchestra full, rich and mellow. Yvie was standing just below the orchestra making notes on the score as they played and occasionally conferring with the conductor, who was dressed casually in a butter-yellow polo shirt and black trousers. He didn't look very scary at all.

Andy and I slipped surreptitiously into seats at the back of the stalls. The orchestra struck up "Who I Was Born to Be." As the music floated around me, all the raging tempests seemed to settle. It's such a familiar tune, it felt bizarre to hear it being played by professional violinists, cellists, percussionists, woodwind, brass, trumpets, even a harp!

"It's my song," I whispered to Andy.

The words began to flow softly from my lips as if I had no choice but to sing it.

"Don't sing to me!" Andy hissed, exasperated. "Get up there and do it!"

"All right, then," I told him, gathering my courage. "I'll give it a go."

The stage was quite high above the stalls and Andy had to hoist me up. It wasn't the most dignified way to greet the conductor, but he was a very nice man with a gentle smile. Without further ado, he tapped his baton.

As I heard the orchestra behind me playing the opening notes and I filled my lungs, it was as if I had been in pieces and was now whole again. I could do it! The relief was so exhilarating, I couldn't stop myself doing a little jig of joy during the orchestral bars building up to the final chorus. At the end of the song the orchestra applauded me, which was a fantastic feeling. We went straight into "I Dreamed a Dream," and after that "Wings to Fly," the song that means so much to Japanese people. It was as if I'd been singing in front of an orchestra all my life.

"I want to do it again!" I exclaimed in the people-carrier on the way back to the hotel. I was buzzing with the wonderful high of performance, but as I turned round to beam at everyone, I could see they were totally shattered by the effort of getting me there.

"You are the girl with the curl, aren't you?" said Yvie, with a smile.

Every artist pays tribute to their fans, but in my case I really wouldn't be here without them. Yes, I could hold a note. Yes, I had the nerve to risk making a fool of myself on *Britain's Got Talent*, but my story really began with the hundred million people who watched my audition on YouTube, breaking all records, and making my face so well known that the two elderly Japanese ladies who were sitting next to me and Andy in the noodle bar where we had lunch knew my name and wanted a photo.

Note to self: Udon noodles are not the best

choice of food if you have false teeth and people are staring at you!

That afternoon I spent some time with a group of fans so dedicated that they had come to Tokyo to see my concert from as far away as America, Canada and Australia. When Syco got wind on the forum that this was happening, they thought how nice it would be for me to meet them, so they arranged for us to have tea together at the hotel.

What a great bunch of people! As I walked into the suite, with its panoramic view of the city, I was embraced by their warmth and good humour. They were all wearing pink badges that they had made for the occasion, printed with images of me and the Budokan and cherry blossom, and they all had red scarves, just as the fans had done when I sang in Rockefeller Plaza. Some of them had actually been there on that chilly November morning when I launched my album. In fact, two of the ladies had met for the first time in Rockefeller Plaza that day even though they live only three streets away from each other in Atlanta, Georgia. It is very heartwarming to hear that people have become friends because of me.

I said hello to each person individually and tried to find out a little bit about their stories. Some were retired, like Linda, the lady who coordinated the trip. She didn't look nearly old enough to be retired, but she told me that being a fan of mine had made her retirement wonderful. Others had jobs from which they'd had to take time off in order to come to Tokyo. One lady said she'd had a hard time persuading her management to allow her to come, but she'd stuck up for herself.

I began to get the sense that seeing me having the courage to go for it at my audition somehow gave these women courage too. I tried to hold on to that thought so that it would make me brave when it came to the concert.

Lisa, the lady who calls herself my greatest fan, was also there. Her husband and four children were all on holiday in the Cayman Islands, but she had chosen to come to Japan instead. I was worried about what her husband would think about this, but she reassured me that he understood. Apparently he'd said, "That girl has more moxie than anyone else, and if anyone's worth supporting, then she is."

I'm still not sure what moxie is, but I think it's probably a good thing!

I was showered with thoughtful gifts and presented with a most beautiful bouquet of long-stemmed red roses. When a huge cake covered in strawberries and cream was wheeled in and everyone sang "Happy Birthday," it was all I could do to stop myself crying.

There were an awful lot of candles on that cake, but my breathing exercises came in useful again, because I managed to blow them all out in one go.

"Make a wish!" they chorused, but I felt so blessed at that moment, it would have been wrong to wish for anything more.

I woke up with a start in the early hours, taking a split second to recognize my surroundings. What on earth? An enormous, king-size bed. Where on earth? Tokyo. Why on earth? It was my birthday and . . . Oh my God! I turned over and pulled the duvet over my head, trying to fool myself into going back to sleep. It didn't work.

As I lay there watching the dawn break over the city, I thought back to my last birthday, 1 April 2009. I'd woken up in the room where I had slept since I was a child, with nothing planned at all. I couldn't recall if I'd actually seen anyone that day. The only thing that had been special about it was the secret knowledge that I was going to be appearing on *Britain's Got Talent*. At that stage I'd never seen the tape of my audition. I had no idea what it would be like.

At breakfast, Andy told me that I had received a royalty cheque over night. I didn't ask how much because money was the last thing I wanted to think about, but he said it would definitely be enough to get the white piano I'd always wanted. The next surprise was when Alex from Syco came to wish me happy birthday with a gift from Simon Cowell—a beautiful bracelet made of white gold and diamonds.

"I'm never going to take it off my wrist!" I told her.

"Ahh, isn't that lovely!" she said.

"It's not so much lovely as I don't want it to get nicked!" I told her. "Anyone who wants this will have to chop my arm off!"

In an effort to take my mind away from the impending concert, we went out sightseeing.

The cherry-blossom season had officially started. For Japanese people, the flowering of the cherry blossom is a metaphor for the fleeting nature of life, and for one week before the petals begin to fall like drifts of delicate snow, cherry-blossom fever grips the city. People celebrate with cherry-blossom viewing parties underneath the blossom-laden bows. On my birthday, it seemed as if the whole of Tokyo was out walking in the park. I had my picture taken a hundred times under a canopy of the palest pink blossom.

We visited another of Tokyo's famous sights, the Shibuya crossing, a six-way intersection of streets, where everyone is on the move, and the buildings glitter with constantly changing electronic images. It couldn't have been more of a contrast with the almost-sacred tranquillity of the Imperial Palace gardens, yet it felt as typically Japanese.

With my mind absorbed in the traditions of a totally different culture, the hours between breakfast and lunch flew past, but as the concert drew closer a very familiar and terrible feeling of ice-cold dread began to trickle through my veins.

The Budokan is a stadium built for martial arts during the Tokyo Olympics in 1964, and it is still used for that purpose, but it has also become a legendary venue for rock concerts. Not only the Beatles played there, but so did Bob Dylan and David Bowie. More recently, it has hosted performers as diverse as Céline Dion and Judas Priest. It is situated just on the other side of the Imperial Palace from the gardens we had visited that morning, and the car had to move slowly because of the crowds thronging the glorious cherry-blossom avenue.

We arrived in the early afternoon and I did a rehearsal with the orchestra while the vast stadium was empty. Everything was going fine until a couple of hours before I was due to perform, just as Michelle was beginning to apply my make-up, when I was suddenly overwhelmed by the enormity of what was facing me.

When you're in a dressing room backstage, you still get a sense of the arena filling up even though you can't see it. You can feel the anticipation growing. The first half of the concert included three Japanese stars of the opera and music world, singing popular arias from *Carmen*, *Aida* and *Miss Saigon*. The minutes ticked away. Michelle put my make-up on. I cried it off. Michelle put it on again. The seconds ticked away.

Finally, it was time. Andy was standing at my

dressing-room door. I knew that ultimately the choice was mine. I could run away now and get the next flight home, or I could go out and show everyone what I was made of. I tried to imagine the smiling faces of all the Japanese people who had shown me so much respect and kindness; I tried to envisage my red-scarfed ladies who'd come from all corners of the globe and were waiting excitedly in the stalls. I looked at Andy, who'd put in so much work to get me to the place I was now, and at Yvie, who'd shown such professional dedication at a time of personal grief. They were both waiting patiently for me to be ready, perhaps wondering if I ever would be.

I took a deep breath, and nodded at Andy to take me to the stage.

Some people would think that stepping on to the stage was the easy bit, but my knees were knocking as I walked across to the mic. The lights were very bright. I couldn't see the far reaches of the stadium, but I had a sense of the thousands of faces out there looking at me. Most people would think that opening your mouth to sing to a crowd of nine thousand was the difficult bit, but as soon as I heard the music all my fears and worries ebbed away. Amazingly, there was no croakiness in my voice as I went straight into "I Dreamed a Dream." It sounded very powerful with the stadium full and the orchestra blasting behind me. The crowd was much bigger than any I had sung to before, and the energy coming from the audience as they applauded gave my spirits a great fillip. As I started singing "Who I Was Born to Be" I began to relax and become aware of the red scarves waving just to my left. The words of the song soared out like a rallying cry. This is what I was born to do.

I went off to get a few sips of water before returning to the stage to sing "Amazing Grace," but I cannot tell you how that song sounded because I was trying so hard to contain all the emotion that welled up inside me. Just five days before, I had sung the same hymn without accompaniment to a small, sad congregation in a wee grey stone church on the other side of the world. I looked down into the stalls. Yvie was in her usual position just below me, her sweet face tilted heavenwards, almost as if she was trying to keep the tears in her eyes.

At the end of the hymn, nine thousand people applauded, but the two of us exchanged a poignant smile, both knowing who we were thinking about.

My final number was "Wings to Fly." It is a much higher, more floaty song and requires a different placement of the voice. For the first time in the evening, I squeaked the first couple of notes, but fortunately was able to correct myself. I could tell that the audience were on my side, even with that mistake, and that made me relax and enjoy the words:

Want to spread my wings and fly
Away into the sky
How I dream to be so free
No more sadness no more pain
No more anger no more hate
How I dream to have those wings and
    fly into the sky

The best surprise of all came after my performance when the presenter of the show was interviewing me through an interpreter. What she was saying sounded like "Blaa blaa blaa Susan Boyle, blaa blaa blaa Susan Boyle!"

Then the orchestra unexpectedly struck up behind me. It took a moment for me to recognize the tune and to realize that the whole stadium was now singing to me.

Happy Birthday to you!
Happy Birthday to you!
Happy Birthday, dear Susan!
Happy Birthday to you!

39
Rosary

Over the last year I have been lucky enough to receive many wonderful gifts, far too many to list here. All the flowers and balloons and toys are fantastic; the albums of messages and prayers have meant a great deal to me and brought me comfort in times of stress; and I am constantly surprised and delighted by the hand-made gifts that people have put so much thought and effort into, such as the very detailed and accurate pencil drawing of me and my mother which a disabled girl had copied from the photograph she'd seen on the Internet. I'd like to thank everyone who has thought about me and prayed for me for your incredible kindness and generosity.

In May 2010 I returned once again to St. Bennet's, this time to receive a very special presentation. In the beautiful little oratory, His Eminence asked a lovely lady called Maria Dorrian to explain the extraordinary story of how a set of rosary beads had been created specially for me.

Maria works in Scotland for St. Padre Pio's Friary, which is in San Giovanni Rotondo, Puglia, in Italy. She is a fan of mine and one day last year she was involved in a thread on one of my fan sites where my faith was being discussed. Maria continued the conversation with a volunteer from the Marian Information Center in Las Vegas, who expressed interest in bringing the relics of Padre Pio to Las Vegas. From that introduction, Maria accompanied the relics to many churches there and met the Bishop of Las Vegas and members of the congregation.

As the link in the spiritual journey that people from different sides of the world were experiencing was Susan Boyle (although I knew nothing about it at the time), the idea of the rosary was conceived. The Marian group in Las Vegas asked their members each to supply one bead from their own rosary, with other beads coming from Maria herself and from her close friends in Scotland, Holland, California and Connecticut.

Maria then contacted Cardinal O'Brien to ask him if he would give a bead from his rosary too. He gave one from the rosary on which he'd prayed at the Vatican while awaiting his audience with Pope Benedict XVI.

A lady called Collette from Nevada took all the beads and created an exquisite rosary, which includes a silver locket containing a piece of cloth that covered the wounds of Padre Pio's stigmata. The crucifix is from the shrine of Medjugorje in Bosnia-Herzegovina. The rosary was blessed at the tomb of St. Padre Pio.

Maria invited the Cardinal to present me with the

rosary and, accompanying it, a leather-bound book with a hand-written message from each donor, promising to pray for me in my singing vocation. I was overcome with emotion to hold in my hands the product of so many prayers from people around the world. Using my unique and precious new rosary, we recited the five decades and sang hymns to Our Lady. At the Cardinal's request, I sang "Ave Maria," pouring all my gratitude and humility into the prayer.

Afterwards there was a lovely tea laid out for us. As we relaxed and chatted, Friar GianMaria, who had travelled from Padre Pio's shrine in southern Italy, said that God uses certain humble people, often from insignificant little towns, to make a spiritual impact on the world and that I was one of those people who leads people to God and Our Lady.

"I haven't done anything!" I protested.

I'm just an ordinary person, but I have always believed that I am on a path that God has created for me, so if this path is one that brings people together, then I am very glad and grateful to Him.

40
Moving On

As I come to the end of my memoir, I am sitting in the living room of Yule Terrace where I have always lived, trying to pluck up the courage to make another journey, to my own new house. It is in Blackburn, where I feel at home, but I'll have more space for a piano, and it's somewhere I'll feel safer. I was a wee bit spooked when a lad broke into my house earlier this year, and my family and friends keep telling me that I'm too vulnerable in Yule Terrace.

There are so many memories all around me here, especially of my beloved mother. I often find myself wondering what she would have made of it all. I know she would have been so proud of me recording an album and singing with an orchestra in Japan, but she would have been equally delighted by the generosity and support I've been shown closer to home. In June, in the nearby village Polbeth, I was invited to the Gala Day to crown the wee Gala Day Queen. Gala Days are joyous occasions for the local community, and it meant a lot to me to be asked to play a part. It was a beautiful sunny day as well, and I felt as if I spent the whole time smiling. I know that would have made my mother very happy.

Somebody told me recently that I had come seventh in a poll of the most influential people in the world. I suspect the result was swung by some of my more ardent fans voting fast and often, but how daft can you get? As I sit here in my living room, I can almost see my mother's face lighting up at that news and hear her peals of laughter.

But I have learned that you can't hold on to memories for ever because that is like holding on to the person and preventing them from enjoying the life that God has prepared for them.

> *And so here am I*
> *Open arms and ready to stand*
> *I've got the world in my hands*
> *And it feels like my turn to fly.*
>
> *And though I may not*
> *Know the answers*
> *I can finally say I'm free*
> *And if the questions*
> *Lead me here, then*
> *I am who I was born to be.*

There are still many questions I constantly ask myself. Am I doing things right? Am I becoming a better person?

In a way, this first year has been my growing up. I was innocent at the start, and I was unprotected.

I probably received more attention than any other unelected person for many years. I accept that it goes with the job, but at times it was an almost unbearable pressure.

Now I have people around me that I trust and am willing to be guided by. My confidence is growing and with it, I hope, my professionalism. I like to think I have become more of a lady.

I still have my moments of doubt. Doesn't everybody? That's only human. I know there's still a long way to go in my evolving journey.

I want to continue to grow as an entertainer myself and become better at it, but I am also starting to look at different avenues to explore, like seeing if there are ways I can give other struggling artists the chance to achieve their dreams.

Some of the most satisfying moments this year have been when I have been asked to sing to help other people, such as recording the single in aid of the rescue effort in Haiti, and performing "Wild Horses" for Sport Relief. I hope I will be able to do more charity work, giving financially and benefiting those who have a disability.

If there is one thing I would most like to think I have achieved this past year, it is to have made life a little easier for people with a disability. In my dictionary there's no such word as "disability." Those first three letters imply that you're limited, that a fence has been built around you—not by you, but by what people think of you. If you take those first three letters off, then you've got "ability," and the gate is open.

You should always focus on what you can do, not on what you can't do—and remember, there's no rush. People want things straight away these days and there's a lot of pressure to get on, but some people need a bit more time to fulfil their potential.

If my story means anything, it is that people are very often too quick to judge a person by the way they look or by their quirks of behaviour. I may not have quite the same sense of humour as other people, but at least I do have a sense of humour, and I've needed it! As a society, we seem to have very tight restrictions on what is considered "normal." I am happy to admit that I have had some difficulties, but I also have many blessings: the gift of a voice that makes people happy; the certainty of my faith in an uncertain world.

I hope that my story demonstrates that you shouldn't just look at the label, you should always look at the whole person, emotionally, physically, mentally and spiritually.

One of the things that is most different about my life now is that I never know what is going to happen next. If my life was a wee bit monochrome before, now it is a rainbow of colour and contrast. I've learned to embrace and relish that uncertainty instead of fearing it. In the past few weeks, I have been offered a guest role as dinner lady in the hit

American television series *Glee*; I have also received an invitation to sing for the Pope when he visits Scotland in September. The first would be great fun, the second would be a privilege and an honour so profound I could never even have dreamed of wishing for it.

As my friend Frank Quinn has said on many occasions, "You are writing your story, Susan. It's about achievement and belief in yourself."

I have no idea what the next chapter is going to be, but I do know that I'm looking forward to whatever the future holds.

A Reflection

God of New Beginnings
I come before You with an open heart and
outstretched arms
Seeking guidance as I reach beyond myself
To find your love in everyone I meet and
everyone I sing for.
I ask that my arms might embrace your
Spirit
And that my eyes continue to see You in
others
As I celebrate your love.
I ask for the strength and patience to be a
person of peace and an instrument
For justice and respect for all people,
especially people with a disability.
I wish to keep my life simple and always
keep in mind the simplicity of your
message: Your love for all of us
Through your divine strength I open in a
new way,
Committing myself to always try and walk
your path and share in your work.
I thank You for the gift of people, the talents
of all people and my own gift of music
and song.

It is through respecting each other that we experience oneness with You.

Keep me close and never let me stray from You.

Let me always be a person of hope and certain of your powerful and gentle presence.

Amen

Acknowledgments

I would like to express my gratitude to everyone who has been involved in my story, especially to each and every one of my family, my friends and my fantastic fans. I am especially grateful to my sisters, Mary and Bridie, and my nieces Kirsty, Joanne and Pamela for sharing their memories for this book. Kirsty and Joanne have been a great support throughout the year, and I want to thank them very much for that.

I would like to thank Lorraine Campbell and Fred O'Neil for contributing to the book. I am also grateful to Charles Earley for supplying details about the West Lothian Voluntary Arts Council.

I am grateful to Mark Lucas and the team at LAW, and to Doug Young and everyone at Transworld who has been involved in the publication of my book.

Thank you, Ossie, for organizing everything so well.

Thank you, Yvie and Steve, for your professional expertise and friendship.

I am indebted to my friend and teacher Frank Quinn, who has cheered and inspired me, and to His Eminence Cardinal Keith Patrick O'Brien for his support and hospitality.

I am very fortunate indeed to have Andy Stephens as my manager, and I am constantly grateful for his good sense, good humour and great company. Thanks, Andy!

Finally, my heartfelt thanks go to Imogen Parker, whose patience, sensitivity and sense of humour made the daunting task of telling my story a very enjoyable experience.

Song Credits

Photo Credits

Center Point Publishing
600 Brooks Road ● PO Box 1
Thorndike ME 04986-0001 USA

(207) 568-3717

US & Canada:
1 800 929-9108
www.centerpointlargeprint.com